The American Lyceum

The American Lyceum

TOWN MEETING OF THE MIND

CARL BODE

Southern Illinois University Press, *Carbondale and Edwardsville*

Feffer & Simons, Inc., *London and Amsterdam*

Arcturus Books Edition, November, 1968

Copyright © 1956 by Carl Bode

Preface to this Edition,
Copyright © 1968 by Southern Illinois University Press

All Rights Reserved
Library of Congress Catalog Number 56–5163

The research necessary for the writing of this book
was made possible in part by two grants-in-aid
from the American Philosophical Society.

This edition printed by offset lithography
in the United States of America

Preface to This Edition

IN THE past decade the role of the lyceum movement in nine-teenth century American culture has been recognized more and more. Its contribution was many sided; its spectrum was broad. At one extreme it stimulated an interest in American science. At the other it helped to shape a distinctive prose style in American literature. In between it performed numerous other services. Its leaders were among the most colorful figures on the American scene. However, no book besides this one (the first comprehensive study to be made) has yet appeared and so *The American Lyceum* is now reprinted. There are some minor corrections I should like to make: on page 80 *1836* should be *1838;* on page 107 *Caroline* should be *Catharine,* as it also should on page 261; on page 215 Dr. Boynton's first name, *John,* should be supplied, as it should on page 261. Major corrections, I realize, doubtless may be called for too; but even if I had a chance to change the general method and approach, I do not believe I would do so. This was one of the first books to describe an American institution from an interdisciplinary point of view; it still seems to me the proper point of view. As to the value of the institution itself, I content myself with quoting Henry Thoreau, who wrote in his journal for August 29, 1852, "The one hundred and twenty-five dollars which is subscribed in

[Concord] every winter for a Lyceum is better spent than any other equal sum."

CARL BODE

University of Maryland
March 1, 1968

Contents

Definition

From *A Dictionary of American English*

[† Indicates that the word or sense clearly or to all appearance originated within the present limits of the United States]

LYCEUM. [1786—]

† 1. a. An institution through which lectures, dramatic performances, debates, and the like are presented to a community.

b. The association which sponsors such an institution.

1820 *Amer. Jrnl. Science* II. 366 Abstract of the proceedings of the Lyceum of Natural History, New-York. 1835 S. *Lit. Messenger* I. 273 In all the cities, and many of the larger and middling towns . . . there are Lyceums. 1842 *Knickerb.* XIX. 437 He belonged to the village lyceum and had a chance to listen to all the lectures of the season. 1865 *Atlantic Mo.* XV. 370 Our plain-speaking gentleman who makes his yearly circuit among the lyceums. 1894 WISTER in *Harper's Mag.* Aug. 387/1 'Louise, why

don't you quit her outfit?' 'Resign from the Lyceum?'

† 2. The building in which such lectures, etc., are given.

1833 COKE *Subaltern's Furlough* X, The college has . . . two chapels, and a lycaeum, (in which are the recitation rooms). 1847 HOWE *Hist. Coll. Ohio* 477 On the left [are] the Cuyahoga river, the lyceum and Presbyterian church. 1889 P. BUTLER *Recollections* II Even in those early days Wadsworth contained . . . a lyceum where the young men discussed the questions of the day.

† 3. The program sponsored by a lyceum.

1854. 'O. OPTIC' *In Doors & Out* (1876) 306 There were balls, parties, and lyceums in Tiptop. 1858 *Harper's Mag.* April 699/2 The Lyceum—or the course of miscellaneous winter lectures in towns and villages all through the country—has now become a fixed American institution. 1877 *Ib.* Jan. 285/1, I don't care for your lyceums here winter times. 1900 BACHELLER *E. Holden* 139 Thet there is talent in Faraway

---

Poking fun was as much an American trait a century ago as it is now; here an unknown artist has caricatured a lyceum lecture on weather given in New York about 1841. (*Museum of the City of New York.*)

township . . . no one can deny who has ever attended a lyceum at the Howard schoolhouse.

4. A school. *Obsolescent*. . . .

† 5. Attrib. with *amusement, association, hall,* etc.

1831 *Mass. Statutes* 4 March, They are hereby made a corporation, by the name of the Lyceum Hall, . . . for the purpose of affording means and facilities for the prosecution of literary and scientific studies. 1843 'CARL-TON' *New Purchase* II. 174 The common school system, and the lyceum system. 1865 *Atlantic Mo*. XV. 363 There are library associations or lyceum associations, composed generally of young men. 1881 *Harper's Mag*. March 628/2 During the days of his lyceum lecturing, no man was more popular [than Dr. Chapin] upon the platform. 1883 *Century Mag*. Aug. 636/1 Encourage Lyceum amusement courses in the towns.

That the term *lyceum* failed to satisfy everyone who used it is abundantly clear. More than once in the early years of the lyceum system the word was defined apologetically or even irritably. The first critical reaction can be summed up in the belief that it was a poor word but better than none. One reason for its adoption was suggested by the *Columbian Centinel* for 15 November 1828, which pointed out the advantage of the fact that it was confined to no particular class. Unlike *mechanics' institute*, it had a universal—and neutral—quality. As the years went on, *lyceum* became fixed in the language and few further animadversions were cast against it. It continued to stand, grandly if a little vaguely, for learning.

We shall follow nineteenth-century usage. Though in the 1850s *lecture system* appeared because it was by then a more accurate term for the second phase of the lyceum's development—away from informal, mutual education—many people clung to *lyceum*. We shall use *lyceum* to refer to the movement in either its first or second phase and *lecture system* only in connection with the second phase.

The Dynamics of the Early Lyceum

1

The Crossing of the Sea

A S the busy second quarter of the nineteenth century began, it would have made little difference to some young clerk or mechanic, lyceum-bound, that scholars still quarreled about the exact location of the temple of Apollo Lyceius in ancient Athens. Or that they were far from unanimous about whether the epithet *Lyceius* referred to the eastern country of Lycia or to an animal, the wolf. The clerk's more learned elders might have told him, however, that in one respect at least the authorities agreed. They agreed that immortality had touched the temple, for next to it Aristotle had taught his philosophy. The grove or garden in which the philosopher had walked back and forth as he spoke with the students was named the *Lyceum,* and the term was kept alive by virtue of this association. Throughout the literatures of the various European countries a reference to this lyceum can, every so often, be found. In the eighteenth century the Italians and the Swiss adapted the name for universities in their country. The French employed the term *lycée* for a whole class of schools as well as attaching it to single institutions. But such continental precedents meant nothing to the forward-looking American of the time when our native lyceum emerged.

He was, however, aware of England in a variety of ways. His attitude then as now was a mixed one. Its chief elements were distrust and grudging admiration, and he paid some attention to significant movements in the British Isles.

One such was the growth of the 'mechanics' institutes.' The first (if there is ever a genuine first) was probably the one founded in

1800. It grew up when a kindly young professor, Dr. George Birkbeck, of the Andersonian University in Glasgow found that he was wasting his time. The stories about this vary in their details, but it is evident that he either had to assemble his own set of scientific instruments or else had to have them repaired. As the story was retold in a well known weekly for London workmen, the *Mechanic's Magazine*, he was forced to supervise the manufacture of the set. That necessitated his going in turn to the smith, the glassblower, the carpenter, and the rest, for the various steps in construction. To each man he had to explain how he wanted everything done. This was the more tedious for Birkbeck since all the necessary information could have been available to anyone attending his lectures at the Andersonian University. The workmen in fact told him 'how glad they should be, could they too have lectures delivered to them.' As a result Birkbeck admitted a few of the most intelligent but there were many others for whom there was no room. He thereupon announced a new class in the 1800–1801 Andersonian equivalent of today's college catalogue. 'I shall deliver a series of lectures,' he said in describing the course, 'upon the *mechanical properties of solid and fluid bodies,* abounding with experiments, and conducted with the greatest simplicity of expression and familiarity of illustration, solely for persons engaged in the practical exercise of the mechanic arts.'

In that sentence he summed up what was to become the principal intention of the British mechanics' institute movement.

Birkbeck's classes soon established themselves as a highly successful department of the Andersonian University. By 1804, however, he apparently decided to redirect his career. He ended his few years of teaching and moved to London to practice medicine. Yet he did not forget his old interests. He helped in 1809 to set up the London Institution for the Diffusion of Science, Literature, and the Arts. At least twice, in 1820 and 1823, he delivered a course of lectures. The first time he spoke on natural and experimental philosophy, the second time upon the atmosphere. Early in 1823 some mechanics who had split off from the Andersonian classes formed the Glasgow Mechanics' Institution and asked Birkbeck to become the patron. He agreed and so had a share in starting this school too.

A fresh call to action came in London when the *Mechanic's Magazine* carried a proposal, in the issue for the week of 11 October 1823, for starting a London mechanics' institute modeled on the Glasgow society Birkbeck had sponsored. Anyone interested was asked to leave his name and address with the publishers of the magazine. Birkbeck himself was the first to respond. The entire issue of the periodical for 15 November was given over by the editor to an account of the public meeting that followed the announcement. For the meeting the planners engaged the 'large room of the Crown and Anchor Tavern,' one of the biggest in the city; and it was filled. More than 2000 mechanics were present, along with a sprinkling of civic-minded gentlemen.

Dr. Birkbeck, characterized by the editor of the *Mechanic's Magazine* as the 'first and best friend' of the British mechanic, was called to the chair. He made a short address outlining his Glasgow experience and the good that came of it. He praised the mechanics who had studied under him during his three seasons of lecturing there and then ended with an appeal that Gray's 'Elegy' (which he mildly misquoted) should never again tell the truth when it said: 'But knowledge to their eyes her ample page, Rich with the spoils of time, did ne'er unfold.' He sat down amid applause and then actual organization began. The London Mechanics' Institution needed no further impetus to embark on its long, useful career.

The amiable doctor was the first leader to be acquired by the British mechanics' institute movement. The second was one of the liveliest political figures in the British life at the time, Henry Brougham. He and Birkbeck had been classmates at college in Edinburgh, and a generation later when Birkbeck was chosen to lead the London mechanics' society just mentioned, Lord Brougham became one of the first trustees. Gaunt, sarcastic, and egotistical, with a long, forward-thrusting nose, Brougham made his brilliant way into law and politics after his Edinburgh days and finally emerged as Lord Chancellor. His reputation as a powerful though flamboyant advocate spread through the United Kingdom. He enjoyed a colorful career in Parliament. Popular causes consistently won his support; and in the course of time

Brougham found himself to be a symbol in his native land, in America, and on the continent of Europe, of the fight against caste and special privilege. Popular education was especially dear to him, and the people knew it.

The early progress of the mechanics' institutions is surveyed in a speech Brougham made in 1824. Dedicated to Birkbeck when published, it is entitled 'Practical Observations upon the Education of the People.' The word 'Practical' is worth keeping in mind, for it represented the keynote of the movement. Among other things, Brougham gives a picture of Birkbeck's London institution. By the time Brougham prepared his speech, 1000 workmen were enrolled at twenty shillings a head. Courses of lectures on mechanics, chemistry, geometry, hydrostatics (by Birkbeck himself), the application of chemistry to the arts, astronomy, electricity, and, surprisingly, on the French language were offered the very first year. And a lecture room, books, and scientific 'apparatus' —a term we shall see again and again in the records of the early American lyceums—were being procured.

Brougham precedes his account of the mechanics' movement with an emphatic brief in its favor. After suggesting just how book clubs and other devices to help workmen learn by reading can be put into operation, he turns to lecturing. The instituting of 'lectures is, of all the helps that can be given, the most valuable, where circumstances permit; that is, in towns of a certain size.' He goes on, 'Much may thus be taught, even without any other instruction; but, combined with reading, and subservient to it, the effects of public lectures are great indeed.' Lectures include experiments and demonstrations. They are therefore visual as well as audible. The fields that lend themselves best to such a mode of instruction are 'mechanical philosophy' and chemistry.

He also makes two recommendations of particular importance. One is that the workingmen rather than the gentry should pay the running expenses; the other, that the workingmen should have control over the institutes. Either they would be democratically controlled, Brougham was convinced, or they would die.

Thus the British movement began and expanded. By 1826 it had taken root in France too. Here the British influence is clear, for we know that the French nobleman, Baron Charles Dupin, who was to lead the movement in his own country, became enthusiastic because of his visits to the Glasgow and London societies. On his return to France he vigorously and successfully undertook the task of adapting the British institutes to French needs. The best summary of Dupin's achievement can be found in the preface to the English adaptation of his *Mathematics Practically Applied* which Birkbeck personally prepared. From it we know that Dupin was able to submit a report to his government proclaiming that there were by the fall of 1826 classes for workingmen in La Rochelle (380 students), Nevers (200 students), and elsewhere; and centers were about to be set up in Lyons, Metz, and Versailles, among other places. By December Dupin could write with elation that, thanks to the help of government officials, ninety-eight towns were 'endeavoring to rival each other in their zeal for imparting the new instruction to the working classes.'

The method of government sponsorship was not the way the institution took in the United States, however. Of that we are sure. But when it comes to describing how the idea moved across the ocean from Britain to this country, we are on less certain ground.

Nevertheless, we do know that in most respects the first American lyceums conformed to the British pattern. For both countries the main purpose of the movement originally was to provide practical scientific instruction for workmen, and to have as a result a more intelligent worker as well as a better product. The main methods were the use of lecture-demonstration courses organized by public-spirited citizens and the assembling of local libraries of technical books. And the main financial support was by an initial contribution and thereafter by course fees.

The American movement followed closely after the British one. The London Mechanics' Institution opened in January 1824. The first American lyceum was started late in 1826. Actually, just about enough time elapsed for the British idea to be disseminated through the Isles and for alert Americans to read and hear about it and to adapt it to their own purposes. Everyone realizes that there is nothing new in a group of persons gathering together and listening to educational lectures. But when those gatherings follow the same general plan and when they multiply far beyond their original number, then a social institution is in the making. So it was with the British mechanics' institutes; so it was to be with the American lyceum system.

One other similarity should be mentioned. That is the fact that the top leadership was restricted to one or two individuals. In Britain the movement had defined itself under the guidance of Dr. Birkbeck and Lord Brougham, and in France, Baron Dupin. In America the movement received its driving impetus not from many persons but from one, a man named Josiah Holbrook.

The circumstances in Holbrook's life before 1826 which prepared him for the highly important part he was to play are not difficult to determine, in spite of the fact that there is no reliable account of his early life. We know that Holbrook was born in 1788 and that his upbringing was that of a prosperous Connecticut farmer's son. He entered Yale College in 1806, at the age of eighteen. A student older than most, his academic record was good but not exceptional. What stayed in his classmates' memory was his intense interest in science. During his last two years at Yale he served as a laboratory assistant for the college's finest scientist, Benjamin Silliman, professor of chemistry and mineralogy. Keen-eyed, leonine, Silliman was a noteworthy figure. A pioneer in making a place for the sciences in America, he taught at Yale for many years, lectured widely especially after the lyceum system was developed by his onetime assistant, and established and edited the first American scientific periodical. 'Silliman's Journal' was, in fact, the popular name for the *American Journal of Science*. Incidentally, a good many of the articles that he printed in his magazine dealt with applied rather than pure science. Working for a person such as Silliman, young Josiah was exposed to fruitful influences.

After graduation he farmed a little but disliked it and spent hours in learning about Connecticut minerals and becoming a well informed geologist. He went back to Yale when he could to hear Silliman lecture. He started one manual labor school, which he seems to have run badly, but he later founded another which— in its combination of labor and simple scientific learning—was a true ancestor of the lyceum seminary. And for several years before he led the lyceum movement, he gave scientific lectures in New England villages and towns.

He gave up his second school in the fall of 1825 and then, as his son Alfred later said in his *Reminiscences,* 'commenced his career, the establishing of lyceums.'

We have no record of the immediate events or impulses that moved Holbrook to undertake his mission, just as we cannot find any exact chain of events to connect the first American lyceums with their British predecessors.

There were of course many ways in which news could travel. American newspapers carried intelligence about European developments, and we can be sure that at least a few American newspapers reported on the mechanics' institutes as these started to flourish abroad. Books were lacking about the new institutes, but there were some tracts and speeches that certainly circulated in this country, the speeches of Brougham being a good example. The best and most probable source, however, was the magazine— and one type of American magazine in particular. It could be characterized as a nineteenth-century combination of *The Reader's Digest* and *Popular Mechanics.* It was like the *Digest* because it drew most of its material from other magazines, though it did not ordinarily condense it. It was like *Popular Mechanics* in its subject matter. In England there were by 1825, when Holbrook's seminary disbanded, several such publications. By the same year there was at least one American imitator, with several more to come.

The first English periodical for mechanics was the *Mechanic's Magazine.* Its first number is dated 30 August 1823, and the volume in which it is bound is prefaced by Dr. Birkbeck's enthusiastic praise of the weekly as 'the most valuable gift which the hand of science has yet offered to the artisan.' It contains many references to mechanics' institutes and especially to the one in London. The drawings and diagrams are numerous, and the over-all scope is wide. The lead article, for instance, for the issue of 7 February 1824 is 'Improvement on the Common Lathe.' Then come such items as 'On the Combination Law' (which was aimed at unions of workingmen), 'Hunt's Roasted Corn,' 'Reply to "The Salt-Herring Eater"' (Dutch herring tastes better than English!), 'George's Clock-Wakener and Lighter,' and 'Answers to Inquiries' and 'Inquiries.' The final section is a catchall of 'Discoveries and Improvements.'

In February 1825 the initial American version of the magazine for mechanics came out. The opening number was called the *Mechanics' Magazine* too, but by the fourth number the word *American* had been prefixed. The preface to Volume I was frank in assuring the readers that the original intention had been to copy the noted English periodical. However, that *Mechanics' Magazine* was found to contain too much London matter the preface explained, and so the plan was changed. The editors decided instead to write some of their own material, they added blandly, but soon took the curse off this decision by appropriating 'selections from other journals of a somewhat similar character.'

A glance at the contents of any issue during the first year shows that the *American Mechanics' Magazine* trod hard on the heels of its English progenitors. However, in February 1826 it was transformed into a new and considerably different periodical, the *Franklin Journal and American Mechanics' Magazine*. Dr. Thomas Jones, who had founded but not previously edited the magazine, now took over the active direction, acquired a patron for the journal, and changed its policies. The patron was the Franklin Institute of Philadelphia. Established two years earlier, it represented an attempt by a group of Philadelphians to foster scientific education particularly among those unable to pay for it. The reorganized magazine began immediately to abandon the practical applications of science in favor of academic learning. Soon topics such as 'Specific Gravity' and 'Mechanical Jurisprudence' stretched out through several issues.

The manifesto of the American lyceum system appeared in October 1826. Josiah Holbrook, now thirty-eight and in his prime, composed it. That he might have sent it to the *Franklin Journal* had its sphere of interest stayed the same is not improbable. However, he submitted it to a new periodical in a different field, the *American Journal of Education*, which appeared in January 1826. In its initial years it was guided by the alert, high-minded William Russell, who had been born and brought up in Glasgow. Almost as soon as the *American Journal of Education* made itself known, in its third number in fact, Russell published a substantial article on British mechanics' institutes. Actually, Russell's 'Address' to the reader in the first number of the magazine demonstrated his sympathy with the institutes. He told his readers he foresaw stirring times for public education. Interest was, he felt, already aroused. He sensed the wide implications of the institute movement. 'In this era of great and rapid revolutions in society, nothing has yet appeared which seems likely to be attended with more extensive and lasting effects than the formation of mechanics' institutions. . . . We shall endeavor to make our pages the vehicle of information on this interesting subject'; and he did. Later in the address he talked briefly about the nature of his audience, making it clear by what he said that here was another way in which his periodical would be the proper place for Holbrook's kind of community-wide and society-wide proposal. 'We have no intention,' Russell asserted, 'of furnishing a work for the use of teachers exclusively. . . . Our wish is to benefit the WHOLE COMMUNITY.'

Holbrook's article must have pleased Russell. He seems to have accepted it promptly though he failed to find space for it right away. It occupied about three pages when it came out in the October number and was not signed. Russell's headnote identified the unnamed author merely as 'an individual whose attention has been long and peculiarly directed to the subject on which he writes, and who has contributed extensive and efficient service to associations modeled on a plan similar to that which is now presented to our readers.'

What followed was no great literary or political document. Its immediate perceptible results were small, yet it laid down the lines of direction which the entire movement followed during its opening years. Reinforced later both by Holbrook's printed propaganda and his magnetic personal appeals as he toured the country, it proved eminently satisfactory as a plan for many and diverse communities.

'I take the liberty,' wrote Holbrook, 'to submit for your consideration a few articles as regulations for associations for mutual instruction in the sciences, and in useful knowledge generally. . . . It seems to me that if associations . . . could once be started in our villages, and upon a general plan, they would increase with great rapidity, and do more for the general diffusion of know-

ledge, and for raising the moral and intellectual taste of our
countrymen, than any other expedient which can possibly be devised. And it may be questioned if there is any other way to check
the progress of that monster, intemperance, which is making such
havoc with talents, morals, and everything that raises man above
the brute, but by presenting some object of sufficient interest to
divert the attention of the young from places and practices which
lead to dissipation and to ruin. . . .'

His 'Society for Mutual Education' had two objectives. Surprisingly enough, he was more than a little hazy about their scope
and so the two aims overlapped. The first one, furthermore, turned
out to be double itself. It was 'to procure for youths an economical
and practical education, and to diffuse rational and useful information through the community generally.' He wished to educate both young men and the rest of the people, putting the
young men first, but there was a degree of difference in what he
wanted them to be taught. And that difference forecast the changing emphasis that would be found when the lyceum movement
took root, for it would start as practical instruction for the young
apprentices or clerks but would gradually become general instruction for the entire town.

Holbrook's second major objective was 'to apply the sciences
and the various branches of education to the domestic and useful
arts, and to all the common purposes of life.' He said nothing more
about who was to be taught, but when he came to what was to
be taught, he placed science first. This priority appears again in
Holbrook's recommendation on the purpose of the society's meetings: 'mutual instruction in the sciences . . . or any other branch
of useful knowledge.' And he is specific in naming the branches
of science ('mechanics, hydrostatics, pneumatics, chemistry, mineralogy, botany') while lumping all other branches of knowledge
together.

Having suggested who and what were to be taught, Holbrook
went on to explain the means to be employed. He first mentioned
lectures but opened the door for other methods such as demonstration or discussion too—'regular courses of instruction by lectures
or otherwise' was his phrase. He recommended the purchase by
the society of 'books, apparatus for illustrating the sciences, a

cabinet of minerals, and other articles,' the money for these teaching aids to come from dues. Holbrook proposed the moderate sum of a dollar a year, with the stipulation that the payment of ten dollars in a lump sum would make anyone a life member.

The officers he suggested the society elect were the customary ones except for five curators. These curators turned out to be quite important because besides caring for the society's educational property they became the persons who chose the lecturers.

Lastly, Holbrook set his hand to creating a hierarchy of lyceums (though he did not use the word *lyceum* yet). He began with the local society for mutual instruction by proposing that it elect three delegates to represent it at a county lyceum and become part of its board. Each county board in turn was to appoint one member to the state 'Board of Mutual Education.' Then Holbrook took his longest leap and suggested that it might be an advantage 'to have also a General Board embracing the United States.'

'The present, then, is the moment for making an effort to propagate the system,' Lord Brougham had advised in his 'Practical Observations.' Holbrook did just that. His lecture tours had already showed him places where the salient opportunities for a lyceum existed. It was plain that Worcester County, Massachusetts, was one of them. He evidently preferred to start there instead of in his own neighborhood in Connecticut. For one thing, Worcester County already had some organizations, such as the Worcester Lyceum of Natural History, which might be converted into his kind of lyceum (though this Worcester Lyceum did not join him after all). Then too, Worcester included both manufacturing and agriculture among its economic activities, and so amply furnished Holbrook with the required mechanics and farmers. In Worcester County lay the community of Millbury; there, a month after his proposal was published in the *American Journal of Education*, he started Millbury Branch Number 1 of the American Lyceum.

Millbury's skilled workmen made their living in a number of small factories that produced guns, broadcloth, harness leather, ammunition, morocco linings, and iron bars and plates. Before a gathering of about forty of these men plus some neighboring farmers Holbrook laid his plan one evening early in November.

The result was historical—for they organized themselves, with his guidance, into the first of thousands of lyceums.

This fruitful meeting no doubt spurred Holbrook on, since he swiftly set about organizing other lyceums in the neighboring towns. By 22 November the Worcester *National Aegis* could report that 'Mr. Holbrook, an intelligent and interesting lecturer on different scientific subjects, has established in many of the towns in our county, associations for mutual instruction and information in the arts and sciences. One of these associations is to be established in each town.' The newspaper described the members as young men from the various classes of society, though mostly consisting of mechanics. The dues were set at one dollar, 'a trifling sum,' which would go for the purchase of books and apparatus to illustrate the sciences. All that the young mechanics needed, the *Aegis* felt, was the opportunity for instruction. They would surely avail themselves of it. In concluding its half-column the paper endorsed the lyceum as a rehabilitator, 'a powerful influence in effecting a reformation in . . . morals.'

The movement took hold readily. On 26 January delegates from lyceums in Brookfield, Holden, Leicester, Millbury, Oxford, Rutland, Shrewsbury, and Southbridge met in Leicester. A high proportion of ministers and doctors rather than young workingmen appear among the delegates listed. The Honorable Nathaniel P. Denny, a respected lawyer and politician, was elected chairman of the session. The delegates reported on how their lyceums were getting along and then resolved to form a county board, the first county lyceum in fact if not in name. Very probably Holbrook sat in on the meeting, for when a committee was chosen to draft a county board constitution he was named to it. The *Aegis* printed the constitution. Its first article christens the organization the 'Board of Delegates of the American Lyceum of Science and the Arts, for the County of Worcester,' while a following one states that the aim shall be the 'improvement of intellectual and practical education.' The meeting did not dissolve without voting that 'the thanks of this Board be tendered to Mr. Josiah Holbrook for his assistance at the organization of it, and for his able and successful efforts in establishing the several lyceums which we represent.'

Although the county buzzed with lyceum activities, the County

Lyceum itself did little—thus setting the pattern for later county lyceums! Its inaction was understandable, though, since it performed only as a supplement to the local lyceums. Its next session was not held until 3 October 1827 at Shrewsbury. The notice appeared in the *Massachusetts Spy* as well as the *Aegis*, in sober contrast to the advertisements, on the reverse of the *Aegis'* page, for aromatic snuff, Cobb's Spelling Book, military goods, and assorted merchandise. The Worcester County Lyceum managed to continue for several years. Holbrook attended the October 1829 meeting. There he showed several maps and announced that he was going to give one to each lyceum in the county. His efforts were aided by the main speaker at the meeting, an eloquent young Worcester lawyer named Emory Washburn, who later developed one of the best legal minds of the century. He talked on education, and in addition there was a free discussion specifically on the 'common-school' system. A history of Worcester remarks that 'prominent citizens from various parts of the county' went to the gathering. But if there were any leather-aproned artisans present or farmers with dirt on their shoes, it fails to say so.

Reversing the suggested procedure, Worcester members of the County Lyceum met the next month to form the town lyceum. It started with about half a hundred members. In 1830 there were 276 members; in 1831, 126 (the novelty had worn off); in 1832, 191; in 1833, 171, in 1834, 181; and in 1835, 190. In their ups and downs these membership figures represent not only the career of Worcester's lyceum but also the course many another lyceum was to follow.

Such were the first steps, with Holbrook's guidance, that the lyceum movement took in the United States. Profiting from the cultural milieu of eastern Massachusetts, the lyceum idea expanded still further. Urged on by Holbrook and his new supporters, it was only a matter of time until it reached the intellectual center of the state, Boston.

'An institution is the lengthened shadow of a man,' once wrote the most venerated lyceum lecturer of them all. It was close to being true for the lyceum. There is no doubt that the one man to whom the greatest credit should go for beginning and guiding the lyceum system was Holbrook. He looks like a fanatic in his pictures. Lips compressed and brows bent, he stares sternly at the beholder. What fails to show is Holbrook's deep humanity. William Russell, who became his trusted friend, composed the vignette of him printed in Barnard's *American Journal of Education.* After remarking that Holbrook often experimented with metals 'in the blacksmith shop,' Russell continues: 'On one occasion, the writer of this communication met him issuing from such a scene in the streets of Brooklyn—his working-coat both shabby with age and badly torn; his face begrimed with smoke and soot, and his hands in the same condition; but his eye gleaming, from under its heavy, massive eyebrow, with delight at the result of his operation, and his whole soul buoyant. . . . As he left the ferry for his office, he pursued his way along Broadway, utterly unconscious of the state of his outward man, but evidently in an inward "glory and a joy" as deep-felt as that of the peasant-poet in his raptures of inspiration.'

Once the lyceums began to spread in Worcester County, Holbrook's idea was planted elsewhere. He himself soon moved to Windham County in Connecticut, where he seems to have proceeded with his evangelism. But no one locality could contain him for long; we have concurrent records of his appearances elsewhere in New England.

On Friday evening, 7 November 1828, the first organizing meeting in Boston was held. It took place at the Exchange Coffee House, with the great Daniel Webster taking the chair. At the meeting Holbrook explained exactly how lyceums had been started in Massachusetts and the neighboring states and extolled 'the good effects which had already been produced by them.' He added that their immediate result had 'uniformly been to awaken a spirit of inquiry among all classes of the community' about practical science in particular.

Then a set of resolutions—Editor Russell had devised them earlier—was read and adopted. Among them, one expressed interest in organizations for popular improvement, including mechanics' institutions, while another applauded the American Lyceum as the general association for such popular improvement and for the advancement of public education. A third recommended the formation of a committee to outline the best ways of promoting the lyceum idea. Appointed to the committee were G. B. Emerson, a busy, stern-eyed Boston educator; Russell; and Holbrook.

Two weeks later, the committee reported and urged the establishment of a lyceum for Boston. At once the city showed interest. The newspapers, with the *Columbian Centinel* in the lead, swelled the already considerable public support. The founding of the Boston Society for the Diffusion of Useful Knowledge was the result. It adopted a constitution during the winter of 1828–9 which made the education of young men the paramount objective. The dangerous age was from seventeen on, 'when the mind is active and the passions urgent,' the framers of the constitution felt; and so they proposed to channel those energies properly through 'lectures and other means.' The Society swiftly prospered and soon attracted other groups besides the frisky young by presenting lecture courses with a general appeal.

The first series was so over-subscribed that after each lecture the managers had to ask that it be repeated the next night. All lectures were read in the hall of the Boston Athenaeum; the charge for the course was two dollars for adults, one dollar for minors. For the season of 1829–30 exceptionally distinguished lecturers were announced, headed by Daniel Webster.

A project of more importance for the state of Massachusetts than for Boston alone had meanwhile been described in the *Centinel,* and elsewhere, earlier in 1829. The issue of 21 March gave front-page prominence to a meeting in the State House whose aim was to promote the American Lyceum. Members of the Massachusetts legislature 'and others' attended. The news story reported the framing of a questionnaire designed to reach officers of lyceums already in existence, ministers, school committeemen, and any other friends of popular education.

Is there a lyceum in your town or village (and if not, will one be started)? Has your lyceum any lectures? Has it a library? What is the state of the public schools in your locality? Those were the questions the circular asked. The effect of the circular cannot be gauged precisely, but it received wide publicity in Massachusetts and no doubt spurred other communities to form lyceums.

In Connecticut the *Windham County Advertiser* described the multiplying lyceums enthusiastically. 'Almost every mail brings intelligence of the formation of one or more of these noble institutions,' it announced. 'We doubt not,' the paper added, 'that at no distant day lyceums will be established in every section of the country, and that they will constitute the chiefest resort for amusement and knowledge among all ranks.'

2

The Gospel of the Lyceum

A S the 1820s neared their close the lyceum system had taken its definite form. Mutual improvement at the grass-roots level, especially by means of lectures, was already the aim of branches of the American lyceum set up in almost a hundred New England communities. Massachusetts was leading the way, but according to the *American Journal of Education* early in 1829, Connecticut, New Hampshire, Vermont, and Maine each had some lyceums. Several county lyceums were meeting, usually twice a year; and although no state lyceums had met so far, there was at least in Massachusetts a statewide committee. The lyceum was already demonstrating its public acceptance as an educator in New England and was soon to spread its gospel through many other parts of the country.

In this country a student of the colonial period will, a few times at least, come across an organization of some kind that called itself a lyceum. In the Federal period there were others. The Lycaeum of Delaware, for instance, was meeting twice a month early in 1798. Mississippi's Society for the Acquirement and Dissemination of Useful Knowledge received its charter in 1803. New York City's Lyceum of Natural History opened in 1817; Detroit's Lyceum began in 1818. The Wolfeboro, New Hampshire, Lyceum came in 1820 and the lively Athenaeum of Natchez, Mississippi, in 1821. The New York Mechanic and Scientific Institution, which was to be cited as an example to encourage the organizing of the London Mechanics' Institution, was incorporated in 1822. Indeed, societies like these can be traced right down to the day of the notable meeting at Millbury. Most of them, however, only faintly foreshadowed the lyceum as we have defined it.

A few did more than that. One of the best examples is the Maryland Institute in Baltimore. A leading citizen, John Latrobe, assumed most of the burden of organizing it. By January of 1826 the Institute, having leased the Concert Hall and changed its name to the Mechanics' Hall, was ready for action. The Baltimore *American* printed the opening lecture in full. It was given by W. H. Freeman; he reminded his audience that the primary aim of the Institute was the promotion of the mechanic arts. The intentions in particular, said Freeman, were to 'form an extensive library, to collect cabinets of minerals and models, to procure philosophical and chemical apparatus, and to establish professorships in the several branches of science.' Moreover, lectures were to be given on all useful branches of learning, a drawing academy formed, and annual exhibitions held at which awards and premiums were to be offered. The lectures went haltingly at first. 'We wanted to get up a course,' Latrobe said, 'but it was heavy work. I contributed two on the law of apprentices which put, I think, a large part of my audience to sleep.' The next season, though, the lectures went much better. After that the Institute had its vicissitudes but kept up nevertheless, and made a definite contribution to the lyceum movement in the Baltimore area. Elsewhere a few other societies either anticipated or paralleled parts of Holbrook's plan.

But what did not exist before the time of Holbrook's efforts was the lyceum as a social institution, the lyceum as in fact a crusade. In 1829 an eager Boston schoolmaster wrote a note to his brother. It was Clement Durgin, co-principal of the Chauncey Hall School; and he made this request of his brother, who taught at Sanbornton Bridge, New Hampshire: 'Please to ask Capt. Clark or Esq. Clark or Esq. Clement if they know anything about little societies that are forming in various parts of the country called lyceums. If they have a desire to know anything of them? If they want information I will with pleasure furnish it. They are associations for mutual improvement in the sciences and may be made productive of great good.' Few were writing with Durgin's enthusiasm before the advent of Millbury Number 1.

Every leaflet that did more than outline the mechanical arrange-

ment of a lyceum said something about the benefits of the institution. Holbrook swelled the pages of his propaganda pamphlets by
expatiating on the lyceum's advantages. At many lyceums the very
first of the lectures scheduled was on the advantages of the lyceum. Many more lyceums, once set up, included in their annual
courses the same sort of lecture. New Bedford, Massachusetts, for
instance, heard Thomas Greene's 'Address Delivered before the
Members . . . at Their First Meeting, December 18, 1828.' His
address presents a characteristic appeal.

Young Greene foresees many good things coming out of the
establishment of the New Bedford Lyceum. A richly rewarding
exchange of knowledge is the primary one. Every member is an
authority on something, and the rest can learn from him. The
physical facilities for learning will be furnished by the Lyceum;
they should include scientific apparatus and a cabinet of specimens
to be used in studying natural history. Over and above such items,
the teaching facilities should be the community itself and so
should lead to a better understanding of New Bedford. Greene
points out the kinds of subjects that could be studied most ad-
vantageously in this sea-going town, the theory of naval architec-
ture and the improvement of navigation among them. But the
greatest advantages are moral and fraternal rather than intellectual. Through its constructive activities the Lyceum will improve
the behavior of the young people of the community and they will
no longer fall into looseness. And everyone will learn to know his
fellow townsmen better and therefore esteem them more. Greene
strikes the note of brotherhood strongly, making it the climax of his
address. 'From all the divisions, ranks and classes of society, we
are to meet . . . to instruct and to be instructed. While we mingle
together in these pursuits . . . we shall remove many of the preju-
dices which ignorance or partial acquaintance with each other
fostered.'

Newspaper editorials were often equally explicit about the advantages of lyceums. So of course were the formal statements,
carried in many papers and a few magazines, of committees which
wanted to promote the lyceum idea. Russell's *American Journal of
Education* made up for the indifference of some other magazines

by the vigor of its interest. It not only printed articles of its own on the lyceum, it also reprinted scores of newspaper reports.

As an instance, under the heading 'Popular Improvement' Russell helpfully published four pieces on the lyceum idea in his August 1828 issue. One came from a correspondent of the *American Journal*, another was excerpted from a piece of propaganda of Holbrook's, and the other two were clipped from the *Richmond Visitor and Telegraph* and the Boston *Recorder*. The clipping from the *Recorder* dealt especially with the benefits of the lyceum as a social institution. Lyceums will furnish young people 'with places of resort where they can cultivate, not only their social, but their intellectual and moral faculties; where their social intercourse and amusements shall be turned in such a channel as to refine their feelings, enlighten, elevate, and dignify their minds, and soften and purify their hearts.'

So it was that in Russell's magazine, in newspapers, in leaflets and circulars, the briefs for the lyceum and statements of its benefits were widely circulated. But though they came from many different hands, their arguments were much the same. And all of them were those that Holbrook himself was using. He foresaw every advantage that could be claimed for the lyceum and he advertised them without exception.

Consequently, the archetype of all published material was the Holbrook leaflet. It became the gospel of the lyceum in print. Holbrook propagated it as vigorously as he knew how. Time passed, and his publications grew fuller as his leadership in the thriving movement allowed him to add chapter and verse to his earlier generalizations. He expanded his persuasive briefs in two ways, first, by adding details about the hierarchy of lyceums and second, by inserting a good deal of additional matter on the advantages of the lyceum.

His first proposal in print was the one which the *American Journal of Education* ran in October 1826. There it occupied a little less than three pages. The next publication, and the first in leaflet form, is dated November of the same year. It had a new and longer title: *American Lyceum of Science and the Arts, Composed of Associations for Mutual Instruction and Designed for the General*

Diffusion of Useful and Practical Knowledge. It had at least two, and probably more, issues.

This leaflet was aimed at the community level. On the first page there is a blank for the name of the local branch of the American Lyceum, with the suggested constitution printed next. After the mechanics of starting a lyceum have been explained, some of the advantages are described under the rather neutral title of 'Considerations.' Six are suggested there: (1) that lyceums can diffuse education 'more generally,' (2) that the information lyceums diffuse is practical, (3) that lyceums have a 'good moral tendency,' (4) that lyceums have 'good political tendency'—that is, they provide an educated electorate who will defeat the demagogues, (5) that lyceums are economical, and (6) that they will aid in the improvement of the common schools.

In its number for December 1828 the *American Journal* printed a seven-page article which was headed 'American Lyceum' and embraced 'the substance of several statements submitted to the meeting recently held in Boston,' for considering the lyceum. The article is another and considerably different list of the advantages of the lyceum—but they are Holbrook's too. Now seven instead of six are named: (1) the improvement of 'infant schools,' (2) the improvement of 'common district schools,' (3) the improvement of academies, (4) the establishment or support of 'seminaries and in particular of a central lyceum or lyceum school,' (5) the encouragement of libraries, (6) the stimulation of geological and agricultural surveys, and (7) the stimulation of the writing of town histories.

A new, expanded edition of the leaflet appeared as the year 1829 began. Another followed, and then others. It was now the *American Lyceum, or Society for the Improvement of Schools and Diffusion of Useful Knowledge.*

These fast-multiplying editions betokened the vigor of the lyceum; it had clearly caught the people's interest. Perhaps the most widely circulated and most influential form of the catalogue of advantages and aims was the one included in the first 1829 edition of Holbrook's pamphlet. These, in Holbrook's own words, are the things lyceums are designed to bring about:

1. *The Improvement of Conversation.* An immediate and uniform effect of a lyceum . . . is the introduction of good topics of conversaton into the daily intercourse of families, neighbors and friends. . . . Subjects of science, or other topics of useful knowledge, take the place of frivolous conversation, or petty scandal, frequently indulged, and uniformly deplored, in our country villages. . . .

2. *Directing Amusements.* Few subjects are more important, and none, perhaps, so much neglected, as amusements. Young people always have had, and it is believed and hoped they always will have, places of resort for social enjoyment. From the neglect of parents, and other persons of influence, to furnish them with occasions and opportunities to meet for exercises calculated for the instruction and improvement of each other, as well as for the enjoyment of social affections of a generous and elevated character, they resort to those calculated to corrupt and debase their minds, while they afford them no pleasures, but those of the most groveling character. Instead of having placed before them at their meetings, books, apparatus, minerals, plants, and other objects calculated to acquaint them with the works and the laws of their Creator . . . they are presented with shelves of loaded decanters and sparkling glasses, so richly filled, and so neatly arranged, and for *their* enjoyment too, that to neglect them would be vulgar and unmanly. . . .

3. *Saving of Expense.* No principle in political economy is better established by experience than that a liberal support of religious and literary institutions is calculated to promote the pecuniary as well as the intellectual and moral prosperity of the community. . . . The expense of a year's entertainment and instruction at the meetings and the exercises of a lyceum is from fifty cents to two dollars. The expense of one quarter's instruction in a dancing school, including extra clothes, pocket money, &c. cannot be estimated at less than ten dollars for each pupil. . . . Many young men have paid two dollars for a horse and chaise to ride upon the Sabbath, with too manly a spirit to mention it as an expense, who would be ready to confess themselves too poor to pay the same sum for a weekly course of the most useful instruction, through the year. . . .

4. *Calling into Use Neglected Libraries and Giving Occasion for Establishing New Ones.* It has been a subject of general regret that public libraries, after a short time, fall into neglect and disuse. Where a course of weekly, or other stated exercises, has been carried on in connection, or in the vicinity of a library, an occasion for this regret has never been known to exist. . . .

5. *Providing a Seminary for Teachers.* In the United States more than 50,000 daily teachers, and from 150 to 200,000 weekly teachers of Sabbath schools, are engaged in forming the character of the rising generation and molding the destiny of our nation. Raising the qualifications of this responsible and important class of the community is an object of such vast moment to the prosperity of our country that for several years past it has been the frequent theme of conversation, addresses, sermons, and messages and speeches to legislatures. . . .

6. *Benefiting Academies.* Many academies, young ladies' seminaries, and other institutions of a similar character, have been greatly benefited by the exercises of lyceums. . . .

7. *Increasing the Advantages and Raising the Character of District Schools.* Public schools have been benefited, not only by the facilities offered by lyceums for the improvement of their teachers, but by the opportunities they present directly to some of the eldest members of these schools, to receive a course of weekly instruction, of a higher character, and under better advantages, than can be given among the promiscuous assemblage of children and the great variety of objects which these schools usually embrace. . . .

8. *Compiling of Town Histories.* Several lyceums have undertaken to procure histories of the towns where they are placed. In almost every town there remain a few of those patriots who purchased at so dear a rate the independence we now enjoy. And it would, perhaps, be difficult to determine to whom it would afford the purest and richest entertainment, to themselves in relating the tales of their wrongs, their battles, and their successes, or to their children and grandchildren, in listening to them. . . .

9. *Town Maps.* A few lyceums are taking measures to procure maps of their towns. . . . After a survey and draft are made, it is ascertained from artists, that 200 lithographic prints can be procured for twenty-five dollars. And what family would not be willing to pay 12½ cents for a correct map of the town where they reside?

10. *Agricultural and Geological Surveys.* Many lyceums have explored, thoroughly and minutely, the mineral productions not only of the towns where they are placed but of the surrounding country. . . . And when it is considered that the geology and mineralogy of our country are intimately connected with agriculture and internal improvements, the importance of having them fully and minutely explored must appear too great and too manifest to require one word to explain or enforce it. . . .

11. *State Collections of Minerals.* Some of the states have com-menced collections of minerals deposited in their capitols. When towns or counties are making surveys and collections for their own use, it will be easy to furnish specimens for a general collection, which might be arranged according to towns or geological divisions. . . . Such col-lections would be useful not only to science but to agriculture and in-ternal improvements, by placing before legislators and others specimens of their own productions and a knowledge of their own resources in the mineral kingdom, by which industry would be encouraged, and individual and public wealth and prosperity increased.

So argued Josiah Holbrook.

3

The Favoring Elements

T HE lyceum could rise as spectacularly as it did because it found a whole new era ready to welcome it, the Age of Jackson. The year that marked its official beginning was 1828, when the hatchet-faced old general won the office of President of the United States. In a few respects the year marking its end has not yet come; in most respects, however, it came in 1840 with the defeat of his lieutenant, Martin Van Buren, for re-election as President. Those factors at work between 1828 and 1840—political, demographic, economic, social, psychological, cultural—are the ones for us to probe.

Politics had a pervasive influence in preparing a climate in which the lyceum could prosper. But this influence was consistently indirect because politics, as a controversial subject, was barred from the lyceum with ostentatious firmness. Again and again it is, like religion, singled out in lyceum constitutions as something to be shunned. The currents of political controversy were diverted, naturally enough, from the lyceum to the debating society. That was the most popular place, especially in the eyes of the young men, for political argument.

Although the lyceum never became a political forum, politics in the broad sense of the democratic revolution—the Age of Jackson—had notable significance for the lyceum movement. As the second quarter of the nineteenth century opened, the mechanic, the clerk, the hired man could look back on a series of remarkable victories. Now he was able to march triumphantly into polling places always barred to him before. Now he could

27

decide issues previously closed to him. By 1828 four of the north-eastern states had thrown out property qualifications for voting. Two of them, Massachusetts and New York, had rewritten their entire constitutions. Virginia would do so the year after Jackson's election. By 1828, moreover, half a dozen western states had been admitted to the Union and each had provisions for voting of the new and liberal kind. In all but one of the states in the nation, presidential electors were by then named directly by the people instead of by the legislatures. Among the New England states only Rhode Island, led by its rich reactionaries, would not bow to the times.

The widened franchise was generally followed by a fresh interest in public education. As long as it was only the people with property who were allowed to vote, the public schools were sure to suffer. The argument that a democracy must educate everyone or else run the risk of mob rule apparently made little impression on those people. Through their early spokesmen such as Fisher Ames and later ones such as Chancellor James Kent they advanced various answers in logical terms to the argument. Beneath the logic lay the feeling, no doubt, that they could do better for themselves by keeping the vote restricted. Their feeling was justified at least in part, for as soon as the poorer people were enfranchised, they were able to vote themselves public schools and tax the richer people for them. The poor, however, did not always act promptly in taking advantage of their newly won opportunities. And small property holders as well as large welcomed this occasional tardiness. The farmer with a few acres was often, if short-sightedly, as hostile to taxation as the hard-bitten New England squire or the southern plantation owner. It took time for some to see that the extended franchise would result in improved public schooling for all classes of American society.

The ultimate triumph of tax-supported public education was just as clear-cut as, and much more lasting than, the political triumph of Jacksonian democracy. But during the time of the lyceum such education suffered many temporary defeats and enjoyed few spectacular successes. Massachusetts education was typical in that respect. In colonial days the ministers led the fight for general literacy because their sermons concentrated on the explication of the Bible and because the daily reading of the Bible was part of the religious fabric. 'It being one chief project of that old deluder, Satan, to keep men from the knowledge of the Scriptures,' said the school ordinance of 1647, every town with fifty or more householders was to appoint—and pay—a teacher to make the children literate. Yet later ordinances, particularly the one in 1789, relaxed that requirement and lowered the standards for public education instead of raising them. And the law of 1789 remained on the books until the beginning of the 1820s.

Throughout the 1820s and even into the 1830s the forces working against free education remained active. Yet the logic of events interfered greatly with their effectiveness. The population of the country swelled, and much of it concentrated in the small towns and cities. The population of Massachusetts increased 41 per cent between 1820 and 1840 but the population of Boston increased 115 per cent. Lowell, prime example of the mill town, had a population of 4000 in 1830 and 10,000 only two years later. These figures are all the more dramatic since New England in general failed to match the over-all population gains of the Middle Atlantic states and the West. It was the rise of manufacturing of course which created towns such as Lowell and which, in turn, helped public education. This was not because most of the manufacturers were particularly civic-minded—they were not—but because, as the history of American education has shown, large numbers of underprivileged people will vote improvements for themselves while small numbers often will not. The public schools have almost always fared better in the city than in the country.

A look at the census of 1840 will underline this point. New England and the Middle Atlantic states had the largest population of people in towns in the entire Union. The three southern New England states had the largest proportion within those two regions. And among those three New England states, Massachusetts had 389,000 people living in towns (53 per cent of the total population). The larger the number of towns, the higher the percentage of children in school—that was the way it generally worked out. New England's proportion of children in school was nearly twice that of the Middle Atlantic states and six times that of the states in the South!

Some factors which helped the public school helped the lyceum. Both institutions rode along on the great democratic wave of the Age of Jackson. And both contributed something to swelling it. The public school and the lyceum helped each other too. Until the 1840s, in fact, when the professional educators lost interest in the lyceum, it enjoyed the assistance of the school teachers as well as many of the friends of public schools. During its formative days it likewise enlisted in its cause many foes of tax-supported education.

It was a curious combination of factors which served to keep the lyceum as educator unscathed. To begin with, the lyceum would not cost much. It would cost nothing at all for those who were not participating, and no taxpayer would be forced to contribute to setting up a lyceum. The price of admission was consistently low, the average for a single season ticket in the early 1830s being $1.50. Family rates were similarly low. The overhead was not a large item as a rule. Hall rent, lights, heat, announcements, and—slowly and grudgingly—a fee for the speaker were the main expenses. Concord, Massachusetts, could run its fine lyceum on about $100 a year (it took a long time for it to climb to $125) and it probably struck the median for that time. Up to 1845 five or ten dollars went to the visiting lecturer, over and above expenses for travel; the over-all average lecture fee for the thirty-five years of the lyceum system was perhaps fifteen dollars.

And the lyceum was harmless. At the very beginning it was designed for artisans and farmers, but since it taught the practical application of science—which would result in better workmen and more efficient farmers—it did not threaten the higher economic groups in the way a political forum would have. Then, as the lyceum programs began to change into those heterogeneous courses of lectures on travel, history, biography, foreign affairs, and the art of living, the audience also changed. The broadened programs came as the result of audience demand. A housewife would never throw on her cloak and leave a warm house to hear about the chemistry of paint, but she would step through snow drifts to hear about 'The Romance of the Sea' or 'The Life and Death of Napoleon Bonaparte.' There was no economic threat to the rich in such topics either.

Both politics and religion unwittingly provided problems for public education. The schools all too often became a party issue in the state legislature or in the county. And the early close connection between religion and education grew uncomfortable long before the rise of the lyceum. Nevertheless, the lyceum was able to obtain advantages from religion as it did from politics. They too were indirect of course; the official ban against religious matters in the lyceum held throughout its existence. But they were, on analysis, of considerable importance.

To take a general point first, the main vehicle for Protestant Christianity at this time as well as later was certainly the sermon rather than the service. The transferring of ideas through a homily was something to which everyone was accustomed. The organization, length, and style of the lyceum lecture closely resembled that of the religious homily. Sometimes in fact, as an observant Massachusetts woman wrote, 'the lecturing was called "Lay Preaching," and the lectures "Lay Sermons." ' No doubt, spoken communication won approval all the more readily if the intention was also moral or at any rate beneficial to the hearer. There could be little objection to a lecture that improved the listener's morals—or, for that matter, his ability in business. After all, one of the salient elements in New England's religious tradition (and New England was the cradle of the lyceum) had been the belief that the good would prosper materially as well as spiritually through the blessings of God.

Furthermore, of all professional men, ministers found the lecture platform the easiest to stand on. The great majority no doubt approved thoroughly of the purposes of the lyceum. Some, like Concord's venerable Dr. Ezra Ripley, took the lead in founding their local lyceum, and many more were glad to give lectures. A survey of lecture notices and programs still available shows that the names of ministers led all the rest. A typical season's course of ten lectures might include five by ministers, with professors and politicians coming next. It was often through the kindness of the minister that the lyceum met in the church basement, in what was later sometimes called the church's lecture room. Many a minister also gave an occasional course of inspirational lectures to his own congregation. The favorite time was Sunday night, the favorite topic, advice to young men. It was a rare minister who felt that he had nothing to say to them. Roorbach in his extensive *Bibliotheca Americana* records the publication of manifold courses which, typically, begin by affirming the literal truth of the Scriptures and conclude by warning earnestly against females of easy virtue.

Such factors helped to gain public approval for the new institution and to protect it from sharp attack. Then too, veteran community leaders generally gained control of their local lyceum. They both protected it and tamed it. Although the typical lyceum was conducted 'democratically,' that is, by majority vote, most of the men elected as officers or curators were of substance and standing in the community. Generally they had prospered in the past, so they thought well of the past and had in addition no desire to alter the present or divert the future. They felt comfortable just as they were. They could be counted on to see that controversial questions were not subjects of lectures or even of debates while they were in control. Occasionally they were defeated but not often. Crusty old Squire John Keyes once moved in the Concord Lyceum that the 'vexed and disorganizing question of abolitionism' should be kept out of the Lyceum's affairs. In the Concord of Emerson and Thoreau the squire's motion lost, but in the vast majority of lyceums it would have passed.

Thus the lyceum was a socially approved institution. Translated into concrete terms, that meant that the townspeople both could and should attend it. If there was ever an American dogma during these decades, it was the desirability of personal improvement. In the first years of the lyceum this did not necessarily mean that public schools should be set up everywhere, and for everybody, out of tax money; rather it carried the idea that improvement, like charity, should begin at home. The mechanic should learn to be a better mechanic, the clerk a better clerk. But as a man went up the social scale the concept of improvement widened; general and cultural information began to assume a more important place. Whatever the individual's social level, the local lyceum offered something during its season which could contribute to the betterment of every one of its members. Therefore it was their obligation to attend. Since flesh is weak, some did not always do so. Those who did, however, knew their going was the proper thing. Had there been many conflicting claims on the audiences' evenings, the lyceum would still have had priority. But there were almost no other claims. Only the largest cities had any number of additional attractions. The theater and the concert were nonexistent throughout most of the country; nighttime was, in terms of public entertainment, a void. The narrow streets were dark. Into this void stepped the lyceum, to the frequently recorded gratitude of the light-minded as well as the more sober folk in the villages.

Although this was still a time that esteemed the spoken word, reading became increasingly popular. Literacy improved. Unfortunately we do not have exact figures for the United States until the census of 1840, but at that time the variation in the literacy rate from region to region was astonishing. In his pioneering *Progress of the United States in Population and Wealth*, written just after this census, George Tucker gives the proportion of illiterates (white and over twenty) in different parts of the country as of 1840. 'If the other divisions be compared with New England, the number who cannot read and write is . . . three and a half times as great in the Middle states; seven times as great in the Northwestern states . . . and nearly fifteen times [as great] in the Southern states.' The census shows that state by state the variation was of course greater still, from a state such as Connecticut where only one person in 574 was illiterate to a state such as North Carolina where one in every nine could neither read or write. Furthermore, the chances are that the variations were even larger before 1840.

After 1840 the government's figures become both fuller and more exact. Then they clearly show the gap in literacy between the sections closing. The South moved up, teaching more of its cotton-clad children every year. New England slipped, not because it began to neglect its white-frame schoolhouses but because of its deluge of illiterate immigrants. But this did not happen until after the lyceum system established itself.

Meanwhile, in the most important regions for the budding lyceum it is safe to conclude that more and more people could read and write. A community that read was not necessarily a community that supported the lyceum, yet the two things as a rule went together. They formed part of the same general cultural context.

Most contemporary accounts, whether well informed or not, agree on the heightened importance of the printed word. People thought that periodicals were especially important. Now they could be seen lying open not only on the mahogany table of the rich merchant but on the pinewood kitchen table of the thrifty farmer or industrious mechanic. As the *American Almanac* for 1834 observed grandly, 'Periodical publications, especially newspapers, disseminate knowledge throughout all classes of society and exert an amazing influence in forming and giving effect to public opinion.' The *American Almanac* had a considerably better record for accuracy than most sources, and this 1834 edition estimated, probably correctly, that the number of newspapers had risen to no less than 1,200. It made no over-all calculation about magazines. Another and also reasonably reliable guide, James Hall's *Western Monthly* for October 1833, maintained that 'There are published in the United States six quarterly publications, two once in two months, twenty-two monthlies, besides very many semi-monthlies, and more than a thousand newspapers.' The magazines were sharply localized. 'Of the forty larger periodicals,' according to the *Western Monthly*, 'twenty are published in New England, sixteen in the Middle states, two in the South, and two in the West.'

The newspapers, naturally, were more evenly distributed. A look at the census of 1840 will again help to give us a perspective. There were by that time 138 daily newspapers, 125 which came out two or three times a week, and 1,141 which appeared once a week. There were, besides, 217 other periodical publications. 'Such a diffusion of intelligence and information has never existed in any other country or age' was George Tucker's patriotic verdict. The newspapers were especially valuable. They reported on lyceum activities and summarized lectures. And they announced lectures much more efficiently than word of mouth could have.

In general the magazines had far fewer ties with the lyceum system than did the newspapers. The main ones were the occasional article on lyceums and the reprinting of a small number of lectures. One struggling little group of magazines, however, tried to make up for all the sins of omission of the rest. They were the educational periodicals, with the *American Journal of Education* and its successor the *American Annals of Education* by far the most notable.

Within this group were magazines of at least two kinds. The first was the one especially concerned with the public schools. The best example is the *Connecticut Common School Journal*, which the able Henry Barnard edited from 1838 on. It conceived of the lyceum simply as an aid to the public elementary school movement. The second was the magazine interested in adult education, in self-education. Most of these magazines proved to be sadly short-lived. The most enthusiastic, and for information on the lyceum proper the richest, among them was Holbrook's own *Family Lyceum*. Typically, it lasted only from July 1832 to August 1833—barely more than a year. Other periodicals of this kind which were also involved in the lyceum movement included the cosmopolitan but ill-starred *Magazine of Useful and Entertaining Knowledge*, 1830–31, edited by two New York lyceum leaders. It was followed by the only two magazines to show any longevity, the *American Monthly Magazine*, 1833–8, which printed reports on the meetings of the national lyceum, and the *American Magazine of Useful and Entertaining Knowledge*, 1834–7. And finally, this time merely a flash in a publisher's pan, there came Holbrook's ambitious *Self Instructor and Journal of the Universal Lyceum*, January–February 1842, and the *Lyceum Reporter and Critical Miscellany*, which ran from May to August of the same year. Published in either Boston or New York, this second little cluster of magazines had a broader educational scope than the schoolmen's (or for that matter the mechanics') magazines. They helped the lyceum manfully. Their editors, harried men in rumpled clothes, were united in sensing the potentialities of the lyceum movement and so they supported it through announcements, news articles, and editorials. They were more than chroniclers of its activities; they were its frequent supporters.

Books too had a place in the culture of which the lyceum became a part. Nonfiction was especially important yet its role has seldom been assessed, the main obstacles being its great bulk and the difficulty of finding records of it. The records of every title will of course never be recovered but it happens that enough records survive (still unpublished in the Library of Congress) to allow for substantial generalization. They are in the copyright books, tall folio volumes, which the clerks of the federal district courts filled with copyright entries. The pages of these volumes show that religious and moral tracts, on the one hand, and manuals, on the other, were the two most popular kinds of nonfiction. The manuals represented self-education and showed people how to do things themselves. The tracts illustrated the interest in Christian conduct which had lagged at the start of the nineteenth century but which quickened in the '30s. Both kinds—and this was significant—would be reflected in the topics of lyceum lectures.

A random reading of the district court copyright volumes shows of course many other kinds of titles too. They make the sober mosaic characteristic of that time. In Buffalo, for example, the court clerk entered these among others for a representative year, 1833: Duncan McKercher's *The Spirit of Humanity*, Emma Willard's crusading *Advancement of Female Education*, the Reverend N. C. W. Cannon's devout *The Rock of Wisdom* (he is set down as 'A man of color'), and G. W. Pattison's *Lectures on Geography, Astronomy, Natural History, &c.* In Boston the clerk entered among other things, a book on contraception, newly revised, by Dr. Charles Knowlton. He called it *Fruits of Philosophy; or, The Private Companion of Young Married People,* and its existence illustrates the danger of sweeping generalizations about any period of our history.

Other Boston entries are less surprising. *The Cook's Own Book,* Robert Thomas' *The (Old) Farmer's Almanac,* Peter Parley's widely used *Method of Teaching Arithmetic to Children,* and Harvey Newcomb's *A Practical Directory for Young Christian Females* are recorded in the clerk's elegant hand. So is *Outre-Mer: A Pilgrimage beyond the Sea,* Longfellow's anonymous, first book of any literary importance. In Philadelphia we find records of W. M. Gouge's shrewd *A Short History of Paper Money and Banking,* Stephen Simpson's Plutarchian *The Lives of George Washington and Thomas Jefferson,* 'Several clergymen's' *The Spruce Street Lectures,* and *The American Lady's Medical Pocket Book and*

Nursery Adviser—all of which are representative titles. In Providence, one book recorded by the clerk of court was Oliver Angell's *The Select Reader . . . for the Higher Classes in Academies and Schools*; and for Kentucky one of the few entries was J. D. Paxton's forthright *Letters on Slavery*.

There in the copyright record books is a cross section of America's reading for 1833; there as well as anywhere we can discover, in regard to the printed word, the cultural setting for the lyceum.

'I like the lyceum,' the Reverend Asa Rand announced while helping start the first society in Boston, 'because it is *adapted to the genius of our population*' through 'its *social* and *republican* character.' He was exactly right. Indeed, he could have gone farther, for the lyceum provided a remarkably good vehicle for the times in general. He could justly have observed that it harmonized with the whole spirit of the age. During Jackson's two terms both public services and privately supported civic services increased. Humanitarian forces grew. Prison reform, temperance, women's rights, free education, trade unionism, abolitionism, better care for the insane, and the 'social Gospel'—these were all public causes which aroused fervent interest then.

The lyceum fitted in well with these causes. In a period of cosmological optimism, of belief—but not ecstatic belief—in the goodness of human nature, and in the lively and inquiring spirit, the lyceum had ample and appropriate services to perform.

From Mutual Education to Random Lectures:
The Lyceum through 1845

'Branches of the lyceum,' the *American Journal of Education* trumpeted in its first number for 1830, 'are now organized in nearly every state in the Union, and a deep and general interest manifested upon the subject.' Though the *Journal* was exaggerating somewhat, the number of lyceums at this time was remarkably large and in the next few years would become still larger. The result is an embarrassment of riches in source material. To make it easier to handle, it will be divided both geographically and chronologically. There is a solid basis for the geographical division. Of the four great sections of the country, three of them—New England, the Midwest, and the South—were steadily growing more self-conscious. Sectionalism was on the march. The South appeared particularly aware of its individual interest. Only the Middle Atlantic states, split into two parts, lacked this unified consciousness. New York, Pennsylvania, and New Jersey were oriented toward the North, while Maryland and Delaware favored the South. Notwithstanding, the general rationale for regional division is evident enough.

The basis for chronological division is less solid. The bounds are easy to set. It is not hard to see when the lyceum movement began—we have already done that. Nor is it difficult to see when it ended, for the Civil War put a natural stop to the progress of the movement. But the changes during the thirty-five years in between were gradual ones, without any sharp breaks. There were changes, however, important ones—and the source material needs to be divided to discuss them efficiently. Because the year 1845 was the halfway point in the history of the lyceum, that year has been picked out as the dividing point. It approximates the time when the first great phase of the lyceum, 'From Mutual Instruction to Random Lectures,' was succeeded by the second, the crystallization of the lyceum into the lecture system.

4

New England:
Hub of the Lyceum

I T was in New England that the lyceum developed best, and Massachusetts was clearly pre-eminent within New England. Thanks to Holbrook's brilliant and persuasive leadership, the Massachusetts lyceum flourished inland first, for he was there. Forty bumpy miles lay between inland Millbury and the port of Boston to the east, and it took a little time for the lyceum to travel them. But it did so, with phenomenal results. After the initial cluster of lyceums around the busy community of Worcester came into existence during the second half of the 1820s, lyceums started to spread in every direction. North, south, and west of Worcester, however, they met obstacles.

To the west, in central Massachusetts, the chief one was the physical environment. Forests and lakes left little room for the kind of village life in which the early lyceum would thrive. Lyceums could sometimes do well in isolated, or even frontier, communities; but they could not be too isolated, too much depressed by the need to fight for life. There was a difference of degree between the isolation which stimulated villagers to start their own project of mutual education and the isolation so great that it stultified them.

To the north the lyceum met similar foes. Only in southern New Hampshire and perhaps on the coast of Maine could success be anticipated. Yet success turned out to be slow in coming even in New Hampshire; there it had to await the assistance of increased population and improved transportation. In point, Peterborough, Portsmouth, and Manchester were the three places where lyceums might have been expected soonest. Although the Peterborough Lyceum began early, near the end of 1828, the Portsmouth Lyceum did not start until five years later—and Manchester failed to support a typical lyceum until the mid-1840s. The total showing was not impressive.

When we move up from Massachusetts into Vermont we find again characteristic northern obstacles to the lyceum, notably, poor roads, a difficult climate, and a rather meager culture. In spite of those things Holbrook energized the state in 1830 and left for the time an active lyceum movement behind him. He had help, it is true. The movement in Vermont temporarily attracted at least one other seminal personality, the civic-minded farmer Thomas Palmer, and succeeded in arousing some interest in at least two important newspaper editors. These three men smoothed the way for Holbrook with signal results. But after Holbrook departed and the men he left behind him lost much of their zeal, the previous obstacles made themselves felt again, though not as strongly as before.

In one part of Maine the lyceum received a generous reception. Although most of the state was mountain, wood, or water, the populous seacoast was dotted with towns that showed evidence of intellectual interest. On estuaries or rivers further inland, villages could also be found where lyceums were established. Despite the fact that the lyceum in Maine had its share of shortcomings, it fared much better than a casual observer might have expected. There stretched from Kennebunk to Augusta a territory which the lyceum could enter with some prospect of permanence.

The obstructions which the lyceum met when it moved south from its point of origin at Millbury were generally different from those it encountered to the north. To the south lay Connecticut and Rhode Island. There the physical environment no longer furnished any obstacles, for the frontier had by the beginning of the 1830s moved considerably westward from Rhode Island and Connecticut. In its place, the lyceum came up against social barriers, and formidable ones too. Chief among these was the conservatives' notorious indifference to education. With its traditional relish for an unlearned ministry rather than a learned one and with its long established belief that the schools—if there were to be any—should fall within the control of the church rather than the state, Rhode Island naturally turned its back on the public school movement. In fact, there were no public schools outside of Providence until the beginning of the first period of the lyceum; and there was no working state-wide school system until Henry Barnard managed with herculean efforts to create one in the late 1840s. Nor did the rise of manufacturing, though it brought with it the massing of workers which usually started drives for tax-supported education, offer much immediate help.

Connecticut had similar, though not the same, reasons for greeting the lyceum movement with pious apathy. Psychological factors are usually the most difficult to isolate. Yet it is certainly worth suggesting that the impulses which had led settlers to establish the Connecticut valley theocracy and then to found conservative Yale College also kept the lyceum from succeeding. A kind of spiritual—and civic—thrift characterized the men of Connecticut. They fought newness and hugged their considerable resources to themselves. Publicly supported education, including the lyceum, had a hard row to hoe in Connecticut.

But when the lyceum turned east from Millbury, during the late 1820s, it was received with an enthusiasm which mounted until it was not to be equaled anywhere else. Only Cape Cod stayed aloof; the rest of eastern Massachusetts opened many a lyceum. And when the movement reached Boston, it found its natural home. By 1832 Josiah Holbrook could count fifteen full-fledged lyceums there. The quality varied, with only one or two approaching the intellectual eminence of the town lyceums of Concord and Salem; but the very weight of numbers was important. With Boston as its intellectual center of gravity, the lyceum movement in eastern Massachusetts soon enjoyed unparalleled success.

Throughout the whole state, in fact, the flourishing of New England culture was unusually friendly to the lyceum. So were the different elements within the class structure. The upper class—the merchants, manufacturers, and professional men—offered the lyceum movement a larger degree of leadership than did their peers in any other part of the nation. At the opposite extreme to them were the anti-intellectual plantation aristocrats of the South. The Massachusetts middle class, the backbone of the lyceum in the long run, was large, literate, and alert. And in the lower economic classes there could be found an unusual number of ambitious young men for whom the lyceum meant a chance for advancement.

Another reason the lyceum prospered in Massachusetts was that it had more small towns than any other New England state. They were close together and growing fast where water power invited industry to come in. A good deal of small manufacturing was already in process when the lyceum began—witness the manufacturing in Millbury itself. The major manufacturing event for Massachusetts, however, and indeed for all New England, during the first period of the lyceum was the coming of the textile industry. It drew the people from the farm to the town. The appeal of cash money, a change of scene, and a different kind of responsibility resulted in a steady flow of both women and men into the New England cotton mills. Lowell, Lawrence, and Holyoke—to take the main places—thrived because of two things: water power from the rivers and labor from the farms. Lowell made itself especially attractive, at the outset, for women. Its mills were famous for their pretty and supposedly contented 'mile of gals.' Other kinds of industry helped to build up other towns. And urbanization also took place, but to a smaller extent, in those parts of the states directly adjoining Massachusetts which possessed similar economic advantages.

In Massachusetts the supply of growing communities which the lyceum movement needed was always adequate; but it was different in the rest of New England. In the first years of the lyceum system, the period when it meant local, mutual education, any New England community from a village up was a potential site for a lyceum. But in the late 1830s and early '40s, the time when courses of lectures given by persons from outside became fashionable, most villages in the other states had not become big enough to follow the trend, for the six New England states were growing very little indeed. In 1830 they had a total of 1,955,000 people and ten years later 2,235,000. Judged in relation to the growth of most other states, this was a substantial loss. Much of it was accounted for by rampant 'Ohio fever.' Chilled by the New England climate, discouraged by the barrenness of New England soil, many families were emigrating. They went to the Ohio Valley or through the Erie Canal to northern Ohio (especially the Western Reserve) and the southeastern part of Michigan. If we admit the inference that it was the more ambitious New Englanders rather than their less ambitious fellows who went west to improve their prospects, we can see why the lyceum in New England itself, though it grew well, did not grow as well as it might have. What saved Massachusetts, population-wise, was the fact that her manufacturing towns gained their population not only from her own farms but from other parts of New England.

For one additional perspective on New England's lyceum, we can see how it developed chronologically. The history at its beginning was one of strong enthusiasm in eastern Massachusetts, some interest in Vermont and Maine, and little interest in the three remaining states. During the 1830s, in all states the initial interest, whatever the extent to start with, gradually diminished. Connecticut was an exception. Its apathy temporarily disappeared with the coming of the national lyceum convention to Hartford in 1838. Elsewhere in New England the decade beginning with 1838 was an uneasy one for the lyceum. The effects of the panic of 1837 lingered, and in spite of its low cost the lyceum turned out to be a luxury in the eyes of many members, who consequently dropped out. If by the early 1840s some lyceums were still being founded, a larger number were failing. But eastern Massachusetts, the utopia of the lyceum, maintained its ample strength in this decade of flux.

Throughout the rest of New England the larger communities remained the chief supporters of the lyceum. Within most states the best support came—as the first period of the lyceum ended—from the biggest two or three cities.

Such was the general shape the lyceum took in New England. Some of the details are to be found in the pages that follow.

Today when we think about the lyceums of Massachusetts, particularly of Concord or Salem or Boston, we are apt to remember only the great men who spoke and the grave audiences who listened. Yet that was not the whole picture of course. There was, for example, the young lady from Brookline. Her favorite lecturer, she wrote breathlessly in her diary, was a phrenologist named Dunkin. 'Enjoyed it so much,' she exclaimed about one of his lectures. 'So excited I could not sleep.' And again, after a comment on another lecturer the same season, she wrote that Mr. Dunkin 'spoiled us for any other lecturer. . . . It is like hearing sweet music to listen to him, besides feasting one's eyes on his beauty.' Dunkin came back to Brookline the following season. How could he help it?

What was probably the most intellectual of all town lyceums, the Concord Lyceum, held its official opening session on 28 January 1829, with the patriarch of Concord, Dr. Ezra Ripley, as the prime mover and first president. It became one of the few to outlive the Civil War. For lecturers it drew mainly on the neighborhood, but that was the most distinguished neighborhood in the nation. Emerson lectured before the Concord Lyceum more often than any other person, and he served three terms as curator before the end of the first period of the lyceum. Thoreau was elected to office by the membership five times during this same period, and he did his share of lecturing too. Along with such townsmen, the professors of nearby Harvard and pundits of Boston were frequently called on to speak. Although many men unknown to us appeared on the Concord platform, the proportion of impressive lecturing was remarkably high. The lecture topics, however, were not extraordinary to begin with. Even Emerson spoke in Transcendental tribute to the universal popularity of science. And in testimony to the love for novelty which marked even Concord at the outset, a favorite attraction for the first years was one Nehemiah Ball with his magic lantern. But later with its growing interest in speculative and inspirational subjects Concord anticipated rather than conformed to the trend. The record book for 1828–59, now in the Concord Public Library, demonstrates that the citizens were exposed to perhaps the finest education any lyceum could have provided.

The almost equally noted Salem Lyceum held its first meeting in January 1830, but Salem's interest in lectures went back much farther. As early as 1771, for example, a man named David Mason announced two addresses on electricity, the price one pistareen a lecture. There were also lectures of a more quixotic kind. A Mr. Powell of Boston once notified all interested that he would 'deliver the moral and satirical lectures on human hearts by Dr. Dodd, and a dissertation on noses, "the whole to be concluded with a hornpipe."' Then again, there was a much later lecturer, Colonel J. C. Symmes, who argued on a Salem platform in 1826 that the earth was hollow, with tunnels at the North and South Poles leading to the vacant center. He was 'ingenious in support of his position.'

The establishment of a lyceum in Salem, on a serious level, meant for the most part institutionalizing what already existed. By setting up formal machinery, however, the community facilitated its lecturing. Officers were chosen; curators and secretaries began their work. The Salem Lyceum was to have, as a matter of fact, one of the two most distinguished corresponding secretaries in the country: Nathaniel Hawthorne (Concord's Thoreau was the other); but that was not until 1848. Salem was large enough and lively enough, incidentally, to support two nights of lecturing a week instead of the usual one.

Although the town itself certainly possessed a number of gifted lecturers, they were called on less and less frequently as the lyceum grew older. They palled and outsiders were invited instead. Among the outsiders the most frequent speaker was Emerson. In a *Historical Sketch of the Salem Lyceum*, H. K. Oliver says of his lectures: 'For variety of subject, aptness in treatment, great intellectual display, and profound power of thought, I can imagine nothing superior.' Especially good—'most impressive and winning of attention'—were the lectures on manners and on Napoleon. Another whom Oliver praised was Daniel Webster. As of 1836 it was Webster 'in his full development, in his massive and superb presence and quiet self-possession—with the clear utterance of his rich, deep-toned, and musical voice, and his grace of delivery, the outward manifestations of the marvellous intellect within—these all conspiring to hold to an almost breathless listening.' Others appearing included the Swiss naturalist Louis Agassiz, the pioneering anthropologist George Catlin, the Shakespearean critic H. N. Hudson, and many more.

And what of the lectures themselves? The tenth course (1838–9), to take one at random, was inaugurated by a series on 'The Character, Customs, Costumes, etc., of the North American Indians' by Catlin. Listed below are those that followed.

Salem Lyceum Lectures, 1838–9	*Lecturers*
Causes of the American Revolution	Jared Sparks
The Sun	Hubbard Winslow
The Sources of National Wealth	C. H. Brewster
Common School Education	C. T. Torrey
The Capacity of the Human Mind for Culture and Improvement	Ephraim Peabody
The Honey Bee	H. K. Oliver
Popular Education	R. C. Winthrop
Geology	Prof. C. B. Adams
The Legal Rights of Women	Simon Greenleaf
Instinct	Henry Ware, Jr. (Emerson's friend)
Life of Mohammed	J. H. Ward
Life and Times of Oliver Cromwell	H. W. Kinsman
Memoirs of Count Rumford	A. C. Peirson
The Practical Man	Convers Francis (the Transcendentalist)
The Poet of Natural History	J. L. Russell
The Progress of Democracy	John Wayland
The Discovery of America by the Northmen	A. H. Everett
The Satanic School of Literature and Its Reform	Samuel Osgood
The Education of Children	Horace Mann

The series on the Indian illustrate the fresh notice taken of him from an antiquarian point of view. The three lectures on science— slightly fewer than average for the time—each represent a different phase of popular interest. Oliver's lecture on the honey bee no doubt stressed the specific application of the facts he offered; the lecture on geology exemplified the fresh concern with this science which was already threatening the accepted Biblical view of the creation of the world; the lecture on the fabulous scientist Count

Rumford illustrated both the interest in science and the interest in biography that marked the time.

Salem's love of history revealed itself in the presentation of lectures on the American revolution, on the lives of Mohammed and Oliver Cromwell, and on the discovery of America by the Northmen. Education received its proper share of attention through three lectures, one being by the noted Horace Mann. The last major topic in the course might be termed 'humanity philosophically considered.' Within its scope probably fell the lectures on 'The Capacity of the Human Mind for Culture and Improvement,' 'Instinct,' and 'The Practical Man.'

The richness and variety of the Salem offerings show the strength of that lyceum. Many another community could do almost though not quite as well. In the tradition of Nathaniel Bowditch, Salem usually ran a little more heavily to science (and pseudo-science) than most other towns; otherwise the mixture was about the same. Well could the Salem annalist Joseph Felt imagine the past age saying to his of the 1840s, 'How vastly do your sources of information exceed ours—how greatly has your age outstript that in which we lived!'

In Boston the craze for lectures reached phenomenal proportions throughout the 1830s and 1840s. During the winter of 1837–8, for example, twenty-six courses of lectures were delivered in Boston according to Harriette Smith's history of the Lowell Institute. She did not count any course composed of less than eight lectures. And she estimated that these twenty-six courses were attended by 13,000 listeners!

Besides the ample number of relatively stable lyceums there were the assorted churches, clubs, and societies which gave a course of lectures every now and then in the church basement or the club rooms or the society hall. Finally, many courses were undertaken by free-lance lecturers. There had always been some of this in the cultural life of Boston, but the heyday of the free-lance began with the coming of the lyceum. Everyone from respectable Harvard professors to phrenologists or outright quacks could hire a hall, sell tickets, and hope to clear a profit. Even Emerson, as a matter of fact, occasionally operated this way. Sometimes these lecturers made no money. Other times they made almost enough to support themselves through the summer doldrums.

In this array of lyceums and lectures two societies stand out clearly in retrospect, the Boston Lyceum and the Lowell Institute.

The fourth annual report of the Boston Lyceum, as printed in Holbrook's *Family Lyceum* for 25 May 1833, offers a characteristic picture of that already celebrated organization. It listened to sixteen lectures throughout the year. Most of the speakers were native—in Boston as in Concord there was an abundance of talent. The topics were mainly general: music, the eye, physical education (just emerging into popularity), the blind, political economy. There were other kinds of programs too, most notably the five regular classes held during the year in elocution and debate, astronomy (the science considered most in harmony with divine creation), geography and history, French, and rhetoric and composition. On all this fare the Boston Lyceum grew even stronger. Five years later, as of May 1838, the *American Annals of Education* announced that it attracted as large an attendance, almost 2000 persons a week, as any society of its kind in the country.

The most aristocratic of all lyceums was founded in 1839. It was the Lowell Institute of Boston, which also paid the handsomest of fees. John Lowell, Jr., who died in India in 1836, endowed it with nearly a quarter of a million dollars. Bearded, turbaned, and given to smoking a hookah while on his travels in the East, he was by no means a typical member of his highly conservative family. But his cousin, John Amory Lowell, manager of the Institute for more than forty years, was. Consequently, from the beginning the selection of lectures and lecturers was 'made from a broad and comprehensive knowledge of the safe thought and intelligent study of the time.' That meant that social problems found little room on the Lowell platform. Yet science, far more controversial a century ago than it is now, was freely admitted. Even when it questioned Genesis, it could be heard. Among the noted men, scientific and otherwise, who gave courses during the first five years were Silliman, the educator Mark Hopkins, the English geologist Lyell, and the historian Jared Sparks.

A lyceum could prosper in a city such as Boston or a town such as Salem or even, less ostentatiously, in a good many villages of

Massachusetts. But at the county and state level its life was brief. The Worcester County Lyceum was the first and the Middlesex County Lyceum the most active among the county lyceums, but they both soon withered. The state lyceum, organized out of the Massachusetts Central Committee on Lyceums, did little but send delegates to the national lyceum's yearly conventions of the 1830s.

The highlights of the lyceum movement in Connecticut were two Young Men's Institutes, one in New Haven and the other in Hartford. The New Haven Institute perfectly illustrates the adaptation made by some of the already existing societies to the lyceum movement. When eight young workingmen formed their group in August 1826, they gave it the lofty title of the Apprentices' Literary Association. They declaimed, read, debated, and began a modest library. Two years later there were forty-two members, and classes in arithmetic, geometry, geography, grammar, and bookkeeping. At this time the name was changed to the Young Mechanics' Institute. As of 1831 the main emphasis was on class instruction, a good deal of it coming through the exchange of knowledge in the classroom by members themselves. In its later form, the society proceeded to secure the support of leading Yale professors and citizens of New Haven; but an address given at the annual meeting for 1834 by a leading member named Levi Francis demonstrates that he was speaking to an audience still made up of workingmen. The speech is boldly pro-labor and pro-union, the kind which would have antagonized New Haven conservatives. In the years after Francis' address, lectures became more popular, classes less so. The lectures were given in part by the members and in part by such public-spirited professors as Silliman and the versatile scientist Denison Olmsted and such townsmen as the prominent lawyer Henry White. The last stage in the society's evolution is evidenced by one more change of title, as of August 1840, to the Young Men's Institute.

Throughout its years the lecture courses at the Institute broadened and escaped from some of the early concentration on practical science. They became an important part of the culture of New Haven and lasted into the Civil War. Combined with the

Institute's large circulating library, they provided a broad education for people Yale never reached.

Along with New Haven, Hartford represented the best in Connecticut's intellectual life. Hartford had a lyceum before 1830 which took up the study of school textbooks and the qualifications of teachers. Although it apparently possessed little vigor, the reverse was true of the Young Men's Institute. Founded in 1838, it not only arranged courses of lectures but also established several interest groups, particularly debating classes. The Hermenian Society, the Wadsworth Literary Association, and the Institute Debating Society Number 1 were among its wards before 1845. The manuscript records of the Young Men's Institute trace the history of an aggressive organization. Henry Barnard became the first president and, later, the delegate to the state lyceum of 1839 and 1840.

Other lyceums in Connecticut, mostly early, included the Norwich Lyceum and Mechanics' Institute, the Goodrich Association of Hartford, the East Hartford Lyceum, the lyceums of Litchfield and Danbury, the New Haven Athenaeum, the Franklin Institute, and the Mechanics' Society (both the last of New Haven). The high point, relatively, for all such lyceums in the state came in May 1838 when the American Lyceum held its annual meeting in Hartford and so furnished a strong though short-lived stimulus to local pride. At that convention 'more than twenty lyceums in Connecticut were reported from' according to the *Connecticut Common School Journal*. Thereafter the number dropped drastically.

As the first period of the lyceum went along, Rhode Island developed an industrial economy which—in proportion to the size of the state—was often as strong as, and sometimes stronger than, that of either Massachusetts or Connecticut. The mill towns grew; the wealth of the little state increased. But the culture of eastern Massachusetts, especially the leaven which Boston provided, was lacking. Rhode Island education was beneath the Massachusetts standard, from the lowest level to the highest, from the public elementary schools to the private colleges. When the census of 1840 was taken Rhode Island was found, in fact, to have the smallest percentage of children in school of any New England state.

The intellectual life of Rhode Island centered in the city of Providence. It had first of all a Franklin Society and then a Franklin Lyceum. The society started before the Lyceum and was still active as late as 1841 when the *Providence Directory* noted that 'lectures [were] read and experiments performed.' Its opening season ran through the winter of 1829–30, and it continued to sponsor courses every now and then until the end of the first period of the lyceum movement.

According to Francis Hoppin's *Oration* on the Lyceum, the first exercises were lectures and debates. The initial club rooms were in the basement of a house on Benefit Street, 'where a cabinet of minerals, shells, chemical apparatus, antiquities, and a library were commenced.' A cabinet undoubtedly similar to the Lyceum's is pictured in a poem bound with Hoppin's address:

> The cabinet still broods with varnished wings
> Above its nest of rare and curious things—
> The ostrich egg, the fish-hook, and the shell,
> The sculptured chamois from the land of Tell,
> The Pine-Tree shilling with its quaint device, . . .
> The spider with its feelers long and limp,
> Bottled and labeled like a pickled shrimp,
> And sprawling lizards with their fleshless legs,
> Put up in jars like cucumbers in kegs.

The first annual meeting on record was held in January 1833. It must have been something of an event, for the introductory number of an original magazine called the *Lyceum Star and Evening Chronicle* was read, an address was given, and then 'the society adjourned in a body to Mr. Armington's saloon.' In the winter and spring of 1840 the Lyceum took a more serious step by inviting Emerson to give a series of six lectures on 'Human Life.' The other courses that followed featured such well-known lecturers as the blacksmith Elihu Burritt and Henry Giles.

During the 1830s and '40s there were also a good many lectures, particularly in Providence, which were given either by free-lance lecturers or under the sponsorship of organizations which were clearly not lyceums. W. R. Danforth, for instance, advertised that he would speak on 'Reminiscences of Providence' and added the blunt observation that he was not lecturing purely 'for the public good' but because he needed the money—'having been, for the last nine months, out of productive employment.'

Slowly the lyceum system expanded into New Hampshire. The forest and mountains of the northern half of the state erected a forbidding barrier, but the southern half lacked that obstacle and had such towns as there were—and by the late 1830s, fair transportation. Consequently, that was where lyceums ordinarily appeared. It was still the time of the stage coach and horse for the out-of-town lecturer. The natural result was that most lecturers were either local men or from nearby communities. It was not until about 1840 that the railroads began branching out from Boston toward the thinly settled state.

Furthermore, much of the impulse that might have created the lyceum was diverted into another channel, the debating society. New Hampshire showed a love for oral contention; it preferred to argue (except about religion) rather than to listen. The Concord Lyceum, founded in 1830, apparently concentrated on debating. The Manchester Lyceum, founded in 1842, did too for a time, and the typical lyceum cast did not appear in its programs until after 1845.

New Hampshire had, however, a few lyceums which lived up to their name. The first was probably Peterborough's. Its initial committee report and draft constitution, dated 13 December 1828, are still preserved. The aims announced there are mutual improvement and the advancement of popular education. To achieve them the members were to 'hold meetings for reading, conversation, discussions, dissertations, illustrating the sciences, or other exercises which shall be thought expedient, and, as it is found convenient . . . procure a cabinet consisting of books, apparatus . . . collections of minerals, plants, and other natural or artificial productions.' Teachers were to have all the privileges of membership free except voting. The Lyceum heard lectures on such agricultural topics as 'The Best Time for Plowing Sward

Land' and such educational topics as 'The Best Method of Disposing of Small Children Sent to Winter Schools.'

With the founding of the Portsmouth Lyceum in June 1833, we see the emergence in the state of another lyceum as typical as Peterborough's. The *Portsmouth City Directory* for 1834 observes that before 'this useful and popular institution' 'a course of twenty-eight pleasing and instructive lectures was delivered at the Theater.' The weekly lectures, spreading over five months of each year, continued to be presented up to if not after 1845.

Several of the lectures which the members esteemed most highly were published by the Lyceum. The earliest is J. II. Pierrepont's 'History and Philosophy of Medicine,' given on 10 December 1833. In contrast to the showy language of this first lecture, the next one, by C. W. Brewster, went lucidly to the point. 'The citizens of a free republic should do away with any kind of bondage,' and that includes bondage to new fashions, which is ' "the pride of fools and the plague of wise men." ' That was Brewster's thesis in the second lecture, on the changes of fashion, which he entitled 'National Standard of Costume' and which was published in 1837. The third, read by the Reverend A. P. Peabody on 12 November 1844, was on the 'Wealth, Industry, and Resources of Portsmouth.'

To fill out the picture of the lyceum in New Hampshire, it should be added that less than a dozen other local lyceums came into existence; no county lyceums appeared at all; but a state organization operated at least during 1833 and 1834. When Holbrook reported the starting of the state lyceum, he also announced the making of 'arrangements for lyceums in all the counties and towns in the state.' Time and New Hampshire tastes, however, proved him wrong.

Ordinarily one would expect the same story in Vermont. The communities were few. Transportation was poor: most dirt roads were hardly passable throughout much of the year and the first railroad completed in the state was not open over its whole length until 1849. The frontier, made up of equal parts of hard weather and half-cleared, rocky ground, affected social as well as physical life. The various components of a culture that the lyceum liked, such as general schooling and literacy, were present only in small amounts. Yet the lyceum enjoyed a growth that was surprisingly vigorous if quite brief.

Vermont had its own Holbrook—Thomas Palmer. A retired Philadelphia printer, he bought himself a farm in Pittsford, a town of 2000, in 1828. Soon after his arrival he became interested in the welfare of the local public schools and then in the fall of 1829, having heard about the lyceum movement, he canvassed the town on its behalf. His aim was to promote town and county lyceums which were 'to combine the discussion of scientific subjects with that of education,' in the best Holbrook manner. Both the idea and the man must have been persuasive, for his neighbors helped him buy the scientific apparatus he wanted and joined him in starting the Pittsford Lyceum. With its apparatus and weekly lectures Pittsford proved a stimulating example to other towns. According to Bush's *History of Education in Vermont*, 'like lyceums were instituted at Rutland, Castleton, and other places, proving the popularity and value' of the institution.

Palmer continued to serve the movement. He took an important part in a state-wide meeting, held at Montpelier, for the propagation of lyceums. That meeting appointed county committees, and Palmer went on the one for his home county of Rutland. For the next two years his county experienced a burst of lyceum activity. Lectures, committee meetings, essays on education for the newspapers, the sponsoring of teachers' conventions—those were the main manifestations. Holbrook himself addressed the County Lyceum on 21 December 1830 and no doubt found much to praise. A year later he cited it in print in his *Family Lyceum*. By then Palmer was president of the County Lyceum, giving it and the local schools every aid at his command.

Just as Vermont had its Holbrook in Thomas Palmer, it had a duo of William Russells in Ephraim Maxham and Joseph Tracy. In the years from 1830 to 1833 when the *Rutland Herald* was being published by Maxham, it devoted an exceptional amount of space to the lyceum movement. And when needful it editorialized sadly on the fact that Vermonters did not always appreciate the good inherent in the movement.

Tracy, as editor of the *Vermont Chronicle*, showed his enthusiasm for the lyceum just as Maxham did. The aid the *Chronicle* afforded came through publicity about the meetings and espousal of the same things Holbrook advocated. In the fall of 1830 it conducted a brief survey and counted twenty-five lyceums in the state. 'In general,' the paper proudly remarked, 'they have surpassed . . . the expectations of their founders.' But Tracy's devotion to the cause soon ran its course. When the amount of lyceum news declined in his columns a year later, he explained why. It was not that the lyceums themselves had closed up but that the current religious revival had taken so much of his time. He promised to pay more attention to the lyceum movement as soon as the revival allowed him to—but he never did.

Tracy's defection was far from being the only one in the state. In 1832 and '33 the decline set in. Notwithstanding, the lyceum in Vermont always kept some of its early strength. Bennington, for instance in 1841 and '42, sponsored lectures before its lyceum on such uncompromisingly intellectual topics as 'Miasma.' 'Political Economy,' 'The Feudal System in England,' 'Study of the Ancient Languages,' and 'Union of Church and State.'

Forests covered more than three-quarters of the state of Maine during the early days of the lyceum movement. Few were the lyceums which could grow up in such wild surroundings. On the other hand, the sea coast offered real abundance. On its irregular bays and river mouths lived a high proportion of the people. And the people were many; the census of 1830 reveals an unexpected picture, for Maine (with just under 400,000) had more inhabitants at that time than any other New England state except Massachusetts.

The lyceums appearing in Maine turned out to be widely assorted; the Down-Easters liked many kinds. If there was any single thing that characterized the Maine lyceums it was perhaps the touch of frontier roughness. The lecturers by no means always received the best of treatment. The minutes of the Eastport Lyceum for 1831 show, for example, that the lecture committee recommended that the article of the constitution allowing the heckling of lecturers (or as the committee tactfully put it, demanding 'proof of the facts stated by' them) be abolished. Too many members now, the committee said, hesitated to lecture through 'fear of an application of the *screw,* to their utter confusion.'

Typical of the smaller lyceums in the state was the one at Kennebunk. It grew out of a debating club which some of the younger villagers founded in August 1829. At a meeting late in December five local gentlemen agreed to deliver a lecture apiece before them that winter. The first one, given by a minister, was the customary explanation of 'the nature and design of lyceums' which opened many a course. Three of the others were on science, while the fifth was a lecture on the early history of the town. The course turned out successfully. At the conclusion of the last lecture those present adopted a constitution and officially began the Kennebunk Lyceum. It lasted for almost a decade. Through its lectures (mainly scientific), its discussions, its library and set of philosophical apparatus, it served the community well.

Among the few larger lyceums was Bangor's, started in 1829. A typical season once it had really established itself was that of 1836–7. The opening speaker was a widely known Transcendentalist minister, F. H. Hedge, who lived in Bangor. His topic was not Transcendental philosophy, however; instead it was the 'diffusion of knowledge,' probably little different from what Kennebunk had heard when it started its lyceum. Of the ten other lectures in the course, one was on the popular subject of geology while another, on the atmosphere and its properties, was also plainly scientific. A doctor's lecture on physical education, an example of applied science no doubt, reflected the new awareness of that subject. A lecture on 'Ethiopic Nations' drew at least part of its interest from the slavery controversy, while more general political issues may have appeared in three other lectures. One was on 'Classes in Society.' The two remaining seem to have been carefully set off from one another. 'The Conservative Interest' probably presented one side of the political picture while 'The Progress of Popular Reform' presented the other. But this was doubtless not party politics.

Augusta, Belfast, and Portland were the other cities that usually supported lyceums. Portland did a little worse and Belfast a little better than might be expected. The group of smaller communities with lyceums was much more extensive. Even villages like Warren, Winthrop, Jay, and Machias operated them. Here and there throughout the state, but especially along the seacoast, the red-faced, active men of Maine were apt to save a night a week for education.

5

The Middle Atlantic States:
Bustle in New York

THE Middle Atlantic states were a mixed lot. They encompassed the Yankee cities of upstate New York and the tobacco farms of southern Maryland, the Quaker culture of Philadelphia and the growing industries of northern New Jersey. The three major cities of the region were New York, Philadelphia, and Baltimore, with Washington as a rather anomalous addition. From the beginning days of the lyceum New York City set the commercial if not always the cultural pace. In commerce it was challenged earnestly but unsuccessfully by Philadelphia; and so far as culture was concerned Philadelphia took the point of view that New York did not exist. In terms specifically of the lyceum New York nevertheless assumed more and more leadership. For the Middle Atlantic states it became the metropolis of the lyceum movement.

The city's most important advantage, tied up with its strategic location, was size. A city as large and affluent as New York could not help including within its boundaries many people with an interest in adult education. The percentage of them might be minute but the total number would be impressive. One token of the position the city occupied was that throughout the 1830s the national lyceum held its annual convention there six times in a row.

Upstate New York combined with the metropolis to develop a state-wide lyceum leadership of outstanding proportions. Migrants from New England had already settled in upstate communities before the days of the lyceum; and the opening of the Erie Canal in 1825 helped the lyceum in several ways. The constantly increasing commerce through the Canal meant prosperity for the towns nearby. Rising communities with a New England heritage were the result—and the lyceum benefited markedly. Furthermore, since the Canal brought better transportation for people as well as goods, migration from New England after 1825 often took the Canal route. Most of the migrants pressed on beyond the limits of the state but enough stopped off before that to freshen the state's New England culture.

New York City benefited from the Canal commercially of course, but there was also a cultural increment; easier communication with the rest of the state resulted in a closer cultural alliance. In the second period of the lyceum, in the years after 1845, this would be signally demonstrated in the march of lecturers from New York City into the rest of the state. Meanwhile, the results of this community of cultural interest were more nebulous, yet they were there. For example, the state proposed the founding of the national lyceum and after its creation consistently supported the New York City meetings. And, in a more general way, if the sturdy interest in the public school movement shown by upstate New York had no direct connection with New York City, it nonetheless helped to buttress the city's educational position.

No sizable town in upstate New York failed to develop a lyceum and a good many villages had one too though theirs was apt to be weak. The early 1830s marked the peak of lyceum activity throughout the state. The ten years after that were a decade of ups and downs. Notwithstanding, the lyceum stayed alive in the upstate cities. And in New York City it thrived.

The contrast with other states was striking. In spite of the cultural tradition of Philadelphia, Pennsylvania as a whole showed indifference to the lyceum—as well as, significantly, to publicly supported education. Before the lyceum began, the state had experienced some immigration from New England, especially to the north. The New England culture here, however, unrefreshed by later additions, was in great part lost. The Quaker, the Pennsylvania German, and the West Pennsylvania Scotch-Irishman each had a culture which proved able to dominate that of the migrants from New England. When it came to the lyceum, the Quaker turned out to prefer other forms of adult education; the Pennsylvania German waited to be convinced of its cash value; the Scotch-Irishman found taming the frontier more necessary and playing politics more stimulating.

Yet the foregoing needs some modification. The Quakers supported at least a few lyceums, mainly in the Philadelphia area. In general, the Pennsylvania Dutch did not fight the lyceum with the same hostility they displayed toward the public school movement; and when Josiah Holbrook came to the state, apparently in 1834, his persuasive evangelizing turned some of their indifference into support. After Holbrook's arrival the few lyceums already in existence were invigorated, new ones both at the community and county level were started, and the feeble state education movement found a measure of vitality. By the 1840s, however, the lyceum was again in the doldrums, not to emerge until the lecture system began to attract noted speakers to the handful of larger cities.

In its coldness toward publicly supported education New Jersey resembled its neighbor state across the Delaware River. Only industrial Newark gave the lyceum much attention, and that was doubtless owing in part to the closeness to New York City. Camden, at the opposite end of the state, found no such stimulus in Philadelphia. Yet there were lyceums scattered about in some of the state's other larger communities. And in Maryland only the port of Baltimore—almost another New York with its immigration, commerce, and cultural activities—afforded the lyceum the kind of milieu it needed. The rest of Maryland, agrarian in economy and neglectful of public education, had no use for the lyceum. The farmer, whether growing grain on the Eastern Shore or raising tobacco down in Prince Georges County or wresting a living from the northwest part of the state, probably never even knew that the lyceum existed.

Delaware's culture, like Maryland's, was concentrated in the principal city; and even there it managed poorly at first. Wilmington had the meager beginnings of a lyceum in the early 1830s. Toward the end of the decade the situation improved definitely but for the years from 1840 to 1845 the records fail to show any marked trends. In terms of the state as a whole, it must be remembered that Delaware, again like Maryland, bordered on the

South and consequently was influenced by that southern culture in which slavery was dominant. This was no culture for the lyceum. If New York was the best of the Middle Atlantic states for the lyceum, Delaware was the worst.

A word, finally, should be said about Washington. In the enclave of the District of Columbia the lyceum started at the opening of the 1830s, faltered, and then by the opening of the next decade picked up well. By 1845 there was no dearth of lectures there. Though the dominant mores of the city were southern ones, the existence of the national government created an increasingly cosmopolitan culture in which the lyceum could thrive.

◆

'The commercial emporium of the United States,' as *New York as It Is* called the city in 1833, had a bustling cultural life almost from the beginning of its existence. There were several organizations which heard lectures occasionally; and almost every organization of course had speakers at some time or other. For instance, the New York Mechanic and Scientific Institution, incorporated in March 1822, had for its primary purpose 'instituting and maintaining scientific and practical lectures, applicable to the arts.' This was a society which the noted lecturer and chemistry teacher, John Griscom, had a special interest in, becoming the first chairman of its committee on lectures. And this was the society cited as a precedent when the London Mechanics' Institution was being organized.

The result of the existence of groups like this was to offer a ready-made platform for the lecturer when the lyceum movement impinged on New York. Relatively little need arose to create new societies as long as the old ones were useful. One of the main reasons, no doubt, that the older groups adjusted themselves to the lyceum pattern was the interest generated by local pride, for from its first (and organizing) meeting in May 1831 until the sixth annual meeting in 1836, the American Lyceum held its every session in New York City.

The national lyceum had a connection with both New York City and New York state. The immediate move which led to its formation came from the state lyceum convention of 1831. And the main support for the annual conventions of the American Lyceum came from New York City. To the national convention of 1833, for instance, for which President William Duer of Columbia acted as chairman, the New-York Historical Society, the New York Athenaeum, the General Society of Mechanics and Tradesmen of the City of New York (it inaugurated its lecture courses this year), the New York Mercantile Library Association, the New York Young Men's Society, and even the New York Institution for the Blind all sent delegates. That kind of support continued in later annual conventions.

The same accessibility which helped to make New York City the best site for the meetings of the American Lyceum also attracted individual lecturers to the city. Both in the years before our midpoint, 1845, and after, the best known lecturers all spent some time there. The topics which they announced illustrated the national trend. At the outset, the ambitious mechanic could learn from practical talks on applied science. His lecture clubs gave him what he needed. By the mid-1830s, however, numerous complaints suggest that he had become indifferent to such courses. On the other hand, lectures of a cultural or a pseudo-cultural nature, for the general public, increased. The public doubtless imposed its tastes on the curators and lecture managers in New York as elsewhere. As time went on New York City and New York state heard many of the same speakers and listened to many of the same phrases.

It has been said that culture came up the Hudson River, turned west at Albany, and then, looking neither to right nor left, traveled in a straight line to the far edge of the state. The development of the lyceum furnishes some support for this remark, as a glance at the map will show. No one would expect the lyceum to flourish in the Adirondacks or the Catskills. So too for the Finger Lakes area in the center of the state. Those lakes run north and south; that means that they are either outside of or else athwart the main lines of travel. Some of the towns there, such as Bath, were settled very early, yet by the time Holbrook began to make his rounds they were once again isolated communities. Only at the northern rim of the Finger Lakes did the lyceum find any sustained hospitality.

The cultural center of upstate New York when the lyceum movement began was Albany. As early as the end of the eighteenth century it had various societies devoted to the pursuit of knowledge. The fact that Albany became the state's capital helped to consolidate its educational gains. The Albany Institute of History and Art, already in existence by the late 1820s, moved easily and naturally into the lyceum sphere. The other upstate cities soon followed Albany. Troy had its Rensselaer Institute, started by the noted philanthropist Stephen Van Rensselaer as a school 'for instructing the sons and daughters of farmers and mechanics' in practical science. It served the lyceum movement too by offering training for lyceum lecturers—the only place in the nation where this was done. President Amos Eaton of Rensselaer reported to the American Lyceum in 1832 that the Institute had educated seven young men in the new profession. And they were able to use what they had learned; Eaton announced paternally that they had gone out to 'engage in their vocation and [had] been very favorably received.' Moreover, it was a student from Rensselaer who in 1830 started the Buffalo Lyceum, which achieved a long record of service.

Illustrating the ties between the old world and the new, the city of Rochester established an institution in 1826 for the schooling of mechanics which was patterned directly after the Andersonian University in Glasgow. In 1829 the Rochester Athenaeum began its career. It had its failures as well as successes but managed to span both of the periods into which we have divided the lyceum system's development.

Those were the main communities in the state which supported lyceums. They were not always called lyceums of course; moreover, sometimes one society would die and another with a different name would take its place. But the important point is that the communities always found the function of a lyceum useful. They always benefited in some degree from the lectures, the discussions, the libraries, and the demonstrations.

Thus the lyceum system evidenced its good health upstate. But it did much more, at least briefly, than that. For two years it brought about the strongest development of the county lyceums that any state was to see and also resulted in a remarkably active state lyceum. The signal advance in the growth of lyceums throughout the state came in 1830 and '31. It was climaxed by the emergence of the state organization. Two preliminary meetings were held, mainly among teachers; then a general one came in January 1831. Twenty-two counties sent delegates and revealed a strength of both the public school and the lyceum movements at the county level that was phenomenal, if temporary. When the delegates arrived they found Holbrook in attendance, and he worked his usual magic. It is evident from the abstract of the proceedings that the convention fixed on the lyceum movement as one of the best ways to accomplish its principal objective, the betterment of the public elementary schools. No doubt Holbrook was partly responsible for that strategy. He made speeches at two out of the three evening sessions and it is a safe assumption that off or on the floor of the convention he made converts to the lyceum idea. Furthermore, he was named to a three-man committee on the establishment of lyceums in the state. When this committee made its report, the highlight was the recommendation that the group resolve itself into the New York State Lyceum. This it did. Then it in turn made another recommendation, of marked importance to the movement. It proposed the holding of a national convention of teachers and friends of education, in New York City in May, to found the American Lyceum itself. To make this proposal effective, a committee was chosen to write the various other states and get them to send delegations to the national conclave.

To the organizing meeting in 1831 of the American Lyceum, the New York State Lyceum sent three delegates, while in 1832 it sent fifteen—more than any other society. Stephen Van Rensselaer was elected the first president of the American Lyceum; since he had to be away because of illness, John Griscom took the chair in his place and later was chosen president for the succeeding year. Although New Yorkers soon lost interest in their state and county lyceums, they maintained their loyalty to the national lyceum throughout the decade. And they kept their loyalty to their busy town lyceums even longer.

Rich farms, gray-clad Quakers, a spacious and mellow city, German thrift, heavy-backed mountains, and the bustling Scotch-Irish—these suggest the diversity of Pennsylvania as the lyceum movement began. Philadelphia was the inevitable focus for the state's culture. There the predecessors of the lyceum appeared early though the lyceum movement itself never fully realized its potentialities locally.

Most distinguished and enduring of the predecessors was the Franklin Institute. Plans for it were laid late in 1823 and the next year it opened. From the beginning its activities were characterized by remarkable energy. Dedicated to 'the promotion and encouragement of manufactures and the mechanic and useful arts,' it proceeded promptly to effect its aims and in doing so to interpret them broadly. In its first year the Institute adopted its constitution, elected its officers, secured its charter, appointed standing committees (on lectures, finance, the library, the cabinet of models and minerals, and premiums and exhibitions), and began printing its official reports. The first lectures actually came as early as spring 1824; a school for mechanical drawing started in fall; and the gathering of minerals and of volumes for a technical library began in 1826. The same year brought forth two other achievements. One was the opening of the high school. The other, of wider significance, was the taking over by the Institute of the *American Mechanics' Magazine* beginning with the January issue. Monthly educational meetings for the membership, in addition to the regular meetings, were instituted in 1829 and an evening school in 1832. In all these projects, various and useful as they were, there was less emphasis on mutual instruction than on the instruction of a large group by the elite, knowledgeable few. In this respect the operation of the Institute was different from the operation of the early lyceums. But the passing of time brought a change—not in the Institute but in the nature of lyceums in general, for later audiences furnished the receptive mass and professional lecturers the active elite.

About 1834 Josiah Holbrook descended upon Pennsylvania. He had been preceded by his friend William Russell, who had by now given up editing the *American Journal of Education* and was teaching school in the state. Holbrook soon persuaded many a

Pennsylvania farmer and townsman. He demonstrated his usual shrewd sense of psychology by singing the praises of labor schools, for they would be self-supporting. They would cost the thrifty farmers nothing and would nevertheless educate their sons. As Russell later said in his 'Recollections of Josiah Holbrook,' some of 'the former inveterate enemies of education were heard exclaiming, "Yes, if *this* is education, we want it. This will make our sons better farmers; and they will know, when they are selling their farms, whether they are selling coal and lime and iron too." '

Various reflections of Holbrook's vigorous work appeared. Hazard's *Register of Pennsylvania* devoted its lead article in a number for November 1834 to reprinting some of his words. One clipping which Hazard used came from *Niles' Register* and clearly represented the current trend in Holbrook's thought: '*Self-education* and *self-support* is, in all the departments and all the operations of the lyceum system, its most prominent feature.' The appeal to Pennsylvania thrift was obvious. Another and more direct evidence of his energy was to be found in the field of publicly supported education. Through his influence Philadelphia's Lyceum of Teachers issued a call for a state lyceum convention. The convention opened as planned, in August 1835, with lyceums and teachers' groups sending most of the delegates.

Holbrook apparently dominated the convention. He made the introductory address, served on at least two committees, and was selected as a delegate from the new-born state lyceum to the American Lyceum's next annual meeting. Of a sheaf of resolutions passed, one invited Holbrook to act as an agent 'for the establishment of lyceums and the promotion of popular education throughout the state.' Another extended cordial thanks to him 'for his indefatigable and highly successful efforts.'

Besides participating in the national conventions, the Pennsylvania Lyceum played an additional role, especially at the beginning—it encouraged local lyceums. A number organized themselves in the wake of the state convention of 1835. Some were the direct result of the convention; others were not. Once convinced of the value of the lyceum system, a good many Pennsylvania Germans forsook their early aversion and took active part. The *American Annals* for October 1836 reported their lyceums as flourishing. York, Lancaster, Cumberland, Berks, Montgomery, and Bucks counties all had them.

The communities of Pittsburgh, Lewisburg, Jenkintown, York, and Lancaster differed considerably from one another, yet they too sponsored lyceums before 1845—lyceums, it should be added, which bore the configuration of the dissimilar environments which contained them. There were some others too. Notwithstanding, when the *Berks and Schuylkill Journal* of Reading remarked in 1844 after Edgar Allan Poe lectured there, 'As for lecturers, they are out of fashion with our people,' the paper expressed a widespread view. The plain fact is that most Pennsylvania communities showed little interest in popular education for many years. And one manifestation, among several, of this indifference was the lack of lyceums. Only during the brisk years of 1834 and 1835 did education in the state, and with it the lyceum, enjoy any great vigor. Thereafter both proceeded on the momentum of those two years and then continued with declining force until the end of the initial period of the lyceum movement.

Poor transportation blocked the development of the lyceum in some states but not in New Jersey. That state found itself almost a highroad between New York City at the northeast and Philadelphia at the southwest. On the other hand, there were parts of New Jersey in the 1820s and long after that which were so sparsely populated that they could not support lyceums. The two main areas of this kind were the Appalachian Highlands in the northwestern quarter of the state and the sandy southeastern part terminating in Cape May. Most states had an intellectual center, usually their largest city, and here New Jersey was no exception. It had Newark, a vigorous commercial community, close to New York City and to some extent receiving a cultural and educational impulse from it. Newark was big enough, however, to stand on its own feet and doubtless would have had its mechanics' institutes and lecture platforms had the metropolis been far away. This was not true of Camden, at the other end of the state, which lay across the river from Philadelphia and was a smaller, more dependent town.

Newark, by the time the lyceum idea began to spread, was al-

ready much industrialized. Its mechanics and apprentices early
founded debating clubs and working libraries on the English
model. Paterson, twenty miles to the north of Newark, acquired at
least two similar organizations. Its Mechanics' Society started in
1828 with the aim of mutual instruction in the sciences as connected with the mechanic arts. It prospered for five years, built
its own hall (opened in 1834 with an address by zealous young
Parke Godwin), and then foundered under the weight of paying
for it. The members announced desperately that the 'noble edifice
which first meets the eye of him who enters our town, and which
might stand as a lasting monument of the enterprise and genius
of our mechanics, must soon pass into other hands unless this last
appeal succeeds'; but the appeal failed. As befitted the state capital, Trenton saw to it that its lyceum had a certain amount of
ceremony. The *Family Lyceum* for 23 February 1833 reported
that the governor himself gave the introductory lecture of the
season 'in the presence of the beauty and intelligence of the city'
as well as members of the state legislature.

At Princeton in April 1834, the New Jersey State Lyceum was
formed. Plans for it had been laid against a background of public
education which was worsening instead of improving. When in
1831 the legislature had passed a law which set back the schools a
decade, the friends of education took up the challenge, says Burr
in his *Education in New Jersey*, with 'bitter grief and disappoint-
ment.' They seized the lyceum movement as a useful weapon. The
State Lyceum soon attracted prominent citizens from all over the
state and appointed local corresponding committees. It was the
hub of lyceum activity during the next few years. Ultimately, in
January 1838, a state education convention was held in Trenton
which took over some of the work of the Lyceum and managed to
push an improved law through the legislature. In 1843 the Society
of Teachers and Friends of Education in New Jersey was created,
thereby eliminating any remaining need for the State Lyceum as
originally planned.

As in Pennsylvania, the best years of the New Jersey lyceum
were a few in the 1830s, and those were devoted chiefly to promoting the welfare of the public schools.

With the Chesapeake Bay splitting off the eastern third of Maryland and the Appalachians dominating the western third, only the center of the state—and within it Baltimore in particular—offered any foothold for the lyceum. This cosmopolitan community, with its many workingmen, became the one place in Maryland where lecturing succeeded. The recent immigrants to Baltimore (German and Irish), handicapped by little money and inordinately long hours of work, meant practically nothing to the lyceum. But the industrious apprentice, the ambitious shipping clerk, and the inquiring merchant gave lyceums and lyceum-like societies their support.

Even before the movement began, the city possessed the Maryland Institute. It had a library, a geological cabinet, philosophical apparatus, and practical lectures. Apparatus was imported from Paris rather than bought at home—an index to Baltimore's vigorous ocean trade. By 1829 the lectures attracted an average of 200 persons, a fourth of whom were ladies. The lecturers, so one of the later presidents reported, were 'the most intelligent men of the state.' They spoke on 'all subjects which had a connection with the mechanic arts.' In 1833 the library held 3000 volumes. In 1835 the membership numbered 707. Yet underneath, all was not success. Even as early as 1833 two members of the Board of Managers publicly referred to a 'feeling of apathy and an abated concern for the important objects aspired after.' And in 1835 the building which housed the Institute burned, thus ending an organization that was not to be reconstituted until 1847.

This situation did not, however, mean that Baltimore failed to support the lyceum idea. By 1832 the Baltimore Lyceum had been founded. It was a typical lyceum and many citizens simply transferred their interest from the Maryland Institute to it. By the late 1830s the city had numerous other lyceums too. During the years the lyceum thrived there, the *Baltimore Sun* both reflected this prosperity and stimulated it with editorial encouragement. A glance through the pages of the *Sun* for a few weeks in the season of 1839–40, for instance, shows that even before the coming of winter—which the *Sun* officially pronounced to be the time for literary societies of all sorts—the lyceums in Baltimore had reawakened. On 25 October the *Sun* printed a little notice, then termed a 'card,' of the Madison Lyceum advertising that it would meet every Friday evening. The next day the program of the Phoenix Association for that evening was announced. On the Association's schedule were a lecture on natural history by the Reverend J. G. Morris and a discussion of the question 'Is luxury incompatible with republican institutions?' On the first day of November the *Sun* announced a meeting of the Baltimore Lyceum, with a lecture and debate. On 7 November the paper noted that the prolific writer Peter Parley (S. G. Goodrich) would deliver a course of lectures at Clinton Hall on 'Ireland and the Irish.' On 15 November the *Sun* carried a card for the Baltimore Lyceum saying that the next program would be a lecture on improvisation and a discussion of 'Ought the practice of delivering eulogiums on deceased public characters to be encouraged?' The issue of 20 November carried a card from Baltimore's Franklin Institute, advertising that Dr. W. R. Handy's lecture on the organs of the human voice would be delivered before the society the next day; the public was respectfully invited. On the succeeding day an apparently unsponsored lecture by Robert Grant on 'Financial Economy' was announced. The regular meeting of the Baltimore Lyceum was advertised on the 29th. The lecture was to be on phrenology; so was the discussion to follow. And so on.

These and other announcements reveal that Baltimore gave the usual lyceum a turn by consistently combining discussions with the lectures. By this time most audiences elsewhere in the country found one of the two enough for an evening, but Baltimore appetites proved to be hearty.

In spite of the notorious mud and exuberant politicking, Washington in the late 1820s listened to the normal number of random lectures that characterized most cities before the advent of the lyceum system. On 6 November 1831 the national capital saw the beginning of a genuine lyceum. It came to this city of 20,000 (if we add in neighboring Georgetown) from New England, naturally enough, and the chairman of the citizens' meeting was John Quincy Adams of Massachusetts. Mutual improvement and the general diffusion of knowledge were the formal aims of the Washington City Lyceum. In spite of distinguished auspices, it struggled rather feebly to effect those aims. The last act of any importance it accomplished was to send a delegate to the American Lyceum of 1834.

If we can judge by the columns of the local papers, the lyceum picture was a mixed one up to 1839. The casual lectures continued but the systematic courses, the organized diffusion of knowledge, fared badly. One reason very probably was the influence in Washington of southern culture. While Washington did not have the economy of the South, it had its point of view. However, during the years that the lyceum system existed the situation gradually changed. The cosmopolitanism inevitable in a nation's capital grew and modified the city's southern bias. And the Washington which let lecture courses die before the 1840s revived them and supported them increasingly after that time.

The columns of the *Washington Globe* show courses sponsored in the early 1830s by a few organizations such as the Young Men's Mutual Improvement Society, the Union Fire Company, and the Union Literary and Debating Society. The leading lyceums at the end of our first period were the so-called Debating Society and the Capitol Hill Institute; and the E Street Baptist Church was just beginning its sponsorship of outstanding lecture courses.

The three counties of Delaware led the same sort of tranquil existence that Maryland's Eastern Shore did. Only Wilmington, at the northern tip of the state, paid any attention to lecturing. It established the Lycaeum of Delaware just before the end of the eighteenth century. This was, however, by no means the herald of an early spring; similar cultural groups failed to flourish for a generation afterward. The low point came early in the 1830s. After that time conditions improved, and the change is reflected in the files of the *Delaware Gazette and Watchman*. The Young Men's Lyceum began, in December 1836, to insert cards in the *Gazette* announcing sermons on Sunday evenings to which all young fellows were 'affectionately invited.' Throughout the winter and spring of 1837 the Delaware Academy of Natural Science conducted a highly successful series of lectures. Originally announced as free to the public, conditions caused the Academy to charge first five and then ten cents admission. Those conditions, as explained in a letter to the *Gazette*, proved to be the crowding of the lecture room and the 'disorder committed by small boys.' The lectures, all by members, were on such topics as 'The Anatomy of the Eye' and 'Electricity.' In supporting this series the *Gazette* ran a letter from 'Public Good' saying that itinerant lecturers previously had preyed on the 'unsuspecting mechanics and others' of Wilmington and that now was the time to build a lecture hall, do away with the itinerants, and sponsor lectures which were a moral inspiration to young men. Sentiment in favor of having the hall crystallized and it was constructed. Lectures were advertised as being given in it by January 1838.

In the last three or four years of the decade cultural interest clearly increased in Wilmington. The Academy and the young Franklin Lyceum maintained their efforts at adult education; the newspapers gave more space to lectures and schools; there were more booksellers' advertisements; and the number of independent lectures—and itinerant lecturers, in spite of 'Public Good'—grew. What was true for Wilmington was not, though, true for the rest of the state. Delaware, like Maryland, bordered on the South and was strongly influenced by it.

6

The South:
Flurry and Apathy

THE fundamental fact about the lyceum in the South is that it ran counter to the massive economic and social trends—in which slavery became central—of the region, and to their cultural accompaniment. Moreover, the passing of the years during the first period of the lyceum accentuated this fact instead of modifying it. If we group southern society into classes we shall see that each class, in its own way and for its own reasons, failed to offer support to the lyceum.

If there is any personification of the southern upper class, it is in the plantation owner. An outdoor man, a man of action rather than cerebration, a person who cared almost as little for hearing a lecture as for reading a book, he was the opposite of the New England squire or leading citizen who provided so much direction for the lyceum movement in his town. It is true no doubt that in general the Yankee upper class assumed the responsibilities of leadership with mixed motives, and that their kind of American *noblesse oblige* was tempered with the desire to maintain the lyceum as a safe and conservative institution. Notwithstanding, the typical New England town lyceum had an admixture of first citizens among its busy young managers, and the effect was on the whole to give the lyceum help that it needed.

In the South, however, the upper class shrugged off these cultural responsibilities, if it ever felt them at all. That left the middle and lower classes as the remaining potential supporters of the lyceum. But the middle class, and that part of the lower class which aspired to become middle class, diminished decade by decade. Elsewhere they were the mainstays of the movement. Elsewhere the middle class made up the rank and file of lyceum membership; it joined shortly after the lyceum system started, and it paid its dues from that time on. Here, on the contrary, with the surging new strength of the slave power, the average merchant, the owner of merely an adequate farm, the minor professional man, and other members of the middle class found themselves hemmed in. It is true that the picture of the South as a country of nothing but great plantations and humble cabins is overdrawn. Yet it is also true that much of the middle class was worn away and that the South was left by 1845 with substantially more wealth at one end of the scale and more poverty at the other than had been the case in the 1820s.

If the situation was bad for the middle class, it was still worse for the whole lower class, both white and colored. Lyceums for Negroes were naturally out of the question; for the white tenant farmer they were almost equally so. The alert artisan alone remained as a possible user of the lyceum. But class lines in the South were stiffening, and the chances for a mechanic, for instance, to climb the economic ladder gradually lessened. So did his psychological incentives for trying. Translated into terms of the lyceum, this meant that the type of practical education for adults which was extremely important up north during the first stages of the lyceum movement had much less point in the South.

Other factors too, aside from those implied by the class structure, played their part in preventing the lyceum system from developing in the South. In the long run the lyceum achieved its greatest success in the areas that had numerous towns. The South, with its agrarian economy, had fewer towns than either New England or the Middle Atlantic states. The density of southern population also remained strikingly low. In 1840, for instance, Massachusetts had ninety-two people per square mile; New York had fifty-one; while Tennessee topped the South with twenty. The grand average for New England and the Middle Atlantic region was just over forty while the average for the South was only twelve. This difference was sharply accentuated by the fact that the Negroes had to be subtracted for any calculation about the prospects of the lyceum. The percentage of Negroes was considerable in all the southern states. In the frontier states of Missouri and Arkansas it was, as of 1840, least high—16 and 21 per cent respectively—but in South Carolina, Louisiana, and Mississippi there were actually more Negroes than whites.

Overlapping the agrarian economy of the South, especially below Georgia and across the lower Mississippi River, was the frontier. And the frontier was usually antagonistic to the lyceum. The extreme of the southern frontiersman was personified in the 'Kentuck' (not that he did not have some general western characteristics too), who so irritated the British travelers of his time. They met him on the Mississippi river boats as well as on the Ohio. To this shouting, bragging man the lyceum could offer nothing. Among the southern frontier states neither Arkansas nor Missouri, aside from St. Louis, gave the lyceum active support during its first period; while Florida, which did not achieve statehood till 1845, represented both the geographical isolation of the frontier and its low density of population. In the upper South, in Kentucky itself (and in Tennessee)—in spite of the fact that here by very definition was the home of the Kentuck—there was less of a frontier by the time the lyceum system started. The lyceum fared less badly in those two states than it did across the Mississippi in Arkansas and Missouri. Within most of the southern states, it should be added, many frontier-like areas continued to exist during the years before 1845.

Here, then, were great obstacles, demographic and otherwise, even for the village, mutual-education stage of the lyceum. And later, when local talent was exhausted and outside lecturers were normally in order, the difficulties compounded themselves. The villages and towns remained far fewer than up north, and the transportation between them was sadly inadequate. Roads in the interior often proved extremely poor; railroads developed more tardily in the South than farther north; and, as often as not, only the seacoast offered decent transportation to the would-be traveling lecturer.

Moreover, if the lecturer came from the North (and most traveling lecturers did) he would be apt to find less and less of intellectual hospitality as time went on. With the rise in anti-slavery agitation, the South felt compelled to defend all aspects

of its life with augmented vigor. Under fire from outside, southern
sectionalism closed ranks. The political leaders of this sectionalism,
furthermore, within the states if not in the nation's capital, were
anti-intellectual to a degree not equaled up north. Harm for the
lyceum naturally resulted. The entire cultural milieu was affected,
directly or indirectly, and the value of a congenial milieu to the
lyceum was great.

The importance, also, of the public schools and of literacy in
creating such a congenial milieu has been pointed out earlier. The
census figures for 1840 yield the first accurate data on how the
South stood in relation to other parts of the country. As Virginia's
George Tucker calculated the proportions in his *Progress . . . of
Population and Wealth*, in New England Maine had the best
record for primary school enrollment in proportion to its white
population while Rhode Island had the worst. Yet in Rhode
Island it was as high as one to six, in Maine one to three. In the
Middle Atlantic states New York rated best, with one to five, while
Maryland, with one to seventeen, rated worst. In the South
Missouri was least bad, with one to nineteen; and Louisiana was
worst, with one to forty-four.

The difference between the South, on the one hand, and the
New England and Middle Atlantic states, on the other, became
even more striking when the proportion of illiterates (whites over
twenty years of age who could not read or write) was calculated
in the same census. In New England Connecticut had the best
record, with the proportion of illiterates to the total white population of the state running as low as one to 574. Rhode Island was
worst again: one to sixty-five. The Middle Atlantic states came
considerably behind. New York, however, was best with one to
fifty-four. Delaware was worst with one to twelve. Among the
southern states Louisiana, paradoxically enough, rated best; it
had one to thirty-three. North Carolina was worst with one to nine.

We cannot be sure that the South was more literate after 1840
than before. However, such evidence as we have suggests that the
region became steadily more literate from the time the lyceum
movement began to flourish until the Civil War. The surprising
thing is that this trend did not reflect in a constantly growing
southern lyceum. But other and unfavorable trends overrode it,

and so the best days for the lyceum in the South were early ones, the 1830s. Then there was a flurry of interest but it soon changed, through the action of the major social and ecomic trends, into apathy.

Virginia's economy and part of its social structure resembled those of the southernmost tier of Middle Atlantic states rather than those of the deep South and was therefore beneficial to the lyceum. The Norfolk Lyceum opened in March 1827, preceding many such an institution farther north. Founded by a well-to-do citizen named William Maxwell, it reflected both his wealth and his interest in education. A local paper, the *American Beacon*, described the imposing lyceum hall: it had a 'beautiful vaulted room, . . . settees of curled and bird's-eye maple of fine polish' for the audience, 'and a rostrum of about three feet elevation, of the same materials, tastefully finished and carpeted, and furnished with a handsome settee for the accommodation of the lecturers.'

It is hardly surprising that the lecturers failed to equal the splendor of their surroundings. Norfolk's lyceum never showed much strength, but the limitations of the community made that understandable. Actually, the three likeliest cities in the state for lyceums were Richmond because of its size and political importance, Alexandria because of its nearness to Washington, and Charlottesville because it contained the state university. In each, lyceums and lectures made their appearance.

The Alexandria Lyceum started first, in 1834. It had lectures once a week on some literary, scientific, or historical subject— 'politics and religion being barred.' The Charlottesville Lyceum received its charter from the General Assembly three years later. As it grew it concentrated more on debates and essays than on lectures, but it worked steadily to gather a library. Its minutes, incidentally, attest to a punctilio of rare proportions. A William Pendleton, for example, was fined twelve and a half cents for 'passing between a member while speaking and the Chair.' The Richmond Lyceum, formed in 1838, served a prosperous city of nearly 16,000. It maintained itself in spite of the fact that half of that population was colored. In addition to the customary activities, the Richmond Lyceum briefly printed a literary magazine. The elegant *Southern Literary Messenger* tolerantly praised both its poetry and prose and remarked, looking down from a height, 'We recommend the work to the public and especially to the young.'

While most northern and all western states were showing marked economic progress, North Carolina during the first decade of the lyceum system presented a dismal picture. Poor markets, bad roads, antiquated farming methods, and a partly exhausted land meant a scant increase in either wealth or education. The years 1815-35 were apparently the worst ones. Then, from about 1836 times improved and agitation for public schools grew. Somewhat better days created a somewhat better culture. In 1839 the first state public school law was passed. But the advance made during the next ten or fifteen years was only relative. Actually the lyceum was never able either to take advantage of the gradual growth in literacy or to expedite it by the kind of alliance with the public school movement made in Pennsylvania and New Jersey.

South Carolina was better off from an economic viewpoint but in its case a different combination of factors kept the lyceum from realizing its possibilities. The widely praised richness of Charleston's culture showed itself mainly in club life rather than in classless mutual education. Even when a society crossed class lines, it was not a matter of mutual education but of the education of one class by another. The Apprentices' Library Society, for instance, resembled Philadelphia's Franklin Institute in doing something for, rather than with, the lower-class audience. Indeed, the announced object of the Library Society, with its books and lectures, was 'to beget a literary taste among mechanics.'

Once, however, during the middle '30s, Charleston stopped its customary activities and heard the gospel of the lyceum. Josiah Holbrook, moving south in his role of evangelist for the lyceum, arrived there in March 1834. The Literary and Philosophical Society held two special meetings on his behalf. He obviously swayed them both. The Society appointed a committee to prepare an address to the state explaining the merits which Holbrook had so convincingly ascribed to the lyceum movement. The chairman of the committee was Thomas Grimké, a member of a noted and idealistic family, who was elected vice-president of the American Lyceum when it met in May. The finished address, printed the same year, was on *The Classification, Character, and Exercises, or the Objects and Advantages of the Lyceum System, with a View to Its General Introduction into Our Towns, Villages, and the Country at Large.*

Holbrook's influence pervades it, and the plan outlined in the booklet follows the custom he initiated. The constitutions for town, district, state, and national lyceums are as expected. One appendix is devoted, moreover, to 'Facts Communicated by Mr. Holbrook.' It is succeeded by a series of pointers on mistakes to avoid about lyceums which no doubt derived from his observations. But this booklet is more than Holbrook. It is a useful, at times even charming, social document. Through its generous concern with popular education and with the improvement of the mechanic and farming classes, it testifies to a side of southern life that is more than magnolias and pillared plantations. Here the impress of Grimké is evident. However, in spite of Holbrook, in spite of Grimké, the *Address* fell on barren ground; and nothing like a lyceum movement appeared in South Carolina.

Even with a larger artisan class than South Carolina and far less of a genteel tradition, Georgia demonstrated more interest in the possibilities of the lyceum than did its neighbor to the north. Although public education received still worse treatment in Georgia than in South Carolina (the restriction of free schooling to the children of the poor did not end until 1858) the school teachers and the 'friends of education' proved themselves active.

In May 1834 Judge A. S. Clayton, representing the University of Georgia, could stand before the American Lyceum and report the existence of thirteen new lyceums in the state. The bulk of these new ones, and the old ones too, no doubt had a short life; but their very formation was an index to an interest at the time beyond that of most other southern states.

Savannah, farthest north among Georgia's ports, soon proved itself receptive to lecturing. It had its lyceum by 1834 and built a lyceum hall to house it. Macon's Lyceum and Library Society was organized at the end of 1836. In 1839 Columbus' was formed; according to a local historian, it turned out to be 'one of the most valuable societies the city ever had, by furnishing entertainment and instruction to the people.' Moreover, an occasional village as small as Greenville housed a lyceum. The Greenville Lyceum had a hall, a library, and 'a fine cabinet of minerals and curiosities' as of 1843. The local monthly, reporting this with pride, added a challenge, 'We hold up the Greenville Lyceum as a *hint* to other villages. Who will *take*?'

Few, however, did take up the challenge for by then the lyceum was failing. By that time it had practically been reduced to sporadic lecturing in the two or three main cities of the state.

Kentucky, as Tocqueville observed in his trenchant contrast of its economy with that of Ohio, was southern rather than western. Its lyceums could hardly compare with those of its northern and eastern neighbors, yet the state felt something of the early impulse of the movement. The *American Journal of Education* reported in January 1830 that several counties had organized lyceums 'upon a plan which is intended to embrace the state.' A month earlier the Kentucky Educational Society had been formed. It recommended the establishing of 'neighboring associations for self-improvement.' Yet the professional educators failed to utilize the possibilities of the lyceum system as an ally, with the result that public education in general suffered. Louisville supported the lyceum fairly well, and Lexington heard lectures every now and then. But the 'neighboring associations' were almost nonexistent. Little Hopkinsville was a rare exception. It had a lyceum complete with weekly lectures, according to the *American Annals* for July 1831. But the reason, in the eyes of the *Annals*' correspondent at least, was plain. Hopkinsville was fortunate enough to be located 'in one of the best sections of Kentucky, with a moral, energetic, and intelligent population alive to improvements of every kind.'

In Tennessee, as in a dozen other states, Holbrook's coming marked the onset of the only prosperous period for the lyceum. Appearing in late 1831 before the meeting called at Nashville to form a state lyceum, 'Mr. Josiah Holbrook delivered an impressive and instructive address on the subject of popular education and on the systems for mutual improvement.' When he finished, his audience promptly passed a resolution to organize and adopted a constitution. A leading educator, the Reverend Philip Lindsley, became the first president. To assist him a slate of nine other state officers was elected, along with nine curators. Of the curators three had to come from east Tennessee, three from middle Tennessee, and three from west Tennessee. The triple division illustrated the varying interests of the sections—a situation which hurt the lyceum and the public schools both. Though voters in the east Tennessee hills favored tax-supported education, they were always outnumbered by the rural slaveholding sections of middle and west Tennessee.

Enthusiasm for the lyceum proved to be short-lived in any part of the state, however, except for Nashville. There a lyceum had existed before Holbrook came and lectures continued to be given after he left. Though the state lyceum disintegrated, the Nashville Lyceum sponsored lectures and the city of Nashville continued to labor in the cause of public education, as the local papers for the early '30s show.

'Lyceums are becoming common in Alabama,' Holbrook wrote optimistically in December 1832. But if they ever did—and it is to be doubted—it was not for long. The annals of the lyceum there are meager. Mobile had one or two lyceum-like groups in the 1830s, the Mechanics' Association and the Mobile Franklin Society in particular. Toward the end of our first period a few itinerant lecturers made their way, among them a minister who was later to become a famous critic of Shakespeare's plays, H. N. Hudson. During this same time there were a few instances of northern lecturers interrupting their trip to New Orleans by stopping to speak at Montgomery or Mobile. Among them, in 1845, was Benjamin Silliman.

The lyceum movement turned out less badly in Mississippi than in Alabama. How important it was that the length of one state lay next to the great river while the other state was buried in the interior of the South, is hard to say. But certainly it had some significance.

The liveliest county in the state was Adams. Two of its towns, Natchez and Washington, supported the lyceum. Among the predecessors of the movement was the Natchez Athenaeum. Devoted to 'extending the means of intellectual improvement to persons of all ranks and all professions,' it was operating, primarily as a library society, as early as 1821. Four years later the Adams Athenaeum, with headquarters in Washington, was founded. Its first president was the gentleman naturalist Benjamin Wailes. He initiated the move for a library; the other objective he proposed for the Athenaeum was an exchange of knowledge through 'dissertations upon useful and interesting topics' which the members were to prepare. Twice, in December 1832 and January 1833, Holbrook's *Family Lyceum* reported the organizing of a county lyceum, for Adams County, by friends of education in Natchez. As the political and cultural center of Adams County (it was the county seat), it evidently was the logical place. In 1835 another society emerged in the county, the Jefferson College and Washington Lyceum. Far different from some churlish organizations, the Washington Lyceum encouraged the ladies to attend. The local *Gazette* added its appeal, in this case on 11 August 1837. 'If the fashion and beauty of Natchez were fully aware how powerful an impulse their attendance on such occasions could give the cause of learning, they would not fail to attend. It is a pretty evening's drive on the Washington road.' Along with references to the Washington Lyceum in the *Gazette* there are a few to a Ladies Institute and Lyceum, where women could hear every two weeks how important it was that they should be educated.

The story of the lyceum in Louisana is the story of New Orleans; the rest of the state was much behind Mississippi and even Alabama. But New Orleans was the transportation center of the Southwest. In the ten years from 1830 to 1840 its population doubled, reaching over 100,000 and making it the third largest city in the United States. The effect of the influx was, however, only gradually felt. Holbrook managed to visit New Orleans in December 1831. When a group of citizens gathered to consider establishing a lyceum, he spoke before them on its purposes and remarkable advantages. But he spoke too early. The city showed itself uninterested and the effort was abortive. With the coming of northern immigrants and Yankee businessmen in the 1840s, on the other hand, the lyceum received substantial assistance. The core of the support was the Second Municipality. The First Municipality was the old town, the Creole section. With its aristocratic, close-minded culture, it showed little evidence of any regard for those values which formed the basis for the lyceum system. The Third Municipality was the motley and miscellaneous remainder of the city. But the progressive Second Municipality, almost a Yankee enclave, labored on the side of education and public good. Among other things, it established the Library and Lyceum Society in 1844. From this same energy, the People's Lyceum—which had already passed some feeble years—received new life. In the seasons following 1844 the previously rather casual lecturing became better organized, more orderly.

The climax of the period through 1845 was definitely the course by Benjamin Silliman. He made the long journey from New England at the invitation of the local Medical College and several important citizens, who were probably Yale graduates. The expense of bringing the apparatus, as well as the lecturer, to this far corner of the country bulked so large that he had to be guaranteed $1,500 before he left home. He opened his course of twelve lectures on 18 February 1845. Before what the *Picayune* called one of the 'largest, most intelligent, and fashionable audiences ever seen convened in the city,' he spoke on the subject of geology. All his lectures seem to have been scientific, the last ones being devoted to the history of fossil animals. His speaking received praise as 'dignified and commanding,' 'simple and impressive without the affectations of oratory.'

North of Louisana lay Arkansas and then Missouri. Arkansas showed only a glimmer of lyceum activity. And Missouri resembled Louisiana, for both states ignored the lyceum except in their principal cities, St. Louis and New Orleans.

Settled early and excellently located on the Mississippi River, St. Louis enjoyed cultural advantages long before its neighbors.

Missouri itself when the lyceum movement began was a mixed, borderline state, with an uneasy combination of western and southern characteristics. So far as the lyceum was concerned the state proved southern. But the founding of the St. Louis Lyceum, the Franklin Society, and the Mechanics' Institute goes to show that the city, at any rate, took eastern culture seriously.

The St. Louis Lyceum was active by the end of 1832. Among other things it owned a cabinet of 'Indian curiosities' and listened to addresses on Indian history which were later published. It was abandoned after several years but a new St. Louis Lyceum was opened in June 1838. Its object was 'the intellectual improvement of its members by means of debates, essays, and lectures.' Early lecture topics included 'The Age of Physical Science,' 'Scepticism,' 'Geology,' and 'The Peculiarities of American Character and Duty of American Citizens.' Science was always the most popular subject, followed by travel, history, and what the St. Louis Lyceum called 'morality.'

The high point in the Franklin Society's brief existence came in 1835 when an extraordinary speech was delivered by an extraordinary member of the group. The member was the Reverend W. G. Eliot, Jr., the grandfather of T. S. Eliot and a founder of Washington University. Under the heavy title of 'The Obligation Which Rests upon the Present Generation to Establish Literary Institutions in the West,' he offered both a challenge and a warning. Speaking of Missouri as 'this remotest state,' he predicted for it and the entire Mississippi Valley the condition almost of a great nation in itself. To him the West combined the virtues of the East and South, and was intended to act as a balance between them. But the West might easily be corrupted into immorality, selfishness, and greed unless education could be fostered. 'Give such a character to the West, and its greatness would be palsy to the limbs and a stone round the necks of the East and South.' In his conclusion Eliot described one remedy he saw. 'If lyceums or literary societies were erected throughout the West, in every considerable village, they would excite many a young man to obtain a solid, useful education; they would exert a purifying influence upon public morals and tastes, and serve to remind many who are engrossed in money-getting that they have an intellectual treasure within them which ought not to be entirely forgotten.'

Like Missouri, Arkansas during the lyceum period contained elements both of the West and the South. Such evidences of the lyceum as there were restricted themselves naturally enough to the northeastern and central parts of the state. The Ozarks and the young cotton plantations in the southeast of the state offered no soil for lecturing. The fact that the eastern border of Arkansas was the Mississippi River, on the other hand, constituted a potential advantage for the traveling lecturer when his time came. But few lecturers stopped off; the communities were not yet large enough to encourage them.

Little Rock had a debating society, with a library, as early as 1822; it was reorganized in 1835 as the Pulaski County Lyceum. And Batesville, with Arkansas optimism, organized a lyceum which it grandly termed Batesville Number 1. One lecture we know of, probably representative, was given by a local minister on chemistry, 'demonstrated,' according to the *Batesville News*, 'by experiment.'

7

The Midwest:
New England Culture Immigrates

THE rich lands of the Midwest continued to beckon to those
New Englanders who had enough of cold weather, stone
walls, and rocky fields. All throughout the first period of the lyceum the waves of migration advanced. When Holbrook founded
the first lyceum at little Millbury, there was already a belt of
New England settlers in northern Ohio—the old Western Reserve—around the shores of Lake Erie. During the next decade
and a half many more came to join them. Two other places in Ohio
continued to be hospitable to former New Englanders as well.
These were the center of the state, around Gambier, and the southwest, both around Marietta and immediately north of the Ohio
River. The rest of the state was settled by people from the South
and the Middle Atlantic area, with the southern culture predominant in the early years of the century. With this original diversity
of cultures the state as a whole ought to have become a composite.
'Yet,' as Lois Mathews says in *The Expansion of New England,*
'New England tradition had been impressed upon Ohio. . . .
Into the new West the school, the church, and the town-meeting
had been carried.'

Ohio became the New England, indeed the Massachusetts, of
the Midwest. The most vivid contrast between the New England-
Ohio culture, which favored the lyceum, and the southern culture,
which did not, was the one painted by Tocqueville. Much more
than a river separated Ohio from Kentucky, he felt. On the Kentucky side the traveler would see little but a troop of slaves idling

in the half deserted fields; while on the other side he would be impressed by the hum of Ohio's industry and the signs of wealth and abundance. In Tocqueville's estimation the primary reason was the presence of slavery in the one state and its absence in the other.

Other factors too, social, economic, and even political, were involved in the kind of reception the lyceum got; yet in the South those all bore at least some relation to slavery. In the North they obviously did not. The frontier is a prime example of those factors. More often than not, we know, the lyceum found the frontier to be an opponent; so the lyceum normally followed—and at a little distance—the clearing of land and establishment of communities, though there were occasional frontier lyceums. The South, since it maintained a population of relatively low density throughout the years of the lyceum system, kept some of the characteristics of the frontier long after the North. Kentucky's population, in point, was swiftly outstripped by Ohio's. In 1820 both states had between five and six thousand inhabitants. By 1840 Kentucky had added only a little over two hundred thousand while Ohio had almost a million more. And by the same year Ohio had no vacant land left at all. New England institutions, among them the lyceum, consequently could and did thrive in the growing Ohio towns.

Coming to Indiana, on the other hand, the emigrants from New England found Southerners firmly in control and accordingly bypassed the state. It is true that these were Southerners without slaves, and that Ohio also had had its share of them, but the New Englanders considered them to be intrenched in Indiana. Some New Englanders of course stopped when they came to Indiana and settled down, especially in the north, where the former Kentuckians and Tennesseans of the southern part of the state had not penetrated. But in Indiana as a whole, the southern culture overpowered the New England one. The lyceum had little success there.

Among the other things contributing to the stunted state of the lyceum in Indiana was the comparatively sparse population. In the census of 1830 the state had little more than a third of Ohio's population. Each decennial census narrowed the gap, but even by 1860 when Indiana had 1,350,000 inhabitants, Ohio still had nearly a million more. Yet this too is only part of the story, for we know that lyceums prospered in states with fewer people than Indiana. Other factors beside demography entered in. The ever-felt need to hew out a living (work as a creed as well as a necessity), the narrowing sectarianism of the biggest protestant denominations, ('the most powerful single influence in early Indiana,' the Federal Writers' Project *Indiana* asserts), and the indifference to education (not until 1851 was an effective state-wide public school law passed) all must be considered. 'It was not without reason,' the volume adds, 'that Indiana in the early nineteenth century was said to have the crudest and most provincial population in the United States.' If this conclusion is correct, it throws additional light on why later in the century Indiana failed to support the lyceum movement with any zeal.

The lyceum in Michigan, however, could count on a good measure of hospitality. First of all, a strategically located city arose to give Michigan leadership and luster. That was Detroit. From the 1820s on, it possessed a remarkably vigorous intellectual life. Indeed in terms of the kind of culture that the lyceum represented, Detroit became the outstanding city in the Midwest (with the possible exception of Cincinnati) prior to 1845. Furthermore, the year before Holbrook founded the Millbury Lyceum, the Erie Canal opened; New Englanders took increasing advantage of the Canal and of steamboat passage to Detroit and its environs. Throughout the 1830s Detroit's culture was steadily reinforced by the culture the New England emigrants were bringing with them. Pushing beyond Detroit, they peopled most of the southern third of the new state by 1840. There too they planted their institutions.

In Illinois the situation for a time resembled that in Indiana. Tocqueville, again, had said that 'The population of Ohio is already proceeding westward and most of the settlers who descend to the fertile savannas of Illinois are citizens of Ohio.' These Ohioans—New Englanders once removed—and other New Englanders who came directly found the populated part of Illinois under southern control. The state constitution and the first laws were framed on southern models. The political leaders were all from the South. Because they and their fellows had moved up to about the middle of the state, the New Englanders occupied the vacant territory from Peoria north to Rockford. Antagonism between the two halves of the state grew bitter during the early 1840s.

Before this time there were also a few New England settlements farther south in Illinois, particularly around Springfield, Alton, and Pittsfield. The beginnings of the lyceum showed themselves there rather than in the north, because the frontier in northern Illinois was still a major problem. But they showed themselves, it should be noted, particularly in the New England enclaves. When the state lyceum was started in 1831, the delegates came for the most part from them. Chicago, later to be the hub of lecturing for the Midwest, had no importance at all during the early years of the lyceum system.

By the 1840s the fringe of New England settlement was extending into southern Wisconsin but the frontier, once again, was not yet subdued; and so the lyceum had to wait a while for genuine support. For Iowa this was almost as true. As it turned out, neither Wisconsin nor Iowa achieved statehood during the first period of the lyceum and the correlation of that fact with the feeble condition of the lyceum is close.

———◆———

After the original migrations into the Western Reserve, which were concluded by the end of the eighteenth century, Ohio experienced a quarter century of economic consolidation. By the time Josiah Holbrook began to spread the gospel of the lyceum, the frontier was under control, commerce and industry were starting to thrive, and the conditions which fostered lyceums could be found in much of the state. There were now some two dozen lively smaller towns along with a metropolis, Cincinnati. There was a public school system, far superior, incidentally, to Indiana's. In 1840 Ohio had, proportionately, twice as many children in school. The literacy rate was much higher for the total white population in Ohio than in Indiana. There were many more newspapers and even some magazines, including the *Western Messenger*, beloved by the New England Transcendentalists. Lastly,

Ohio already had a number of literary, historical, and debating societies when the lyceum movement entered the state.

Cincinnati's strategic position in Ohio's culture was shown, so far as lecturing was concerned, in the occasional individual lectures and courses beginning as early as 1812. By 1828 the Ohio Mechanics' Institute was being organized. By 1835 the Young Men's Mercantile Library Association appeared. It helped set the pattern—later to be repeated throughout the whole Midwest —of the private library association which sponsored lectures both for their own sake and to get money to buy books. By the late 1840s the platform of the Cincinnati Association had been occupied by a number of the best lecturers from the East as well as the West.

And Cincinnati was only the first among many Ohio communities. One of the most impressive indexes to the strength of the lyceum in Ohio is the acts of incorporation passed by the General Assembly. From 1831, when the Cincinnati Lyceum was incorporated, to 1845, at least sixty lyceums or lyceum-like societies received a state charter. Every town of any size in the entire state is represented. There were even two county lyceums, in Delaware and Stark Counties. If we add those athenaeums, library companies, and assorted literary societies which served at least some of the purposes of a lyceum, the result is still more striking.

Here was a state with a cultural vitality more pervasive than that of any other state in the Union. Massachusetts and New York, with the advantage of the two greatest cities in the nation, certainly were richer intellectually. And parts of both those states, in addition to Boston and New York, showed a remarkable cultural strength. But other parts were, for the purposes of the lyceum, very weak. Western Massachusetts and Cape Cod, the mountainous parts of New York state as well as the Finger Lakes region—those were territories where the lyceum meant little. In Ohio, on the other hand, though it is true that lyceums were even more frequent in some areas than in others, there were few places throughout the state where they could not be found.

With many a field not yet cleared by the time the lyceum movement started, Indiana still presented a picture of a frontier state. Some of the pulsing energy which created Ohio avoided Indiana and ultimately reached Illinois. And the fact that Indiana touched the important east-west channels of travel had less result than one would anticipate. Lyceums were to be rare. In an important letter (printed in the *Indiana Journal* of 12 November 1831) which represents the formal beginning of the lyceum movement in the state, the writers begin by saying frankly, 'We are aware of the hardships and privations to which the first settlers of a new country are exposed.' They go on to make the argument that the way to aid education is through private initiative. In order to help public education the writers—sixty-eight in all including the governor—suggest as the next two steps the calling of a state-wide education convention and the establishing of lyceums in the counties.

Organizing started, then, not at the grass roots but at the state level. The meeting to launch a state lyceum was held in the Hall of the House of Representatives on 19 December with Governor Noah Noble in the chair. A resolution in favor of forming the Indiana Lyceum was passed and thirteen persons were appointed as a committee to draft the constitution. Yet in spite of its distinguished auspices nothing came of the state lyceum. Instead the normal pattern asserted itself and the main city in the state took over the leadership, By March 1832 Indianapolis' own lyceum was ready to commence operations, with Governor Noble as president. The first meeting showed an inordinate thirst for knowledge: not one but three lectures were given. They were about lyceums, chemistry, and music. The program took some two and a half hours. Twenty new members joined. 'May this prosperous commencement eventuate in making our community wiser and better,' said the *Indiana Journal* hopefully.

How much it did so is a question, but the city's continuing interest in lyceum activities was shown by the establishment, two years later, of the Indianapolis Athenaeum. It immediately specialized in long lecture seasons, and cultural rather than practical topics. Perhaps the topics were too cultural, the seasons too long, for the Athenaeum was soon succeeded by the Young Men's Literary Society; and it in turn was followed by the Union Literary Society.

Elsewhere, for instance in Logansport, Vincennes, and Evansville, scattered lyceums appeared; but when the eastern lecturers began coming in toward the end of the first period of the lyceum's history, Indianapolis was apt to be their sole stopping place in the state.

If the settlers of 1830 in Indiana thought they were on the frontier, those in Michigan knew it for a certainty. Throughout all the decades of the lyceum movement, in fact, upper Michigan rarely saw an outside lecturer. Almost all the lyceums that came into being were located, as one would expect, in the southern third of the state. There transportation was better and there most of the settlers congregated. Here again, one fortunately placed city, Detroit, became the cultural heart of the state.

With the establishment of the Detroit Young Men's Society in 1832, the basis for a regular lyceum appeared. According to its *Historical Sketch*, a few young men, 'clerks and employees,' met in a store after hours 'for the purpose of devising means of providing greater facilities for their intellectual improvement.' They were much aware of the fact that Detroit had no library and no daily paper, and that books were scarce and expensive. The men arranged to meet every Friday night throughout the winter months and less often in summertime. Lectures and debates formed the main business of most of the meetings. 'Eastern lecturers then had not,' the *Historical Sketch* observes, 'and in fact could not, find their way to this place, but a series of lectures by able men among our own citizens was commenced and maintained for many years, and until lecturers from abroad fully occupied the field.'

The Young Men's Society did well from the beginning. From a defunct predecessor, the Detroit City Library Association, it inherited a small collection of books. As time passed, the collection increased until by 1842 there were 1,350 volumes. The emphasis on youth in the organization lessened, and the rule that barred persons over thirty from active membership was altered to make it thirty-five. Finally even that age limit was erased. The Society was well led, and several of its young presidents achieved distinction later on.

The Society printed at least a few of the lectures given before it. One was by Samuel Barstow, one of the presidents of the Society, and another by a political leader, John Norvell. Since the great bulk of lectures disappeared without leaving any record behind, it might be worthwhile to look at Barstow's and Norvell's. Speaking on 'Some Moral Features of the Present' in 1844, Barstow found much to criticize in contemporary America. Materialism, he thought, was probably the worst American weakness. 'The mere mercenary love of gain . . . is . . . fast becoming, if it has not already become, the source of most debasing influences upon our national character.' 'Even science,' Barstow adds, 'feels its poisonous breath, and, descending from her starry throne on high, has become the mere slave of Utilitarianism.' As bad as materialism is French socialism in the form of the theories of the radical François Fourier. It degrades the individual, making him merely part of an enormous machine. But there is a way in which these flaws in America can be eliminated, and it is the way of education. 'Man's moral improvement must be cultivated through the medium of his intellect.' The lecture concludes with a vigorous assertion of the immortality of the soul and the consequent dignity of the individual.

Norvell chose 'The Importance of Capacity, Information, and Ability as Qualifications for Public Station' as his topic. He minced no words. Paying little attention to the democratic clichés of the quondam frontier, he spoke strongly of the need for thoughtful, independent legislators. 'In the contests of parties for power,' he declared, 'it has become common to speak of "the voice of the people" as "the voice of God." This is not true. The people consist of erring and fallible men.' Norvell's style is as direct as his approach to his subject.

The gains which the lyceum movement in Michigan, aside from Detroit, were able to make may at first glance appear small. But when the burdensome effect of the frontier is considered, the state accomplished more than average. The strong connecting link, in theory at least, among the local lyceums was to have been the Lyceum of Michigan, organized late in 1830 with Lewis Cass as president and with headquarters in Detroit. It lived, however, no longer than most state lyceums. After it expired, there were several years relatively bare of lyceum activity. But thereafter, with the impetus furnished by expanding trade and increased population, more than one southern Michigan town showed that it could create a lyceum. Kalamazoo had one by the mid-1830s; so did Monroe; so did Niles.

In Illinois as in Indiana the lyceum movement first made itself felt at the state level, but the Illinois State Lyceum lasted at least a little longer than Indiana's. The normal thing, one might suppose, would have been the assumption of leadership in the state by Chicago. In 1831, however, when the first meeting of the Illinois State Lyceum took place, even the friendly light of local pride could not do much to improve the picture of Chicago. No Detroit from our point of view, it was 'a frontier town of the lowest class,' Andreas' *History of Chicago* bluntly says. The southern half of Illinois was in a better cultural position, with its substantial islands of New Englanders.

The purpose of the first meeting, held at Vandalia (then the state capital) was to form 'an institution for the diffusion of useful knowledge.' The specific objects included propagandizing for education, developing lyceums in 'towns and populous neighborhoods,' and collecting materials on Illinois history and ecology.

Not long before the state meeting of the next year, the venturesome Reverend Theron Baldwin attended the American Lyceum convention in New York. There he explained that the Illinois Lyceum was so new that there was little to report. But he added that the very 'fact of its existence is interesting, located as it is on the outposts of the nation.' 'We are anxious,' he said looking trustfully eastward, 'to attach ourselves to the great system, in the hope that some pulsations from the seat of vitality may be felt in these distant extremities.'

The first local lyceum in the state was founded in Jacksonville—and by Josiah Holbrook. It heard lectures on natural philosophy, chemistry, botany, and history. Local history and geography (a typical Holbrook touch) were said to form 'a distinct subject of investigation, with the origin of the [Indian] mounds, whether natural or artificial, and of the prairies.'

Regardless of the fact that Chicago was still mostly submerged in the frontier, the Chicago Lyceum held its first meeting on 2 December 1834. It prospered for a few years but began to go

downhill by 1841 and died about 1843 or 1844, 'from sheer neglect,' according to a disillusioned former secretary. Meanwhile,
the Young Men's Association, a library company, had been
founded. In its first flush of vigor it saw five different slates of
officers put up. Walter Newberry, after whom the Newberry
Library was later named, headed the victorious ticket and became
first president of the Association. It hoped to maintain a library,
procure 'literary and scientific' lectures, and promote the intellectual improvement of the membership. The early lectures were
by local men on 'various topics of the times.'

In 1843 the Chicago Mechanics' Institute began to sponsor lectures on a rather casual basis. The Institute also took over and
operated a periodical, the *Prairie Farmer*; and there it once described the sponsoring process: 'Whenever a traveling lecturer
comes along, if he be an able one and promises an interesting
course, an arrangement is made by which he is furnished with
. . . room, lights, etc., and the members of the Institute admitted
free, other citizens paying what the lecturer may demand.' The
same year that the Institute made its offhand entrance into the
lecture field, the Young Men's Lyceum was established. It had a
short life, however—a reflection of Chicago's relative lack of interest in early lyceum activities.

The situation throughout the rest of the state was all too similar,
though here and there activity could be detected. For example, the
Young Men's Lyceum of Springfield, founded in 1833, had an
erratic career but not one without a highlight. On 27 January
1838 it listened to the young lawyer Abraham Lincoln as he lectured on 'The Perpetuation of Our Political Institutions.' He
maintained the thesis that mob violence was a prime danger to
the continuance of those institutions. When Rock Creek established its lyceum in 1837, one of the spurs was the feeling that
'we have been idle spectators of the advancement of other neighborhood towns.' This lyceum illustrated both the exuberance and
shortcomings of the frontier. There were several more *don'ts* in the
constitution that we find farther east. Also, the official reader of
papers by members of the club was ordered to examine the contents of his box, in which the papers were deposited, 'and on
finding any obscene documents . . . to burn them without further

ceremony.' And, lastly, the president had the constitutional power to assess fines for various offenses, ranging from not less than one candle to not more than six.

Before the lyceum could enter Wisconsin it had to hack out its own clearing, because this was frontier territory during the first half of the history of the lyceum system. Wisconsin was admitted to the Union in 1848, eleven years after Michigan and some thirty years after Illinois and Indiana.

The fact that the lyceum came late to Wisconsin had important results for the structure of the institution there. The philosophic apparatus, the cabinet of specimens, the practical topics, the intimate alliance with the drive for free elementary schools—all these things had come and gone in the East before the lyceum system established itself in this state. The constants, the factors that remained, were the lecturing, the setting up of libraries, and (less often characteristic of eastern states) the prominence of debating. One other constant, of a different kind, was the youth of the members. But lyceums such as these were just beginning to be in evidence in the mid-1840s. Before 1845 the handful of so-called lyceums such as the Milwaukee Lyceum and the Southport (later Kenosha) Lyceum were in reality debating societies.

When the lyceum made its first tentative crossing over the Mississippi to enter Iowa, it did so through eastern migrants who cherished their former institutions. These settlers found that the plains could be subdued more readily than the woods. The result was that lyceums in Iowa had a head start over those of Wisconsin. They confined themselves, as might be guessed, to the eastern side of Iowa, the side closest to civilization. In addition, though their founders often called them lyceums, they were much more apt to be debating clubs. The situation, in that respect, was the same as in Wisconsin. In Davenport, the most prominent community, the Lyceum was founded in 1839 and the Davenport Institute was operating in the early 1840s; but both stressed debating. That was true as well for the Dubuque Lyceum, Iowa City's succession of societies (the Iowa City Lyceum, the Young Men's Lyceum, and the Iowa City Literary Institute), and the Muscatine Lyceum.

Facets of the Lyceum: I

8

This Noble National Conclave

IT had been a long, extremely cold winter in New York and the city had suffered. But now, early in May of 1831, when the American Lyceum was being organized there as a national society, it was well into spring and fine weather. The creation of a 'national department,' as the convention's *Proceedings* later put it, was the next logical step after the creation of county and state lyceums. The immediate cause of this convention, which opened 4 May, was the resolution passed by the New York State Lyceum in January proposing a nationwide body. But even before that Holbrook had envisioned a top-level organization (his 'General Board') to co-ordinate the burgeoning activities of the lyceum movement.

It was time for such an organization. The movement had already become a national one, the *Proceedings* asserted, and it was true. Although official claims about the number of lyceums in existence were apt to be on the generous side, the figures in the *Proceedings* were impressive enough. It was now estimated that 'not less than eight or ten hundred town lyceums, fifty or sixty county societies, [and] several state lyceums' already existed.

Though lyceums could be found in most of the settled parts of the country by this time, the delegates who attended the 1831 organizing session came from New York state and the states nearby. To be exact, thirteen out of the twenty-three delegates listed in the journal were from the state of New York. The rest were from Massachusetts, Maine, Connecticut, and Pennsylvania. The Reverend Alexander Proudfit, a distinguished minister serving as the delegate from Washington County, New York, was elected president of the meeting. Others there who either already had or would have prominent places in the lyceum movement included Holbrook himself (one of the four delegates from the Massachusetts State Lyceum), the widely esteemed John Griscom, the brilliant Professor Denison Olmsted of Yale College, and Henry Barnard, who five years later became the first of Connecticut's state superintendents of education.

The business of the opening day went briskly. Officers having been chosen, and delegates and 'a number of [other] gentlemen' having been admitted as members of the convention, a draft constitution for the national society was submitted, discussed, amended, and then adopted. As given in the constitution, the objects of the national lyceum were 'the advancement of education, especially in common schools, and the general diffusion of knowledge.'

The journal shows that the meeting lasted four more days (and into raw weather)—longer than any succeeding national convention. On 5 May the slate of officers for the coming year was presented, with Holbrook rising to make the nominations on behalf of the nominating committee. The delegates followed the committee's recommendations and chose Stephen Van Rensselaer as president. In addition they elected five vice-presidents. They were the Reverend Mr. Proudfit, Griscom, the already illustrious Edward Everett, Thomas Grimké of South Carolina, and the courtly Philadelphia philanthropist, Roberts Vaux. Thereafter the convention turned itself into a lyceum to discuss the problems of education and the lyceum system.

One of the best ways to assess the thinking of a convention like this is through its resolutions. Out of the eleven passed here, the most important advocated daily Bible reading in school, proposed the establishment of training schools for teachers, favored teachers' meetings under local lyceum auspices, and praised the schoolteachers of the nation '(. . . now estimated at 50,000) as a body on whom the future character and stability of our institutions chiefly depend.' But passing resolutions was not of course enough.

The convention realized the necessity of letting the public know what the lyceum movement was doing and so it readily ordered the publication of the 1831 *Proceedings.* Later proceedings reached print as well. During the next two years at least ten numbers, in fact, came out. One recorded the activities of the annual convention of 1832. The others were printings in leaflet form of essays or addresses which the national lyceum commissioned. A typical instance was Number 2, dated August 1832 and consisting of a paper on the use of the monitorial system in the common schools by Professor W. R. Johnson, the educational historian.

New York's handsome City Hall—'our *proud* City Hall' the old merchant John Pintard called it in one of his letters of this time—again housed the American Lyceum when it met on 4, 5, and 7 May for its annual convention of 1832. (Like the New York State Lyceum, the national group confusingly counted this second annual meeting as its first regular one.) Dressed in the dark, claw-hammer or skirted coats, light-colored pantaloons, and full stocks of the period, the delegates gathered with enthusiasm. The reports they gave were full of the feeling that an admirable cause was being advanced. John Pintard mentioned the meeting promptly in a letter to a grandson in New Orleans and incidentally urged an 'auxiliary' to it there. 'Such institutions,' he wrote, 'besides their positive utility give a character to society, and I should feel proud if my dear grandsons should be instrumental in establishing one.'

The convention of 1832 set the pattern for the remainder, so it will repay closer analysis than those that followed. We can see from the minutes that it performed all the characteristic functions of its kind. Its fifty-six delegates (more than twice as many as the previous year) represented state and local lyceums plus two colleges. Ministers and schoolmen constituted nearly a third of the delegates. Representatives came mostly from New York and New England. However, Ohio sent two and the farthest traveler was Theron Baldwin, the pioneer missionary and schoolman from the Illinois State Lyceum. After a more or less casual scrutiny by the credentials committee, they were all seated and the business began. The nominating committee presented its slate, headed by John Griscom for president, and the slate was quickly elected. Then came reports on the progress of assorted local lyceums. They appeared to be doing very well. 'This Lyceum was represented to be in a flourishing condition' say the minutes about the report on Worcester's society which its Mr. Going made; and so were they all.

The militant educator Theodore Dwight, who was national corresponding secretary, made a thoughtful report which not only surveyed plans and proposals for lyceums in this country but also in South America. Interspersed among the other proceedings were the lectures which had been commissioned. Among their subjects were 'Infant Education' and 'On Learning To Read and Write the English Language.' Motions and a minor amendment to the constitution were passed. Last came a set of three resolutions stating: (1) that lyceums were 'elevating the intellectual and moral character,' 'softening the asperities of party feeling,' 'promoting union and energy in other public objects,' and contributing 'materially to the improvement of common schools'; (2) that every town and village should have one; and (3) that 'naturalists and men of experience in science and the arts be respectfully requested to aid the lyceums' in selecting the subjects in natural history to be studied and in giving instruction in the use of scientific instruments and apparatus. In the marriage of social benevolence with practical scientific instruction this trio of resolutions accurately reflected the aims of the lyceum at the opening of the decade.

The discussions and reports of the succeeding years were crystallized into the annual sets of resolutions just as they had been in 1831 and '32. Noteworthy resolutions passed in 1833 advocated the formation of state lyceums, recommended to all lyceums and schools that they acquire 'cabinets of natural history' and help to establish a national cabinet as well, requested the current president of the American Lyceum, William Duer, to prepare a book on constitutional law for use at lectures and in classrooms, appointed a committee to devise a uniform plan for weather reporting, recommended to all lyceums and schools that they do something for charity, gave a pat on the back to the *American Annals* and the *Family Lyceum,* advocated hiring agents to 'promote the objects of the lyceum,' praised J. J. Audubon for his fine work in ornithology, and advocated courses in physiology, with a $300 prize for the best physiology text to be published.

The resolutions passed in 1834 were fewer in number but not

without their own significance. They showed a sudden love for the device of committees. They urged the appointment of a committee to collect information—on a nationwide scale—about teaching and to promote the establishment of a 'central seminary' for the education of common-school teachers. They requested appointment of a committee to raise money for the national lyceum. They asked for still another committee to study the problem of improving lyceums and making their programs more interesting. Then, without asking for a committee, they thanked Duer for writing the textbook on law proposed the previous year. Lastly they urged local lyceums to affiliate with the national body.

The numerous resolutions passed in 1835 can in general be gathered into three groups. One group stated firmly that 'the subject of female education deserves more attention than it has yet received from the American community' and went on to detail how that oversight might be remedied. Another demonstrated an interest in the lyceum movement in the South, while the third group spoke up for local financial support of the lyceum idea with the thesis that 'Lyceums are calculated to afford a cheap and agreeable means of intellectual and moral improvement.'

The march of the resolutions continued in 1836. This year's lot turned out to be a variegated one, the most important element being the realistic stress on the need of popular support for public education. Another resolution, but not in this category, was apparently passed in uneasy anticipation of the presidential election which was to follow in a few months. All allusions to 'the party politics of the day' (as well as to sectarian differences) should be avoided, the American Lyceum warned, mindful of the coming battle between Martin Van Buren and assorted Whigs.

That the warning had some effect, or at least so the Lyceum thought, can be seen from a resolution of the next year which congratulated the lyceum system on being the most effective allayer of 'party excitements.' Two other resolutions of 1837 reaffirmed former stands. The first was that the lyceum should have paid agents. The second was that weather data should be collected in a more scientific manner.

Eighteen thirty-eight saw in its resolutions a religious cast that had hitherto been missing except at the very first meeting. The

American Sunday School Union had suggested that the national lyceum offer a library of books of an 'entertaining and instructive character' (such as biographies, histories, and travels) printed by the Union to families, localities, and schools. These books were not, it would seem, intended to inculcate doctrine—that would have been contrary to one of the strongest lyceum traditions—but to inculcate morals. By resolution, the American Lyceum expressed its approval of the Union's idea. Still more explicit was another resolution, similar to the one passed in 1831, which stated that 'the use of the Bible in our popular systems of education, as a textbook of moral and religious instruction, is regarded by the lyceum as indispensable.' Other resolutions recommended the forming of teachers' associations and (once again) that the American Lyceum employ one or more paid agents.

In its unwittingly final convention, that of 1839, the American Lyceum laid plans for another kind of organization, which would later expand or even take over some of the national lyceum's functions. The Lyceum resolved that 'it is expedient to hold a national convention . . . for the purpose of discussing the various topics connected with elementary education in the United States.' The place proposed was Independence Hall in Philadelphia, the time the fourth week in November. An auxiliary resolution requested that invitations to attend be sent out through state governors and legislatures.

Such were the resolutions passed in the American Lyceum. Some of them probably had little impact but most, it can be hazarded, amounted to considerably more than wasted breath. As the *American Annals* for August 1839 observed, 'It has often been remarked that some good result has followed every public meeting of this association.' Part of the influence of the American Lyceum came through the fact that it acted as a federal institution. Part came through the high caliber of its officers and delegates, who were either professional educators or energetic laymen. Incidentally, one of the greatest services that the lyceum system performed, both nationally and locally, for the schools was the bringing together of educators and interested laymen.

The persons asked to lecture before the national lyceum made up a catholic and impressive group. They ranged from artists to explorers. Although there was a natural emphasis on education and educators, it was by no means exclusive. The romantic painter and poet Thomas Cole, for instance, lectured on 'American Scenery' to the Lyceum one year, at the same time that William Dunlap, first historian of the arts in America and himself a painter and dramatist, read 'The Influence of the Arts of Design.' At another of the annual meetings the 'Sweet Singer of Hartford,' Lydia Huntley Sigourney, spoke on behalf of 'Raising the Standards of Female Education.' One of the most devoted friends the American Indian ever had, Henry R. Schoolcraft, composed an address for the Lyceum entitled 'The Means for Promoting Civilization and Education among the Western Indians.' The German educator and refugee Hermann Bokum talked on 'The Moral and Intellectual Condition of the German Population in the United States.' About to become the outstanding meteorologist of his day, J. P. Espy lectured on his specialty. Edwin James, an ethnologist and explorer who was the first white man to climb Pikes Peak, read a lecture about 'The Chippewa Language.' The Turk Constantine Oscanyan addressed his audience on 'The History and Conditions of Education in Armenia.' And other speakers of almost equal interest were invited to appear on the annual programs.

The delegates, who elected the officers and listened to these lecturers, themselves represented both local and national leadership in education, and especially in the broadened education for which the lyceum system stood. Among the ones who achieved a nationwide reputation in one field or another were Jacob Abbott, Henry Barnard, Caroline Beecher, Theodore Dwight, Albert Gallatin, Samuel Gridley Howe, Abbot Lawrence, Lowell Mason, John Neal, and Daniel Webster.

Up to 1837 the American Lyceum met annually in New York, but that year (having amended its constitution to sanction the shift) it moved to Philadelphia, the next year to Hartford, and finally back again to New York in 1839. It made plans for meeting again the year after that and even sponsored the additional national gathering just mentioned, for friends of education in Philadelphia in the fall. But no other annual conventions followed. The Philadelphia assembly, which was actually termed a national lyceum by some people, itself scheduled another general convention for Washington, D. C., to be held in May of 1840. That one met too but with little result. The American Lyceum as such was then already dead.

It had, however, performed important services during its decade. It had acted as a focus, a clearinghouse, and a source of enthusiasm, immeasurable but actual, for the work of the lyceum. Its deliberations were at times ponderous, but that was the fashion of the day; and they testified to a genuine devotion. A delegate could rightly call it a noble conclave.

That it looked beyond our borders the American Lyceum proved both by such acts as Theodore Dwight's internationally minded report, already cited, and by the invitations it often made a point of extending to distinguished foreigners. At the same 1832 convention we have discussed, those present were Don Tomás Gener, ex-president of the Cortes of Spain; Lorenzo de Zavala, a Mexican historian and liberal political leader; José Salgado, who had just finished his term as governor of the state of Michoacán in Mexico; and Dr. Alejo Fortique, who was a member of the Venezuelan Congress at the time of his visit to the convention.

Such visitors Josiah Holbrook was delighted to see. In September 1837 he took the ultimate logical step and issued the *First Quarterly Report of the Universal Lyceum*. Here he outlined the way in which the benefits of the lyceum could be extended from this country to the rest of the world. He foresaw the system spreading 'not only to all sections and classes of our Republic, and through the continent of America, but to Europe, Asia, Africa, and the Islands of the Sea.' The fact that the lyceum could be so far flung, he went on to assert, afforded 'proof that it is founded upon the principles, and fitted to the wants, of human nature.'

The cabinets, the apparatus, the lectures, and the rest were, in his eyes, to become international instead of national. Officers, furthermore, were already selected from various parts of the world. Fittingly, Lord Brougham was named president. The *Report* continues with a list of vice-presidents, corresponding secretaries, an 'actuary' (Holbrook), and both corresponding and honorary members. On the list are persons from Scotland, Mexico,

Switzerland, the United States, France, England, and Africa.

One of the major purposes of the Universal Lyceum, the report said, was to provide the 'statistics . . . of the earth.' The aid of scientists, engineers, naval officers, philanthropists, and Christians, in various spheres, was solicited. Universal though this lyceum was intended to be, it was based on small units. The Holbrook hierarchy of lyceums is still present; in this report it works down to the neighborhood social lyceum and, finally, to the Committee of Three, which would be formed to accomplish any small set task such as the construction of a piece of apparatus.

But Holbrook was far ahead of his time. In almost every respect the Universal Lyceum could exist only on paper. Even here it did not exist long; if any other quarterly reports were printed, we do not know of them.

Notwithstanding, Holbrook did not let go of the idea. Five years later, in 1842, he managed to publish two numbers of a little magazine he called *The Self Instructor and Journal of the Universal Lyceum*. In it he still argued for 'diffusing knowledge over the globe,' to him the grand purpose of the lyceum system. In the face of the facts, he maintained that by now there were individual lyceums in operation in every part of North and South America, not to mention in 'many of the islands in the Atlantic and Pacific.' He thought he saw his vision fulfilled. Though he no longer stressed the importance of providing 'statistics of the earth,' he continued to advocate the international exchange of specimens of minerals and other objects 'of nature and art.' However, he was not content with paper plans alone—if he could help it—regardless of how wide they were in scope. He could report through the *Self Instructor* that he had already made at least a start by establishing the 'Universal Exchange Lyceum' in a room on the premises of the New York Society Library. Anyone could go there, Holbrook said, and exchange specimens for his cabinet.

9

The Lyceum and the Public Schools

The lyceum was education, adult education, and so the history of the lyceum is fundamentally the history of that phase of American education. However, the lyceum also took part prominently in the development of another phase of American education, the struggle on behalf of the tax-supported elementary school.

WRITTEN by a friend of Ralph Waldo Emerson's named Warren Burton, *The District School as It was, by One Who Went to It* appeared in 1883. It gives a pungent description of the only kind of school available to many a child during the first quarter of the nineteenth century. Suffering from all the inadequacies that went with local control, the district schools were least effective in the communities where they were needed most. Burton well remembered the tumble-down shanty he was forced to study in when a boy. The wind came through the clapboards. The windows were half broken, with shutters hanging vacantly or else lying useless on the ground outside. In winter the fireplace sputtered with green wood, and even when it worked it roasted the littlest children who sat up at the front of the room, while the rest shivered.

The teaching was on a par with the schoolroom. All too often the schoolmasters showed themselves indolent and ill-prepared. To the young men, teaching was a way to make a little money before or during college—as it was to Henry Thoreau though he happened not to be indolent—or else, and more characteristically, it was a place to pause a while between better jobs. To the young women, teaching was ordinarily a brief career before marriage. The main pedagogical method was rote-learning and routine, with plenty of discipline thrown in if the teacher was able to administer it.

That was Burton's grim picture of the district school in Massachusetts. No doubt it was overdrawn in places. Individual instances of good teaching, good equipment, and good morale could be found here and there in the state. And from another point of view even the sorry school that Burton wrote about could have something said in its favor: at least it existed. Poor as publicly supported education was in Massachusetts before the lyceum system began, it was far better than none. In most states there were for many children no schools at all.

New England was least badly off. Generally, the farther south or west one went, the more neglected public education became. As late as 1830 the Pennsylvania Society for the Promotion of Public Schools memorialized its state legislature and asserted that of the 400,000 children within the state, less than 150,000 were being schooled. 'Multitudes are living, and continuing to live, in ignorance; and multitudes more receive superficial instruction,' the Society said bitterly. In neighboring New Jersey the committee on the state of common schools had reported a few years earlier that 'in addition to the 11,742 children who are destitute of instruction, thousands of children in the state receive only a partial and very imperfect education and in many places from immoral and unqualified teachers.' In terms of public education Virginia, the Carolinas, Georgia, Alabama, Mississippi, and the rest were even worse with only the few larger cities as an exception. Most of those states had some money set aside for the common schools but nothing, it seemed, could persuade their penny-pinching, tobacco-chewing legislatures to spend it. Out west the same situation prevailed. There, however, there was a reason. The settlements were still so new, the country still so much a frontier, that schools had to wait if the incoming families were to survive. Everyone, children included, had to help in the struggle for existence. But even with allowance for that situation, the schools were forced to sue for support longer than they should have. Illinois was perhaps a worse example than the average. According to a news item in the *American Annals* for December 1831 it had almost 50,000 children of school age, and only about a fourth were actually going to school. Yet other midwestern states, aside from Ohio, did not have a much superior record.

In Massachusetts when the lyceum was starting, some male schoolteachers were being paid at the rate of $185 a year (if they worked the whole year—and they usually could not); some of the women teachers were being paid $64 a year; and some mechanics were getting $300 a year. Other states proved still more niggardly. Connecticut's Society for the Improvement of Common Schools made surveys of the situation in 1828 and 1831. The Society reported that the average salary, in addition to board, was about eleven dollars a month for men teachers and one dollar a week for women—and some of the women received as little as fifty cents a week. Throughout the nation the amounts expended for the schoolhouses and the physical equipment they contained were in dismal keeping with the salaries.

The forces that starved public schooling were formidable ones. Hostility to taxation was probably the most potent. Personified in the tight-fisted merchant or the black-coated Whig banker, it opposed taxes in both principle and practice. In his incisive little book, *Economic Influences upon Educational Progress in the United States,* F. T. Carlton analyzes those particular factors. He puts the financial one first. Its argument was classic: it was wrong, economically and ethically wrong, for the wealthy to be taxed to educate the children of the poor. Various other arguments were also advanced by the foes of public schools. The children of the poor would grow up idle and lazy—or discontented—if their education were given to them free and they would not have to labor for it. The number of poor children would increase if their schooling were provided without charge (the rich and the middle class would limit their families because they would want to do their utmost for them). If the children of the poor were made to go to school, it would be an infringement on their hard-won liberty. They would not be free to work, and their parents would lose the labor or the money the children would otherwise con-

tribute. Free public schools would mean the advance of centralized control and bureaucracy. Public schools would conflict with
parochial and private ones (a very telling argument). And each
of these arguments was vigorously employed.

Carlton also lists the specific groups opposed to, or at best luke-
warm toward, public education. As he saw them, they were the
residents of rural districts as opposed to the cities, the taxpayers
(then a small but very influential part of the total population),
the members of the exclusive or ultraconservative social classes,
the Lutherans, Quakers, and other proponents of sectarian schools,
the foreigners, and the proprietors of private schools.

The lyceum system afforded great aid to the public schools by
creating a general atmosphere favorable to them. This should be
emphasized. It did so at the village level; it did so for state legislatures. The many specific services the lyceum performed were
also of importance, but this general one was paramount.

The lyceum found itself able, in one way or another, to meet
or to divert every objection the enemies of public education had
to offer. The lyceum system was the center of an army in which
the elementary public schools were the exposed left flank. When
the lyceum won its battle, those schools profited.

First of all, the lyceum solicited rather than legislated for its
financial support. No one had to contribute unless he wanted to.
Secondly, the sum total of the money it needed to solicit was not
great. The lyceum, as the Reverend Asa Rand proclaimed in Boston, was economical. Next, in spite of the occasional juvenile or
school lyceums, most were intended for youths (and their elders)
rather than for children of school age. Only those who wished
came to the meetings; and the education they received was, furthermore, as a rule of a highly practical sort in the important early
days of the lyceum. It was designed to make better workingmen.
Since those being educated were not children and were generally
supporting themselves, the quasi-Malthusian argument that the
poorer part of the population would increase if schooled free did
not apply. There was in the lyceum system, in addition, no infringement on the rights of parents; typically, the youngest among
the actual lyceum members qualified in terms of those days as

young adults. And it was characteristic of the lyceum that it met in the evenings anyway, so there was no loss of children's working time when children did come. The specter of centralized control was avoided because it was only at the local level that the lyceum showed enduring strength. The control rested at the bottom instead of the top. True, some county and state lyceums managed to stay alive for a few years, and the American Lyceum existed for almost a decade. Yet each of these bodies had nothing but the power to urge or exhort; they could not enforce. Later, as the public school systems developed, some of their opponents would stigmatize centralized control as 'Prussian,' but that epithet was never hurled at the lyceum. The opposition by the parochial schools in certain states, especially Pennsylvania, proved more formidable to the lyceum than most of the other factors. However, with Holbrook's notable persuasiveness, even that opposition was diverted there by his explaining the value of practical scientific knowledge of the kind the religious schools were not ready to provide. The argument, lastly, that public schools would injure the private ones—the dame schools and the academies— was one more which did not apply to the lyceum for two reasons. For one thing, it did not concern itself primarily with children; and, for another, those young men who went to the lyceum were most often clerks and apprentices—persons who could not have gone to academies anyway because of the fees.

Besides the creation of an educational atmosphere more favorable to the public schools, the supporters of the lyceum movement were from the very beginning ready to offer more particularized aid.

'To the Friends of Education' many an early lyceum notice began. From the outset, publicly supported education, of all the aspects of America, was the one closest to the lyceum movement. Until about 1840 the lyceum worked steadily for the welfare of the common school. It did so in a large number of different ways. It made local surveys of children of school age. It expressed an official interest in the schools. It memorialized county commissioners as well as state legislatures. It passed resolutions. It listened to lectures on primary education. It gave school teachers a preferred place in lyceum meetings (they might, for instance, attend a course free while the public was charged a dollar). It called conventions of teachers on the county and state level. It acted at times as a training school (usually called a county institute) for teachers before the days of the normal school. It sponsored a national educational convention. And the lyceum worked for the public school by making common cause with thousands of educators ranging from the national leaders such as Horace Mann and Henry Barnard to the multitude of local schoolmen, forgotten today, who saw in the lyceum both a good in itself and an excellent tool for the advancement of the schools.

The potentialities of the lyceum as an ally of education were realized at once by Editor William Russell of the *American Journal of Education*. First published in 1826, it briefly but significantly added *and Monthly Lyceum* to its title before it became the *American Annals of Education* under its second editor, the handsome, sickly William Woodbridge. Meager though its subscription list always was, the magazine remained the leading educational journal in the country during its fourteen years of existence. Both editors gave the lyceum all the space that anyone except perhaps Holbrook could want. In a sheaf of about thirty consecutive pages taken out of the March 1830 issue, the headings which illustrate the manifold mingling of education and the lyceum are 'An Address Pronounced on the Anniversary of the Concord Lyceum,' 'Columbia College,' 'Salem, Mass., Lyceum,' 'Williamstown Lyceum,' 'Middlesex County Lyceum,' 'Worcester County Lyceum,' 'New Bedford Lyceum,' 'Brooklyn, Conn., Lyceum,' 'Montpelier, Vt., Lyceum,' 'Education in Chile,'' 'The Common School System of New York,' 'Boston Schools,' 'Physical Education,' 'Popular Education,' a letter for the *American Journal* praising American education, 'Tribute to the Worth of Sabbath Schools,' 'Sunday Schools,' 'Infant Schools,' and 'Remarkable Precocity of Talent.'

In half a dozen states, the state-wide lyceums showed their interest in education unmistakably. Most outstanding was the New York State Lyceum. Born in January 1831, it announced as its paramount aim 'the improvement of our system of common school education,' and only after that came the 'general diffusion of knowledge.' The American Lyceum itself trod close behind, for in May of the same year, when the national lyceum organized itself, it similarly put improving the elementary schools ahead of the general diffusion of knowledge.

Among the occasional lyceums intended especially for teachers the most prominent as well as one of the earliest was the American Institute of Instruction. It was for education what the American Lyceum was for the lyceum movement. Founded in 1830 in Boston, the Institute held yearly meetings at which it heard lectures on education that were later published. These annual volumes contain some of the best educational thought—as well as a little of the dullest—of the lyceum period. The lectures for 1836, an average year, which saw print were 'On the Education of the Blind,' 'On Thorough Teaching,' 'On "the House I Live in,"' 'On the Incitements to Moral and Intellectual Well-Doing,' 'On the Duties of Female Teachers of Common Schools,' 'On the Best Method of Teaching Elocution in Schools,' 'On the Influence of Intellectual Action on Civilization,' and 'On School Discipline.'

Dr. Samuel Gridley Howe, currently in charge of the Massachusetts school for the blind, was the author of the first lecture. Although marred, understandably, by the defects in the psychology of the time, the address is distinguished by its high degree of common sense. Do not pamper the blind child, Howe advises for instance, and this advice is followed even today. William H. Brooks's lecture 'On Thorough Teaching' mingles two things, one much less useful than the other. The first is a good deal of grandiose generalizing about how teaching should be done. The second, and more helpful, is a series of suggestions about proper classroom management. 'The House I Live in,' the subject of Dr. W. A. Alcott's address, proved to be the human body. A pioneer in physical education, this cousin of Bronson Alcott told the listening teachers that the rules for good living must come from God because the body is the temple of the immortal soul. J. H. Belcher's lecture 'On the Incitements to Moral and Intellectual Well-Doing' must have been a waste of time. It elaborated the obvious in deadly fashion. Its subject, motivating the student, is perennially important but Belcher had little that was fresh to say about it. Like Belcher's lecture, Daniel Kimball's on the duties of the woman teacher probably did little to instruct or inspire his hearers in spite of its flights of rhetoric. The next lecture was by T. D. P. Stone on elocution. It testified to the steady interest of the nineteenth century in making the spoken word effective. H. R. Cleaveland's address 'On the Influence of Intellectual Action on Civilization' found its worst foe in the breadth of the subject. A mass of generalizations, it tried to give an impression of structure through its numbered points but failed. S. R. Hall, an educational reformer and founder of the first American normal school, gave the final lecture, which dealt with the eternal problem of school discipline. It briskly outlined the correct methods, as Hall saw them, and then comforted the teachers by pointing out that a large part of school discipline should begin at home— and if it did not, then the family was at fault.

A substantial minority among the lecturers from year to year included enthusiasts for the lyceum. They were generally schoolmen also since most of the subjects were treated too technically to interest even enlightened laymen. In form, if not always in content, the American Institute was a national lyceum and served further to demonstrate the connection between the lyceum movement and tax-supported education.

One of the most illuminating gestures toward the improvement of public education was made in 1839 when the American Lyceum sponsored not an institute but the first national convention for the public schools. The call came, as we have noted earlier, out of a resolution adopted by the national lyceum to the effect that it was 'expedient' to hold a week-long convention to discuss elementary education in the United States. The convention was held as planned, in Philadelphia during the month of November. A committee was appointed to implement each of the important resolutions which were passed. The question of how much this so-called National Education Convention and its resolutions accomplished is, once again, not the kind that can be answered specifically. But at the very least, stands were taken and principles for future action laid down.

The first resolution, invoking the spirit of George Washington, urged the citizens of the entire country to take an interest in the public elementary schools. The resolutions that followed were directed at both the federal and state governments. Congress was twice asked for money. In one resolution it was requested to make an appropriation from the rich legacy which the British philanthropist James Smithson had left and devote it to education. In the other it was urged to appropriate to education all, or part at any rate, of the money coming from the sale of public lands. If Congress heard either plea, it gave no sign. At the state level, the sluggish legislatures were requested to establish a 'system of general education whereby free and common schools may be made accessible to all and that knowledge be secured to the people which is the bulwark of social and political happiness and freedom.' In addition, the governors of the states were urged to make the condition of the public schools a part of their annual messages and to find out how the schools in their state could be improved. A related resolution recommended the forming of state-wide education societies or the holding of state-wide educational meetings.

Before it broke up, this convention in turn decided to call for another one. Washington, since it was the nation's capital, was picked as the best place, and committees were named to put the necessary machinery in motion.

The Washington convention met on schedule, beginning Wednesday, 6 May 1840. Under the title of the National Convention of Friends of Education it held its deliberations in the Alderman's Chamber of the City Hall. Replacing John Griscom, the current president was Dr. A. D. Bache, physicist and first head of Girard College in Philadelphia. Delegates from sixteen states attended, although there appears to have been a natural weighting in favor of those from nearby Pennsylvania and Maryland. Both the *National Intelligencer* and the *Globe* carried announcements of the sessions. Both stated that important business was transacted and promised to report it in full. Apparently they found enough space to summarize other meetings including the National Convention of Whig Young Men; and they had room for advertisements of Dr. Taylor's Balsam of Liverwort or Dr. Phelps's Tomato Pills. But their columns failed to include the promised report on the convention.

We know, however, that other educational conventions followed, for a long time sporadically, with a growing tendency among the participants to draw to themselves and to professionalize. Perhaps the only unhappy result—but a truly damaging one—of the educators' becoming professionally minded, with ever-growing insistence on the vocational arcana of teaching, was that they began to think less about the public in its relation to the schools and more and more about the schools alone. Specialization was setting in. The schoolmen concentrated on founding their own associations and neglected to support the lyceums. As late as 1845 Henry Barnard, then Commissioner of Public Schools in Rhode Island, could still say of lyceums and their adjunct libraries, 'These lectures and books will silently but powerfully help on the improvement of public schools.' Others of Barnard's annual reports besides this one of 1845 show his constant awareness of what the lyceum system had to offer the public schools. But he was a far-sighted and increasingly rare exception among educators.

This drifting apart of the lyceum and the common school movement turned out unhappily for the lyceum too, for it was one of the things that allowed lyceum programs to become more entertaining and less instructive. Both sides lost by the cutting of the ties.

10

Platform Gallery: I

O F necessity, because this book surveys the history of an institution on a nationwide scale, it has been an account of groups rather than individuals. Yet we should remember that real people were categorized by labels such as the New Bedford Lyceum or the Chicago Young Men's Association. These people— a multitude—we cannot individualize, but we can say a little about one or two of their typical leaders and a few of their lecturers. The lecturers we are going to speak about in this first period up through 1845 were representative, each in his own way, of a large number of others.

Timothy Claxton: the Enterprising Mechanic

The ideal type, so-called, of the intelligent artisan who assumed prominence in the early lyceum was a handsome, restless Briton born in 1790 and named Timothy Claxton. Most of what we know about him comes from his *Memoir*. He began as an ambitious country lad who was schooled in Suffolk and then went up to London. There his training developed him into a skilled mechanic as well as something of an inventor. Because he wanted to learn more about science he applied for membership in a middle-class 'philosophical society' but was rejected. He promptly decided to form his own. He sent out printed circulars which asserted, among other things, that none of the existing societies were 'adapted to the capacity of a working mechanic.' Begun during the summer of 1817, his 'Mechanical Institution' met for three years before it dwindled away. The meetings were held weekly, and the exercises, says Claxton, 'consisted of lectures and discussions on subjects relating to the arts and sciences.'

In 1820 he went from London to Russia to work and the Institution seems to have withered because of his departure. After three years in Russia he took ship to this country instead of returning to England. He found a job in Methuen, less than thirty miles from Boston. The first six months passed away, Claxton remarks, 'without my being able to do anything towards my favorite object—the promotion of popular improvement.' In the spring of the next year he was, however, approached by a clergyman who headed an almost dormant reading circle. Claxton was invited to one of its rare meetings. There he suggested lectures and debates in addition to reading. Would he give a lecture, he was asked. He would and did; it was mainly a demonstration, with apparatus, of the properties of air. As Claxton observes blandly, 'This put new life into the society.' He was elected vice-president and during the several years he stayed in Methuen he took a vigorous part in its exercises.

Moving to Boston he placed a notice in the newspapers about founding a mutual improvement society there. After a slow start, the Boston Mechanics' Institution was set up in 1826. It failed to realize its potentialities because its program consisted of nothing but lectures. It had, Claxton later felt, an 'unsocial character.' Probably in 1830, Josiah Holbrook came to the machine shop which Claxton by then operated and asked him about manufacturing scientific apparatus for sale to lyceums and schools. In particular he wanted a simplified air pump. Claxton had it. Holbrook 'frankly acknowledged it to be the very thing that was wanted.' From then on Claxton manufactured 'philosophical apparatus' and was, he himself adds, very successful. When Holbrook called the organizing meetings for the Boston Mechanics' Lyceum in February of 1831, Claxton was elected president. He again proved himself an energetic leader.

His interest both in the society and the lyceum movement continued; during the next four or five years his name comes up every now and then in the records. In 1836 he returned to England to live but even if he had not it would probably have made little difference, for the lyceum movement was outgrowing him. Other, more polished leaders were crowding out Claxton and his rough-diamond kind.

John Griscom: the Benevolent Chemist

John Griscom, though born sixteen years before Claxton, was representative of the new kind of leader who replaced him. While a young school teacher in Burlington, New Jersey, Griscom became much interested in chemistry. According to his *Memoir*, he soon taught it to himself and then to his pupils. The townspeople came next. 'I issued,' he said, 'a handbill proposing to my fellow citizens of Burlington a course of lectures on chemistry.' The course went off well but Griscom decided to look for wider fields. Going to New York City, he started to lecture and teach there. Those he impressed included 'many of the most intelligent and respectable (and, by their virtues, the most influential) of the citizens of New York.' He became a professor of chemistry at Columbia College and a teacher who attracted devoted students from several social levels.

Among those who found his lectures attractive were the ladies. When in 1819 the popular poet Fitz-Greene Halleck published a mild satire on New York society called 'Fanny,' he said of his heroine:

> She was among the first and warmest patrons
>   of G[riscom]'s *conversatiónes,* where
> In rainbow groups, our bright-ey'd maids and matrons,
>   On science bent, assemble; to prepare
> Themselves for acting well, in life, their part
> As wives and mothers. There she learn'd by heart
>
> Words, to the witches in Macbeth unknown.
>   *Hydraulics, hydrostatics,* and *pneumatics,*
> *Dioptrics, optics, katoptrics, carbon,*
>   *Chlodine,* and *iodine,* and *äerostatics:*
> Also,—why frogs, for want of air, expire;
> And how to set the Tappan sea on fire!

Griscom's appeal to both men and women lay in an easy, colloquial delivery, an urbane charm of manner, and the fact that he tried to illustrate almost every point with an experiment.

A trip across the ocean the year before 'Fanny' was published brought Griscom into contact with English education and the forerunners of the mechanics' institute movement in the British Isles. On his return he worked for a number of humanitarian causes in addition to continuing his lectures and establishing a New York high school on the monitorial plan. When the lyceum movement came to his attention, Griscom found it perfectly congenial. The interest in public education, the stress on science, the use of apparatus in instruction, and the employment of the lecture system as the main vehicle were all close to his heart. He continued to lecture extensively until the early 1840s when attacks of bronchitis forced him to cut down his activities.

How prominent he became in the operations of the lyceum system is testified in a variety of ways. Most notable is the fact that when the national group, the American Lyceum, organized itself in May 1831, he became a vice-president and the next year was chosen president. Having attained this eminence, he went on to play smaller roles in the succeeding national conventions; but he was again elected a vice-president during the final two years of the national group, those of 1838 and 1839.

Orville Dewey: Moral Eloquence

'His church in New York was crowded morning and evening, and eager multitudes hung upon his lips for the very bread of life; and . . . he entered also with spirit and power into the social, philanthropic, and artistic life of that great city.' So wrote his devoted daughter about the Reverend Orville Dewey, who in several ways typified the Protestant clergyman who proved a mainstay both early and late of the lyceum system. The contributing cause which sent Dewey into the lecture field was unusual, however: a migraine which made it extremely hard for him to write a sermon yet offered no barrier to his preaching one. But the psychology behind his 'nervous brain' is not as important to us as the result. More usual factors that influenced him were his genuine predilection for lecturing and the undoubted eloquence he possessed which made audiences eager to hear him—not to the extent that his daughter would wish us to believe but still enough to keep him in demand.

During the 1830s and thereafter, this Unitarian minister preached a large number of lay sermons before lyceums. He did on a modest scale what Emerson did on a grand one. And there were compensations for the modesty. Although he lacked Emerson's luminous power of suggestion, he exceeded him in clarity and organization, and in oratorical style, for that matter. Dewey achieved his peak in a course of Lowell Institute lectures which he gave after the end of the first period of the lyceum system. The title he chose for the Lowell course was 'The Problem of Human Destiny.' In discussing destiny he used all the essentials of those platform homilies on moral and ethical matters which he had previously given in many lyceums. Such homilies differed little, in fact, from the Sunday night sermons (the nondoctrinal kind which would not have been appropriate on Sunday morning) he sometimes preached to his congregation. As he said in his *Autobiography*, 'I discussed the morals of trade, political morality, civic duty—that of voters, jurymen, etc.—social questions, peace and war, and the problem of the human life and condition.'

Characteristic of the general run of his 'non-moral' lectures was the one on 'Reading,' which he gave before the Mechanics' Library Association in New York and which was published in 1839. 'The subject of this lecture is *Reading*,' he begins simply. Then he develops the idea that there are two kinds of reading, for entertainment and for improvement. The core of the lecture is his attempt, naturally, to persuade his audience of the paramount value of the second kind. 'Read one good, strong book,' he advises near the end,—'study one problem, one point in philosophy, and you may find that you have powers of which you never suspected the existence.' His style was plain though not familiar. His images were uncomplicated ones. The power of his impression must have lain in the eloquence with which he lifted up his listeners.

George Combe: Bumps and Hollows

No picture of lecturing during this period would be complete without a mention of the phrenologists. Usually they were itinerant lecturers who had to manage their own tours and who found the reputable lyceums closed to them. Their effect, nevertheless, was considerable. Through their pseudo-science they offered a quick, easy way to the understanding of human nature—with the promise that if it could be understood, it might then be manipulated or at least taken into account. The basic premises in phrenology were that the shape and contours of the skull 'paralleled' those of the brain within, and that the brain itself was divided into thirty-odd areas or 'organs,' each with a particular function to perform.

What often drew the respectable merchant, for one, to the course on phrenology was that through it he could tell which clerk to trust or which to discharge out of hand. If the bumps of conscientiousness on the upper rear side of the head were missing—or, worse still, were replaced by hollows—then the wretched clerk could expect short shrift. And the merchant might even tell by the bumps and hollows who would quickly buy from him and who would not. Similarly, the schoolmaster could learn if he wished, by this easy mechanical way, how to adapt his methods to get the most out of his pupils. An inspection of their 'perceptive' phrenological organs would allow him to do that. The rake, by a brief examination of the back of a young lady's neck, could tell whether her 'amativeness' was full-bodied or not— and proceed accordingly. A minister, before reproving a wayward member of his flock, might see how pronounced was the organ of veneration upon the fellow's skull. And so on. The uses of phrenology appeared infinite.

Like most discoveries, and most creeds, it was denounced as soon as it became popular. The temporary effect of the denunciation by medical men and scientists was, however, to increase the pseudo-science's popularity. Its adherents became all the more loyal on being told that they were wrong.

The result was that when one of the two or three most famous of all phrenologists, the Scotchman George Combe, came to this country in the late 1830s, his lecture tour was a triumph. He arrived in New York in September 1838 and then went to Boston to give his first course. It was highly successful, and at the conclusion he was presented with a silver vase of 'chaste and elegant workmanship.' (This was in addition to the lecture fees.) When he returned to New York, his course was equally applauded there. At the end his audience passed a set of resolutions, of which the second and third are especially illuminating. The second, which took an elevated view, read: 'Resolved, That in Mr. Combe we recognize the most successful advocate of phrenological science, the philosopher and the philanthropist; and that phrenology, as explained and illustrated by him, claims in our opinion the attention of all those who would investigate mind philosophically and who desire the diffusion of truth and the exaltation of the moral and intellectual faculties of man.' The third, more pragmatic than the second, stated in part 'That in the application of phrenology to the investigation of human character, and the practical purposes of life, we perceive a new era in mental and physiological science.'

Combe proceeded in acclamation to Philadelphia. There he gave his course in triumph again (the paying audience started with 441 members and ended with 607) and again was the object of complimentary resolutions. The chairman of the committee appointed to convey them to him was no less a public figure than the aristocratic Nicholas Biddle, president of the United States Bank. Combe later gave courses in Washington, D. C., and Wilmington, and in addition repeated his courses in Philadelphia and New York. At the end of the extra New York course, he discovered that there was another, and even more expensive, vase being made for him. Its base was to be ornamented with the skulls of animals.

Combe's platform manner was quiet but effective. In appearance he was rather tall and spare, with a large head and white hair sparsely scattered over it. But even baldness was beloved of the phrenologists, for, as Boardman points out in the preface to Combe's *Lectures,* it allowed the beholder to admire Combe's 'beautifully developed frontal and coronal regions.'

Fanny Wright: the Gadfly of Reform

Claxton, Griscom, and Dewey pretty well represent standard varieties of the lecturer before 1846. Frances Wright can represent the fringe—sometimes but not always lunatic—of extreme individualists who also stepped on the lecture platform. The doughty religionist Orestes Brownson, the quack mystic Andrew

Jackson 'Harmonial' Davis, and the atheist Abner Kneeland were brothers to her.

Slight but fiery, she was among the few daring enough to break the lyceum's taboo against controversy. She saw herself as a true reformer. The sponsor at Nashoba, Tennessee, of an interracial experiment which its opponents loudly called 'Fanny Wright's Free Love Colony,' she lectured in favor of such controversial items as birth control and easy divorce, and against such things as slavery and the divine inspiration of the Bible. She appeared as a rule in some courthouse or hired hall. The regular lyceums shunned her even more than they shunned phrenologists. Feeling against her became so great that she could not speak in peace even on noncontroversial topics. She gave a lecture in Philadelphia which had the innocent title of 'A Geographical and Historical Sketch of the North American United States,' and the mayor forbade her to speak there again!

It was still worse when she turned to politics. In New York she spoke for Jackson and against the Bank. The lecture platform was, it seems, almost torn away underneath her. As Amos Gilbert's *Memoir of Frances Wright* adds vividly though somewhat incoherently about one such experience, 'After the platform on which she held forth was demolished, she has been seen descending from the second story of a building after she had finished a lecture, with thousands of grim faces peering upon her, giving savage indications of murderous intent, so soon as their masters should give the word "go." ' But there was only one Fanny Wright. The lyceum idea could not have survived many like her.

The Lyceum Crystallizes into the Lecture System:
1846 to the Civil War

11

New England:
The Broad Bostonian Platform

I T is easy to exaggerate the continuing importance of New England to the country as a whole during the second period of the lyceum. Many a lecture course could have developed without a sign that the city of Boston was the cultural center of the lecture system. Many a community, large or small, cared nothing for Yankees and Yankee notions. A metropolis such as New York could maintain its own culture without help from outside. So could a state, for that matter, and so could—and did—an entire region; for the South in the years after 1845 saw little in New England culture to copy.

And yet there was a kind of truth in Boston's own view of itself as a fountainhead. The currents of the lyceum, and of systematic lecturing in particular, had their source in Boston if they had them in any place. They flowed from Boston into the rest of Massachusetts, then into the rest of New England, into upstate New York, and then farther westward both by way of the chain of lower Great Lakes to the north and by way of the Ohio Valley to the south. Then they flowed still farther into the West and finally spent their last force on the far side of the Mississippi.

Of course the currents did not always run at an even rate or to the same extent. At the start of the second period of the lyceum's development, New England itself was not supporting the lyceum as it had in the early days. The panic of 1837 had presaged a decade of reduced interest. Some lyceums had continued to exist, others had been founded, but a good many more had quietly disintegrated. By the time, however, that the 1850s opened,

the major economic, social, and cultural trends had effected a re-
surgence of the lyceum. It was now a lyceum from which most
(though not all) of the early elements except the lecture had disappeared, but the lecture proved itself an alluring attraction.
It reigned supreme. The arrival of the panic of 1857 hampered
the lecture movement somewhat, and the Civil War put an end
to it. But for nearly ten years before the panic it enjoyed ample
prosperity.

New England industry, especially in the form of textile mills
and boot and shoe manufacturing, was booming by the late 1840s.
Throughout the decade of the 1850s its progress, in the teeth of
the panic of 1857, was even more impressive. The value of the
cotton goods New England produced in 1850 was $43,786,000;
ten years later it had climbed to $79,360,000. Most of the other
industries shared in cotton's surge. Transportation and communication continued their improvement. The network of railroads expanded particularly along the coast but also into the interior of
New England. Rail connections with the Midwest were built up,
though more slowly; water-borne traffic with it increased too.
The whole national economy reoriented itself. New England and
the bulk of the Middle Atlantic states merged with the West to
become the North. The trade alliance between the South and
West was largely abandoned, except for cotton, in favor of an
alliance between the East and West. For New England, trade
with the West meant both a rich source of raw materials and an
expanding market for manufactured goods. Trade with the
South meant little but raw cotton (although that was certainly
important) and a smaller market for New England manufactures than the West now offered. So New England and the
West traded increasingly with each other, and the wheels in the
New England mill towns revolved briskly. The many manufacturing communities grew larger and provided out of their citizens
the 'auditory' for many a lecture course.

The farms of New England, on the contrary, furnished less
support rather than more for the lyceum. An analysis of the lyceum membership lists still available will show that the farmer
who in the first decade of the lyceum drove his family and himself into town every week for the lecture was becoming a rarity.

By 1845 many of his more ambitious (or, at times, more restless) fellows had already set out for richer lands. His own land and his own mind too—it may be suggested—became steadily less productive. In his interest in lectures, he now compared very poorly with the tradesman, the mill manager, the merchant, or the clerk.

New England's population, whose rate of increase had been sinking slightly in spite of the fact that the towns had been growing bigger, swelled in the late 1840s with the waves of Irish immigration. The Irish by and large clung to Boston and its satellite communities but enough of them filtered into the rest of New England to augment the general unskilled labor force. To the lyceum the Irish immigration meant nothing directly. But indirectly it provided grist for the economic mill and in various ways allowed the middle and upper classes to cultivate the lyceum. As it turned out, industrial and commercial prosperity left a margin for the pursuit of culture among all but the low-paid groups in the manufacturing communities. Appropriately, the lecture courses became more cultural and less informational.

Supplementing the favorable economic trends was the widespread rise in the level of education. The New England public schools after 1850 found themselves winning their fight. Complete victory was still in the distance, but plainly the public schools—and that meant in particular the public elementary schools—were here to stay. Literacy increased still further. The reading public broadened and deepened. More newspapers, magazines, and books were printed. And from this general cultural complex the lecture system benefited.

How much it benefited and precisely where in New England the benefit was most manifest is a matter that can be clarified by a state-by-state analysis. Massachusetts is the place to begin.

———◆———

By 1846 the lyceum situation in Massachusetts was relatively stable. Only traces of the mechanics' institutes, the stress on workaday knowledge, the use of apparatus, and the collecting of rocks remained. Debates and discussions as adjuncts to lyceum programs had also greatly diminished (though debating societies as such continued). What was left was the lectures. By now they were apt to be smooth professional jobs by trained performers, though there were always a few able individualists who also managed to attain platform popularity.

From this time until the coming of the Civil War, the lyceum here and elsewhere would change very slowly. The Massachusetts town lyceums kept their solid strength. By the early 1840s the weak ones had been weeded out. It was no longer possible to boast as Horace Mann did in 1839, that the state had 137 lyceums; but the two score that stayed in business during the second period were strong. In the face of forecasts to the contrary, the lecture system in Massachusetts kept on flourishing. As the *Boston Evening Transcript* said at the start of the season of 1855–6, 'It is quite evident that the lecture system, instead of falling into disrepute, or being displaced by new methods of instruction or culture, as has so often been predicted, was never so universally adopted as at present.'

The *Transcript* went on to explain that this interest in the lyceum characterized all parts of the country where good transportation could be found. To satisfy it, Boston lecturers were in constant demand. 'Some of our friends who engage in the service,' said the *Transcript*, 'have already received upwards of a hundred invitations to lecture.' Then the paper listed the names of nearly seventy lecturers who had been engaged by Massachusetts lyceums for the current season. The names are among the most distinguished the lyceum ever saw, and by far the largest number came from the Boston area.

Among the famous names the *Transcript* printed were those of the witty, sarcastic little Park Benjamin, Thomas Starr King with his almost unparalleled eloquence, the crusading minister Theodore Parker, Wendell Phillips, Richard Henry Dana of *Two Years before the Mast*, Horace Greeley, the clever E. P. Whipple, Oliver Wendell Holmes, the satirical John G. Saxe, Bayard Taylor, and the noblest lecturer among them all, Ralph Waldo Emerson.

Most of the men on the list (there were no women) were ministers; some of the remainder were professors or politicians; and the others belonged to an assortment of vocations. They would

be seen that season in Massachusetts towns as various as tiny
Millers Village and big, bustling Springfield, industrial Lowell
and pastoral Concord. Furthermore, they would travel outside the
state, bringing the message of Massachusetts to places as far
distant as Davenport and New Orleans. Then having—in their
own eyes, it must be admitted—civilized the heathen, they would
return contentedly to the Bay State and to Boston.

The lyceum system in Connecticut continued its rather slow
pace. The Hartford Young Men's Institute kept alive and strong,
however. A typical course of lectures for these years can be found
in the season of 1854–5. It opened with the best possible drawing
card, a lecture by Bayard Taylor, on Japan. Then came 'Patriotism'
by the Reverend Henry Ward Beecher, organ-voiced, assured, and
still untouched by scandal. After that Hartford heard J. H. Wain-
wright on 'Politics and Patriotism,' the Reverend G. W. Bethune
on 'Work and Labor,' G. W. Curtis on 'Success,' W. C. Prince on
'The Triumph of Error,' Josiah Quincy on 'The Mormons,' and
G. H. Clark's poem 'Now and Then.' It must have been a good
series. Similarly, the New Haven Young Men's Institute, benefiting from the intellectual stimulus of Yale College, maintained its
programs and its standards throughout the years. As a matter of
fact it gained ground as time went on. During the season of 1856–7
it sponsored (in the face of the national depression) not one but
five courses. 'The Institute has never before provided the public
with so large a number and variety of lectures,' its annual report
boasted.

The first course for the New Haven public, of nine lectures and
a poem, included Emerson, Whipple, and Beecher on the program. The second was made up of four lectures by Curtis on
'English Authors and Literature,' one by Andrew D. White, who
was to become president of Cornell University, on 'Civilization
in Russia,' and two 'conversation lectures, with readings' by that
celebrated declaimer George Vandenhoff. The third was made up
of six lectures by Professor G. Gajani on 'Italian History, and Re-
formers.' The fourth was a miscellaneous course of eleven lectures open only to members of the Institute and their ladies. It was
staffed almost entirely by local talent. The fifth illustrated both

the importance of the female sex and Yale, for it was a course of twenty lectures on chemistry for New Haven women, given in the laboratory of Yale College by Benjamin Silliman's son and by C. H. Porter, Silliman's one-time colleague. As a dividend, a single lecture by Beecher on 'The Conservative and the Progressive' was added.

Other activities of the Institute this same year included classes in writing, arithmetic, bookkeeping, drawing—especially mechanical drawing for the men and (probably) freehand drawing for the women—and vocal music. The Institute also provided a class in English composition and, apparently, oral English, both for German immigrants. The annual report summed it all up rather too patronizingly, 'The educational department has continued its quiet work.' The library now owned 7,656 volumes. The Institute had 482 annual members and 118 life members. One other salient mark of activity was that the organization had finally moved into its own building. Here before Sumter there were no signs of decay.

That was not true for the few other Connecticut lyceums. When Eleanor Tilton traced Oliver Wendell Holmes's lecture tours of the season of 1851-2 in her *Amiable Autocrat*, she found that he appeared before almost half a hundred Massachusetts audiences —and before only three Connecticut ones, in Hartford, Norwich, and New Haven.

Clearly seeing the value of the lyceum as an instrument for advancing the public school crusade, Henry Barnard (acting in his capacity as Commissioner of Public Schools during the middle and late 1840s) stimulated the forming of more lyceums than any other man in the history of Rhode Island. By the time he left office, in 1849, he could report the establishment of seventeen different courses of popular lectures in as many Rhode Island villages. The establishment of local libraries he also felt to be important; and when he retired, twenty-nine out of the thirty-two towns had libraries of at least half a thousand volumes. But in the villages, interest in the lyceum sagged after Barnard's contagious enthusiasm was withdrawn. In a large city it was a different matter.

In its Franklin Lyceum the city of Providence continued to

have the leading institution of the kind in the state. The annual lecture courses, which were revived in 1848, were more often than not constellations of noted names. Over half of the speakers in the 1848 series would be well known today. Webster, who spoke on 'The Early History of the American Constitution,' Theodore Parker, who lectured on 'The Political Destiny of America,' Holmes, whose topic was 'Medicine as It is and as It Used to be,' Poe, who addressed the lyceum on 'Selections from English Poetry with Critical Remarks,' Agassiz, whose subject was 'Glaciers,' Mark Hopkins, who spoke on 'Method,' and Senator Charles Sumner, whose subject was 'The Law of Human Progress,' all mean something to our time. The others, such as S. K. Lothrop and G. S. Hillard, are men whose significance is lost to us now; but they too contributed their share to making the course an exceptionally fine one.

Toward the mid-1850s several courses of lectures under other auspices were presented in the city. One series given by Professor G. I. Chace of Brown University and sponsored by the Mechanic Institute, was on 'Chemistry Applied to the Mechanic Arts.' A breakdown of it is interesting since it was a late example of the sort of course most popular during the first days of the lyceum movement. As scheduled, the first two lectures were on the constitution of air and water, the third on the composition of building materials, the fourth on making chimneys and furnaces, the fifth on paint, the sixth on animal and vegetable substances used in the arts and for clothing, and the seventh and eighth on dyeing. They serve incidentally to illustrate Rhode Island's cultural lag.

Toward the end of the '50s the state began to make up a little for some of its previous cultural deficiencies. Newport's Association of Mechanics and Manufacturers and its Redwood Library and Athenaeum both sponsored lecture courses. And Westerly 'fairly swarmed with lecturers,' according to one local historian. 'They filled the air with their eager voices of proposal or protest.'

As transportation improved, New Hampshire fitted itself less angularly than before into the pattern of the lecture system. The Concord Lyceum had its vicissitudes but on the whole managed reasonably well. McFarland's *Sixty Years in Concord* says that during an unspecified period (but probably the late 1840s) paid lecturers took the platform. The fee was twenty dollars; the lecturers included Emerson, Holmes, J. G. Saxe, Starr King, and Dr. J. V. C. Smith—all regular performers by this time. One of the records of the Concord Lyceum that has survived shows too what the lecturers were paid from 1851 to 1855. W. E. Chandler, who became Secretary of the Navy thirty years after he kept the Concord minutes book, prepared the list of lecturers and fees. The fees did not vary a great deal; and the names on the program are almost without exception the well-known ones for that time if not, in a few cases, for ours. For example, the 1853–4 season, beginning on 15 November and ending 7 February, brought to Concord: Theodore Parker (at $25), Saxe ($20), Timothy Bigelow ($25), T. W. Higginson ($15), Thomas Hill ($20), Horace Greeley ($25), J. G. Hoyt ($15), and Josiah Quincy ($25).

In Manchester the lyceum movement was split by bitter feeling about slavery. The old-line Manchester Lyceum eschewed political topics and tried simply 'to provide for a course of lectures from distinguished gentlemen from abroad.' These courses were given, in nonpartisan fashion, at the City Hall. By 1856, however, the New Lyceum had been formed. Its attitude was summed up, with considerable understatement, in the *Manchester Directory* for that year: 'The New Lyceum is a voluntary association of anti-slavery views and not particularly apprehensive of the dissolution of the Union.' It sponsored controversial lectures and invited in the firebrands of the abolitionist movement.

At least a dozen other towns heard lecturers, of a less political kind, during this time. Among them were Hollis, Franklin Village, Great Falls, Randolph, Portsmouth, and Dover.

If ever a newspaper tried to breathe life into a lyceum, it was the *Burlington Free Press*. Like most of the rest of Vermont, Burlington was without a lyceum until the paper scolded the community and demanded one. 'Burlington is old enough and big enough to be ashamed of herself for exhibiting such apathy,' the *Free Press* said in October 1851. It called for a lyceum at once, and on a well-organized scale. By the end of the year it was a reality and had announced the fourfold aim of establishing a library, having a reading room to house it, systematically hearing lectures, and participating in discussions. The first course began in January.

The mainstays of this and later courses were local men and University of Vermont professors. The topics ranged from 'Ancient Alchemy' to 'Ethan Allen.' The *Free Press* liked them all. When the subject was alchemy, the paper thought the lecture uncommonly fine. When Ethan Allen was the topic, the paper opened its account with ' "Professor Thompson gave us a very delightful lecture last evening" was the frequent remark in town this morning.' And when a speaker compared the steamboat to a shuttle threading the solid earth and 'weaving a defensive garment through which no power [could] successfully assail THIS UNION,' the paper observed that the comparison was very beautiful.

In spite of the efforts of the *Free Press*, the Burlington society sank out of sight after December 1854. But the last lecture given that year must have been a memorable one. A minister by the name of Todd from Pittsford spoke on 'The Peculiar Characteristics and Dangers of the Present Age.' One of them was the American tendency to heroic remedies for social and political ills. He said he was reminded of a Vermont physician who 'kept a large vial which he called the Tiger, filled with calomel, castor oil, laudanum, and such like cruel medicines; and when he had a bad case which would yield to nothing else, was wont to shake up old Tiger and give a rousing dose, which either put the patient *through* or put him *under*.' While Todd was talking, his audience was disturbed by a cry of 'Fire' as well as by what the paper termed 'uncouth noises from the rooms below.' The audience was, by the way, 'select'—an ominous word for 'much too small'; and the dark days for the Burlington Lyceum were obviously ahead.

In the last few years before the Civil War a handful of outside lecturers were invited into Vermont—among them Beecher, Edward Everett, and Bayard Taylor—but they caused hardly a ripple. Of all the New England states Vermont evidently saw least in the lyceum.

Two conflicting trends met in the state of Maine. One, supported by improved rail and water transportation, was the regularizing of the lyceum system. Better transportation helped several of the larger towns to become part of the growing lecture circuit. In place of local speakers, most of whom had long since lost their novelty, Maine lyceums could now hear such famous itinerants as Emerson, Holmes, Whipple, and Curtis, as well as a few noted native sons such as Henry Giles. Offsetting this trend, however, was the appearance of a genuine apathy about listening to any lectures at all. It was to be expected that the local lecturer, appearing on the platform of his village lyceum, would soon become tedious. Besides, familiarity was apt to breed if not contempt then indifference. But audiences in those cities of the state large enough to support lecture courses also began to dwindle even when the speakers were men of the renown of Theodore Parker or H. N. Hudson. As the 1850s reached their middle, this trend began to cancel the other, favorable one; and so it is not surprising that the high water mark for the lyceum system in Maine came at the opening of the decade.

The best season was probably 1851–2. Almost no evidence of new—or flourishing—small-town lyceums presents itself, but in the larger communities the lyceum fared much better at that time. Belfast heard Hudson, Starr King, John Pierpont, E. H. Chapin, and Parker, in addition to several native sons. Kennebunk heard as many lecturers from Massachusetts as from Maine. Thomaston invited Pierpont, Giles, and one or two lesser figures from either other Maine towns or other states. The Portland Lyceum, recently revived, officially stated as its object: 'to provide for a series of lectures from abroad every winter.' And it did its best.

If other seasons failed to match this one, the lyceum in Maine nonetheless showed more activity than that of any other New England state aside from Massachusetts.

12

The Middle Atlantic States:
New York Dominant

THE most dramatic thing about the lecture system in the Middle Atlantic states was the unchallenged ascendance of New York City. Economic, social, and cultural developments combined to increase its importance year by year. Lecturing in Boston was perhaps more systematic and probably pitched at a generally higher level than that in New York, but New York doubtless heard substantially more lectures than Boston. They were of various kinds but their number was great. Upstate New York also continued to thrive economically, and this fact correlated with the expansion of the lyceum there. The cities along the main lines of communication kept on growing and acquired for themselves an unusually large share of the country-wide prosperity which existed between 1844 and 1857. By 1860 the value of manufactures in the whole state had risen to $378,871,000—the largest in the nation. Massachusetts manufactured $255,546,000 worth of goods the same year —still a huge amount but not to be compared with the product of New York.

Pennsylvania, with a total industrial product in 1860 of $290,-121,000, likewise outstripped Massachusetts and was second in the country. Fortified by industrial prosperity and expanding cities, it put less stress than before on the village and county lyceum societies and much more on the urban lecture-sponsoring societies. Yet in spite of burgeoning wealth, the state straggled far behind New York in its support of the lyceum.

New Jersey, with Newark remaining in the lead, took over a

greater place in the lecture movement than previously. This state's cluster of industrial communities included, as it enlarged, enough people who wanted to hear visiting speakers so that Trenton, Paterson, and Camden also became at least occasional stopovers for stars of the lecture platform. But south of New Jersey, any statewide hospitality for the lyceum ended. It is true that there was not always a relation at the state level between industrial prosperity and prosperity for the lecture system, but in the East at any rate there usually was. For 1860 the value of manufactures in New Jersey was $76,306,000 while for Maryland it was only $41,735,000 and for Delaware a mere $19,893,000. The lectures in the three states were proportional.

Maryland, however, had a good many of its cultural shortcomings made up by Baltimore. The city's shipping and industry acted as the economic basis for a paying lecture system, and the city's intellectual culture provided the necessary milieu. Baltimore maintained its active interest in the lyceum in spite of some politically turbulent days. In Delaware the city of Wilmington alone manifested a measure of interest in lectures, yet even there the interest was none too strong. Geographical isolation remained an important factor. Another factor which retained its importance in Delaware to a larger extent than it did in neighboring Maryland was the influence of southern culture. And both states, but Delaware again more than Maryland, continued to have an agrarian economy—the kind of economy in which the southern cultural pattern fitted best.

Washington now consolidated its reputation as an excellent lecture city. It lacked Baltimore's business wealth but it had the national government—and that turned out to be an even finer source of audiences. The nation's capital became increasingly sophisticated. It demonstrated that it felt no surfeit of lively talk; for it welcomed as many lecturers as any city in the Middle Atlantic states except New York.

As the threat of civil war came closer, lecturing throughout the Middle Atlantic region aside from the District of Columbia began to decline. In the early 1850s it had developed into a pattern of public lectures in the cities, but the panic of 1857 had proved at least a minor setback and the verbal battles over abolition—certainly to be expected in a politically mixed region like the Middle

Atlantic states—doubtless hurt some of the regular lyceums. By the time President Lincoln ordered Fort Sumter to be provisioned, one has the impression that the lyceum system was holding together mainly by an effort of will. Once the war was under way, nothing could keep it intact.

---◆---

When the year 1846 began, the population of New York City had swollen to over 370,000. Because a large part of the increase came from European immigration, the city's cultural life did not grow in proportion to the population. Nevertheless, the city supported more and more lecturing. The main sponsors stayed the same; they were the societies already in existence before 1846. More than a handful of new ones too appeared in Manhattan and its environs; among them were the Yonkers Lyceum, a Franklin Lyceum, and the Merchants' and Clerks' Library Association. Many an uninvited lecturer also visited New York for whatever he could get out of it. He hired his own hall, or basement, and helped to swell the tide of lectures in the metropolis.

New York was the only city that could try to compete with Boston. In the same month and year, October 1855, that the *Boston Evening Transcript* published its list of available outstanding lecturers, Horace Greeley's *Daily Tribune* published one for New York. Greeley's list had forty-three names while the *Transcript's* had sixty-eight. It is true that Greeley's was supposed to be more select, and shorter for that reason, but actually it had a higher proportion of little-known names than the *Transcript* list. A comparison of the two lists, due allowances having been made, shows that New York could not match Boston in either the quality or quantity of its lecturers. But with that one important reservation, New York far outstripped any other city in the United States. And in the range and number of lectures given, New York seems to have surpassed even Boston. New York heard more lectures, if not always as good ones.

For a further perspective on lecturing in New York City, we might examine in detail a representative year, say 1850, from our second period. A good idea of the number and kinds of lectures can be gained from the files of some of the New York newspapers such as the *Daily Express* or the *Sunday Dispatch*. The sheer mass of the references is astonishing.

The Mercantile Library Association began the year (that is, the second half of the 1849–50 lecture season) with Emerson lecturing on 'England' on 22 January. A week later he gave 'The Spirit of the Times.' Following him in the weekly series at Clinton Hall came R. H. Dana on 'Woman,' E. P. Whipple on 'Character,' the Reverend William Ware on 'Florence,' and the Reverend G. W. Bethune on 'Holland and the Hollanders.' The autumn season was opened by Whipple on 'Character' again. The Reverend James Ryder followed with a controversial lecture, 'The Jesuit,' and then G. H. Miles spoke on 'The Crisis and the Struggle.' The Transcendentalist music critic J. S. Dwight lectured on 'The Opera' with special reference to Mozart's *Don Giovanni;* and that apostle of the Middle Ages, the Reverend John Lord, spoke twice, the first time on 'Gustavus Adolphus' and the second on 'The Suppression of the Jesuits by Clement XIV.' George Vandenhoff concluded the year with three nights of readings.

For its part, the General Society of Mechanics and Tradesmen offered three lectures by Agassiz to start the year 1850. They were announced in the *Express* as being on 'Natural Relations between Animals.' Dr. J. W. Redfield succeeded Agassiz with 'Physiognomy: on the Signs of the Selfish and Social Faculties.' The Reverend Mr. Bethune spoke on 'Holland: Its History, Trade, Character, etc.' and J. W. Edmonds spoke on 'The Constitution and Free Institutions of Our Country.'

A somewhat newer organization, the Mechanics' Institute, sponsored a series which emphasized the practical profit of the workers. Several of the topics represent, in fact, a partial throwback to the earliest stage of the lyceum movement. These weekly lectures, as announced in the *Dispatch,* opened with W. P. Wallace's 'The Domestic and Foreign Position of the United States.' They continued with two lectures by Greeley, one being on 'Self-Culture, Individual and Social' and the other on 'Labor, Its Needs and Its Means.' Next C. A. Dana began a lecture on the 'History of Industry' and returned to finish it about two weeks later. Dr. Thomas Antisell gave three lectures on 'Chemistry' to conclude the Institute's season. The fall course opened with a star performer, Park Benjamin. He lectured on 'The Age of Gold.' Then Dana spoke on 'The Workers in Modern Times.' A Professor Hume spoke on 'Electromagnetism, Galvanism, etc.' one week and on the 'Electromagnetic Telegraph' the next. The last two lectures were by the socialist, S. P. Andrews, on 'The True Constitution of Government' and Henry James, Sr., on 'The Rule of the People.'

More representative of the general, mixed course was that offered by the Brooklyn Female Academy, whose series for 1850 was announced in the *Express*. These Tuesday night lectures began on 19 November and carried through to the end of the year. Park Benjamin was scheduled first, on 'The Age of Gold' once again. The others were advertised as John Griscom on Ventilation,' the Reverend J. F. Schroder on 'The Literary History of the English Bible,' Greeley on 'Success or Failure in Life,' a Judge Greenwood on 'The Capacity of Americans for the Cultivation of Music,' and G. P. R. James, billed as 'The Great Novelist,' on 'The Crusades' (a two-lecture performance).

The miscellaneous lectures for the year show the marked variety indicated earlier. Phrenology, Egyptian art, national law, electricity, the European revolution of 1849, and the microcosmos were among the topics. Furthermore, the rich flood of these lectures seems to have continued, on the whole, right up to the Civil War. There was perhaps a slight lessening in their number and there was certainly a new emphasis on the controversial; but those are the only qualifications that need to be made.

Upstate New York developed into one of the best parts of the lecture circuit in the entire country. Without exception, the larger communities maintained lecture-sponsoring organizations. The state capital, Albany, continued to support a Young Men's Association. Henry James, Sr., for example, spoke before it in 1846, on 'What Constitutes the State'; and the Association published his lecture, as it did a few selected others. Buffalo maintained its own Young Men's Association. As of 1850–51 it had about 750 members, a library of some 6000 volumes, and lecture courses ('literary and scientific') during the cold months. Its crest was reached on 27 November 1855 when Parke Godwin addressed an audience of 4000 listeners, the largest—according to a newspaper report—col-

lected up to that time on a 'literary occasion' in the city. The Buffalo
Apprentices' Society, founded in 1833, was still active after 1845;
the Mechanics' Society was too. In Rochester the Athenaeum remained strong. Even in 1857, a depression year, it claimed 550
members; and it had by then a library of 8000 volumes. In Syracuse the Franklin Institute, which sponsored lectures, was incorporated in 1850, but it had its beginning as early as 1837 under the
title of the Library and Reading Room Association. The *Syracuse
Directory* for 1851–2 reports the organizing of another society, as
of October 1850, the Young Men's Lyceum. It was said to be 'in a
highly prosperous condition.' Troy continued its Young Men's Association into our second period, still with a lecture group.

Utica likewise kept its Young Men's Association, though it necessitated some struggling to do so. Membership in 1846, for instance,
was only one hundred compared with double that number three
years earlier. The Utica Mechanics' Association was a group not
listed in directories before 1845. After that it is noted as having
lectures. Two more lyceums emerged in Utica in the early 1850s.
They were the Scientific Association, founded in August 1850,
which sponsored lectures, and another Young Men's Association,
organized in December 1852. The Poughkeepsie Lyceum also continued to be active. The local newspapers for the late 1850s and
early 1860s often refer to visiting lecturers who manned the lyceum
course at the 'Pine Hall,' among them Beecher, Emerson, and
Greeley.

More than one small town, in addition, heard a noted lecturer
whenever it could catch him—in other words, whenever his route
allowed him to stop off conveniently. Under such circumstances
even the village of Penn Yan, for instance, was able in 1855 to attract as aloof a Bostonian as James Russell Lowell.

Cultivated Philadelphia liked to read more than to listen. As of
1852, to take a year at random, it had over half a dozen much used
reading rooms, among them those of the American Philosophical
Society, the Philadelphia Library Company, the Athenaeum, the
Historical Society of Pennsylvania, the Academy of Natural Sciences, the Mercantile Library, the Apprentices' Library, and the
Franklin Institute. And the tendency to make lectures a matter of

casual arrangement and incidental interest that had marked the city before 1846 held afterward. True, in sum total a fair number of lectures were given. Both notable and unknown lecturers made their way to the city and spoke. Notwithstanding, in proportion to Philadelphia's population (about 340,000 in 1852), and its intellectual eminence, lectures were not abundant.

An unusual number of those that were heard dealt with slavery. In Philadelphia the Quakers' general opposition to it offered a better chance for the anti-slavery speaker than he had in most cities. Ordinary lyceums were not as a rule involved, for they might easily have been split by so sharp an issue. Instead, either an anti slavery society or some impromptu organization would be apt to provide for a Garrison or Phillips. Still, by the end of the period even the Philadelphia Lyceum was reported as debating secession 'for several weeks.'

In general, however, many of the remaining lectures were ostentatiously noncontroversial. Turning its face resolutely away from dissension, the *Philadelphia Press* of 28 January 1861—to take a late example—found a good deal to praise in the clever Park Benjamin, who was to speak on 'Fact and Fiction.' It sent him its good wishes: 'As he never makes offensive political observations, wholly alien to his subject, we hope he may have as crowded a house as he always attracts.'

The pages of the *Pennsylvania School Journal* indicate what happened to the lyceum system throughout the rest of the state. The county lyceums established during the brisk years from 1834 to 1838 so thoroughly identified themselves with the promotion of the public schools that no other activity attracted them. By 1852 most of the county lyceums had changed their names but not their educational purpose. Under various titles they now officially functioned as county associations of teachers and 'friends of education.'

That is not to say that all regular lyceums, county or community, disappeared. In fact the *Journal* for September 1852 prints a page about the Chester County Convention of Lyceums the month before. Eight lyceums with a total of forty delegates were represented. As to the sort of program, 'three-fourths of an hour was allotted to each lyceum, at the option of its delegates to select from the addresses, essays, etc., furnished by its members, to be read by the writers.' Provision also was made for recitation, music, and a bit of the drama. The subjects fell into the fields of science, art, theology, and ethics, with the idea of progress receiving special attention.

As the population of the state expanded—from 1,724,000 in 1840 to 2,906,000 in 1860—some communities newly interested and willing to support lyceums appeared. Scranton was one. Its Young Men's Literary and Debating Club was organized 4 November 1857 and maintained itself until the Civil War. It announced its lecturers for the season of 1858-9 as including Isaac Hayes on 'Kane's Polar Sea'; Park Benjamin on 'Amusing Traits of American Character' and (the next night) his poem, 'Fashion'; J. G. Saxe with another poem, this one on 'Love'; Horace Mann, subject to be given out later; the ubiquitous Bayard Taylor on 'Moscow'; Greeley on 'Great Men'; and G. W. Curtis on 'Democracy and Education.' Among the lecturers in other seasons were Beecher, J. G. Holland, Wendell Phillips, and E. H. Chapin. They were all, certainly, well known personalities; this was the star system in action in Pennsylvania.

Besides these new lyceums there were older ones such as those in Pittsburgh, Lancaster, and Lewisburg, which managed to attract support throughout most of the period.

The industrial strength, and the population, of New Jersey continued to grow. The mass of immigrants coming into New York harbor during the middle of the century made Newark in particular an overflowing industrial melting-pot. Trenton, Camden, and Paterson felt the same influx, although to a smaller extent. Here was a great challenge for education, yet so wide was the gap between the lyceum system and the immigrants' basic needs that a little public schooling for their children was all they had the chance to seek. The New Jersey farmer, for his part, showed indifference rather than ignorance where the lyceum was concerned but with almost the same result.

What happened after 1845 was that several already established lyceums continued to serve their communities and a few new ones were founded—not much of a change, really, in spite of many changes of other kinds in the state. Perhaps the best example of those societies that continued was the Newark Mechanics' Association and Lyceum. It survived competition both from citizens trying to form a new mechanics' lyceum and from the Newark Library Association, which after 1850 also sponsored lectures. Other lyceums that kept open included the ones at Orange and Burlington.

Just as it had before 1846, the city of Baltimore occupied a lonely eminence in the lyceum system of Maryland. In spite of social and even bitter political strife in the '50s, lecturing in Baltimore was carried on expeditiously. Yet it is a safe conjecture that without the Know-Nothing mobs and their favorite weapon, the shoemaker's awl, and without the increasing hostility to free speech that some of the southern elements in the city were showing, the lecture system would have become still more vigorous.

The Baltimore Lyceum, after a decline dating from about 1844, rose with renewed vitality in 1847, flourished briefly, and then disappeared at the end of the decade. In its place, the outstanding organization became the revived Maryland Institute for the Promotion of the Mechanic Arts. Formed anew, after a lapse of twelve years, in December 1847 and January 1848, it was incorporated the next year and began a fruitful career. It developed into a genuine educational institution. Lecturing became only one of its briskly diversified activities. The others were: holding an annual exhibition of American manufactureds; opening a school of design as well as one of applied chemistry; and establishing a library, cabinet, and collection of philosophical apparatus.

This institute's history was, in shortened form, that of at least one aspect of the whole lyceum movement; for the Baltimore society, late though it was, started out mainly by providing practical information for workingmen and ended by purveying culture mainly to the middle class. The shift in the lecture topics can be illustrated by a glance at the courses for 1851–2 on the one hand and 1857–8 on the other. The Honorable J. R. Chandler opened the 1851–2 course with 'The Position, Duties, and Responsibilities of the Mechanic,' whereas the Reverend Orville Dewey opened the course for 1857–8 with 'Slowness as a Law of Progress.' Each man set the tone for the season.

The outstanding sponsors in the city in the long run were the Maryland Institute and its competitor the Mercantile Library Association. Baltimoreans could also attend other lectures; these were either single ones or—less often—single courses. They might be given before the Union Fire Company or the Presbyterian Church, the Young Men's Christian Association or the Asbury Sunday School. The topics were of all sorts.

Over the years lecturing in Baltimore knew more feast than famine, as the newspaper references prove. Interest slackened a bit only twice. The first time was in the late 1840s but there was a strong recovery in the early 1850s. Then lecturing leveled off in the mid-'50s, dipped down for the second time because of the depression of 1857 and political warfare, and finally reached a remarkable new height at the opening of the 1860s. In the remainder of the state the normal growth of population and the improvement in communication brought out a few lyceums. Hagerstown and Frederick each had one, and even little Sandy Spring set up what a local historian blandly called a 'pure, high-toned "Association for Mutual Improvement."'

With its love of the spoken word, Washington, D. C., continued to welcome the lecture system. The number of lectures, sponsored or otherwise, listed in the newspapers rose still higher and not until the last few years before the Civil War did they decrease even slightly. Here in the midst of political tensions, lecturing managed to maintain its popularity. The E Street Baptist Church, with its 'Literary and Scientific' courses, the Irving Association, and the Union Literary and Debating Society dominated the scene as the second period of the lyceum opened. Beginning, however, with the season of 1848–9 a new and powerful competitor for them emerged. It was the Smithsonian Institution. In resources it far outmatched the rest. It swiftly acquired the prestige that attaches to a national institution and so could command as good a set of lecturers as anyone might wish. And the lectures were free to the public. The consequence was that the Smithsonian became the scene of the best attended as well as the best lectures in the District. One important qualification should be made, though. The Smithsonian sponsored a high proportion of scientific lectures, as it was supposed to, and so for lectures of a humanistic nature Washingtonians generally had to go elsewhere. It is probably significant that when the Washington Art Association arranged a course in 1859–60, it ran a strong second in popularity to the Smithsonian's.

Other societies that helped to satisfy the city's thirst for lecturing appeared in the 1850s. They included the Island Social Club, the YMCA, and the Methodist Protestant Church of Georgetown.

One item in the *National Intelligencer* ought to be chronicled as a footnote to the history of the American lyceum. It was the report, on 24 January 1849, that Mr. Josiah Holbrook had spoken before the pupils of the third school district. But the days of Holbrook's almost magical influence were over. He had come to live near Washington the previous November. Now sixty years of age but still possessed of great plans and some enthusiasm, he hoped to make the city the national center of the lyceum. His plans, however, brought no result. His important role in the history of American culture was finished years before his death, by drowning, in nearby Virginia in 1854.

In spite of the slightly wider diffusion of culture throughout the state of Delaware during the late 1840s and the 1850s, Wilmington remained the only community to pay attention to the lecture system. There some of the older organizations dropped out of sight but new ones, whose offerings were augmented by independent lectures and unsponsored courses, came in.

The Library Company of Wilmington, in existence since 1787, proved itself by far the most durable of local institutions. In 1846 it absorbed the Franklin Lyceum, previously the main organization of its kind in the city; and in 1857 it absorbed a relative newcomer, the Young Men's Association for Mutual Improvement. But even the Library Company's long lane finally had a turning: two years later it lost much of its own identity and became part of the new Wilmington Institute.

The Institute started out with vigor. It built an imposing hall and quickly attracted over half a thousand members. The *Annual Report* issued in April 1861 could point to some significant achievements. Membership had increased to 666 and the consolidated library now had over 6000 volumes. The season's course, of five scientific and four literary lectures, had just been concluded. The president wrote that they had been 'of the highest order.' On the other hand, the Institute had lost enough money to make the lecture committee feel the course a financial disaster. Determined to recoup, the Institute sponsored a course the next winter that was well calculated to win larger crowds. Listed among the noted speakers were Wendell Phillips. Bayard Taylor, and the famous reformed drunkard John B. Gough. This strategy worked, and the Institute survived, living on through and after the Civil War years.

13

The South: Lowering Skies

SOME of the major economic, social, and psychological trends which blocked the progress of the lyceum system in the South before 1846 not only maintained themselves but gained increasing momentum after that time. Although the slave-holding, cotton-raising economy moved toward the Southwest, it still involved the whole South in various ways. Virginia, to take a pointed instance, contained very few cotton-raising plantations, but one of its more profitable industries turned out to be raising slaves for export to the cotton-producing states. The twin facts that this was an agrarian economy and a slave economy discouraged both the native American artisan and the European immigrant. The southern artisan, fighting an unfriendly economy, either gave up the struggle or else moved north where the opportunities for skilled workers were far richer. The immigrant, skilled or unskilled, saw little profit in competing with slave labor. Consequently, when he landed he stayed up north. Without such leadership as the artisan might have given and without the cultural cross-fertilization that the immigrant would have provided, the southern lower class deteriorated into a mass of poor whites. During the decade and a half before the Civil War its only significant growth was in numbers. The size of the lower class increased steadily, with no gain to the lyceum.

On the other hand, the middle class—the mainstay of the lyceum —became smaller. It lost from above as well as below. It lost from below through the absence of those skilled workmen who elsewhere could rise from the lower class, by dint of their initiative and energy, into the middle class. It lost from above, because there was more incentive to rise to the upper class here. Here a young, middle-class professional man, for instance, trained in medicine, frequently practiced his profession only long enough to acquire a little capital. Then, since the best money lay in raising cotton, he bought an equity in a small plantation and pushed his way into the upper class.

As these things were significant for the lyceum, so was the matter of population. Census figures show that the South continued to lag. The contrast even with New England is dramatic. In 1840 Massachusetts had ninety-two persons per square mile; in 1850 the number had risen to 124, and in 1860 to 153. At the other extreme, South Carolina, making slower progress than any other state in its region, showed only a minute increase. In 1850 it had twenty-two persons per square mile, and ten years later it had merely one more. In those ten years the population of the whole South increased 28 per cent but the population of the North (New England, the Middle Atlantic states, and the Midwest) increased 41 per cent, with the least growth occurring in New England and the most in the Midwest. Moreover, the South had a high proportion of Negroes in its population, and the Negro and the lecture system never touched one another. That meant even fewer customers for the lyceum.

The number of towns, as usual, also had a relation to the status of the lyceum, both before and after 1845. As lecturing became more and more important, the traveling lecturer gravitated toward the clusters of towns, toward the areas with a relatively large number of communities. This was natural. There was little incentive, financial or otherwise, for a lecturer to travel three days to make a single one-hour talk. Because many states in the South lacked both manufactures and commerce, subsisting instead primarily on agriculture, their percentage of town population remained low; and most traveling lecturers stayed away.

Yet the prospect was not entirely forbidding. In spite of the fact that the South continued to have few towns when compared with New England or the Middle Atlantic states, it nonetheless had enough of them in the years after 1845 to offer at least a little opportunity to the lecture system. In particular, the dozen or so leading commercial and industrial cities in the region grew to a point where they contained groups of people ready to pay for the opportunity of hearing well-known outsiders. Railway and road transportation between those cities, as well as elsewhere in the South, also improved.

Certain improvements of an intellectual kind likewise appeared. All other things being equal, a schooled, literate population gave more backing to the lecture system than did any other kind and, as the lyceum became less an instrument of practical—and self—education, the need for an already educated audience, if lecturing was to prosper, grew even greater. Comparatively speaking, the South showed a noteworthy advance both in the proportion of its white children in school and the proportion of adult whites who could read and write. For the New England states the percentage of pupils in 1850 dropped slightly below that of 1840, from 28 to 26 per cent. The percentage of adult illiterates rose; it was 2 per cent in 1850 after having been less than 1 per cent ten years before. These figures on school and literacy do not mean, it should be added, that education in New England had begun to decay. What had happened, rather, was that a multitude of immigrants were now included in New England's population. But even with allowance for that fact, the South showed unusual progress. The number of southern white children in school went up from 5 to 15 per cent from 1840 to 1850. The figures on literacy do not demonstrate the same sort of rise but they prove at any rate that the South was holding its own. In the next decade it bettered its position in respect both to the public schools and literacy. In proportion to the total white population, the number of white children in school continued to climb while the percentage of illiterates went down.

More readers meant more periodicals. North and south, the newspaper and periodical press boomed. Where the census of 1850 showed a total of 2,526 serial publications, the census of 1860 showed 4,051. The aggravated tension between the South and the North reflected itself especially in the thriving of the political press. In New England, specifically once again, the number of publications rose from 394 in 1850 to 428 in 1860. In the South, the number rose from 512 to an impressive 773. But in both regions the increase was largely in political periodicals. There was a definite decrease in literary journals both in New England and the South—something which did not augur well for the lyceum. The decrease, however, constituted at the moment only a minor modification of a favorable trend.

Here, then, was a definite amelioration of the South's cultural condition. The question naturally follows, why was the lyceum unable to make more of a gain? The answer lies in two factors of a rather different kind from those cited earlier as militating against the lyceum. The first is the extreme sensitivity, deepening all through the second period of the lyceum, of the South to the slightest criticism. The Midwest, it is true, also cared little to have eastern lecturers point out its shortcomings. But the South —rubbed raw by the abolitionists—reacted bitterly not only against criticism of slavery but against criticism of anything southern. The South was defending itself against the many-sided attack (as it saw it) of the North. At the heart of the attack was abolitionism but abolitionism was not alone. In economics and its political correlates it was particularly the burdensome tariff. In politics as such it was the onslaught upon states' rights. In religion it was the moral issue involved in slavery which was being raised by northern churchmen. The South gathered its strength to resist attack years before Sumter. As Vann Woodward and Clement Eaton, two outstanding historians of the South, have shown, it set up an intellectual blockade.

The second factor brings us back to class structure. It is that the upper class and the most influential part of the dwindling middle class, unlike those groups in the North, demonstrated practically no interest in the lyceum. The situation is clearest in the case of the upper class. By and large, they were a plantation aristocracy; they were the Cotton Elite. The men who might in Boston have read books at the Athenaeum, in the South rode and hunted. Still interested, to all appearances, in physical activities rather than thoughts, they felt for the lyceum an indifference amounting almost to contempt.

And how they felt was of unusually great importance. More than once, recent historians have been impressed by the way the planter aristocracy proved able to mold the rest of the South to its own pattern of thinking. It was the upper class that played the crucial part in bringing on the struggle for southern independence. Although the South had an agrarian, cotton-based economy, the number of persons who stood to benefit by the maintenance of slavery was surprisingly small. They were chiefly the plantation owners and their political representatives. Almost every state legislature in 1860 and '61 had moderates who wished to stay in the Union, but they never had a chance to be heard because of the surging power of the aristocratic extremists.

Earlier, with able assistance from the pulpit and press, the extremists had managed to crush dissent of most kinds, political, religious, and even cultural. They had brought about a situation where new northern books were seldom found in southern libraries. Similarly, even though the outside lecturers kept up the lyceum tradition of avoiding religious or political topics, the cultural milieu was such by the 1850s that lecturing remained at a far lower level of popularity than it would have otherwise, given the support of the southern upper class. Some lecturing, it should be said again, was done but the kind of culture the aristocracy established kept it from being extensive.

Under the Cotton Elite the South became steadily more anti-intellectual and more militant. As the skies lowered and the war clouds gathered, it was nearly impossible for the South to see the usefulness of the lyceum. The situation varied somewhat from state to state but the main outlines are clear.

◆

Virginia, far enough north and east to retain a place in the lecture system, kept up at least a moderate interest. Although the Charlottesville Lyceum enjoyed debating more than lecturing, Richmond and Alexandria did not. Richmond, in fact, consolidated its position as the best place in the state for lectures. It developed some sponsoring organizations and admitted an occasional free-lance lecturer as well. Poe spoke twice on 'The Poetic Principle' in 1849, ending with the delivery of his poem, 'The Raven.' His lectures did not turn out to be a financial success.

Among the Richmond societies was the Athenaeum, which

probably reached its peak in 1853 when the magnificent Thackeray spoke on 'Swift,' 'Congreve and Addison,' and 'Steele and the Times of Queen Anne.' He made an immense impression on the town and returned readily three years later to lecture on 'The Four Georges.' But Richmond was large enough for more than Thackeray's kind of lecturing. In testimony of this fact, the Mechanics' Institute was founded in 1854. Its aims were to provide—in addition to practical lectures—a library, a laboratory, and even a school of design.

In Alexandria both the Lyceum and the Library Company sponsored lectures. The men who gave them were, however, second-flight. Generally recruited from within the state or else from the nearby cities of Washington and Baltimore, they included no lions like Thackeray, no geniuses like Poe. The pallid Reverend E. Yates Reese of Baltimore was representative of the group. His course of four lectures in the 1858–9 season was announced as 'The Laureate of England,' 'An Evening with the Female Poets,' 'The Poets of the Sanctuary,' and 'Reading as a Fireside Accomplishment.' Lavender and old lace.

Despite North Carolina's economic and educational improvement, the lyceum lecturer, native or not, seldom appeared. Even in the eastern and more accessible portion of the state this held true. Such lectures as the one by a Dr. Williams in Raleigh in January 1850 on 'The Coal Formation of North Carolina,' or the essays read the same year before the Guilford Association of the Friends of Education, or even the series of three illustrated lectures on the Holy Land announced in December 1857 for Wilmington, were marginal to the lecture movement at best. Moreover, it is worth noting that Wilmington's *Daily Journal* of 30 December reported that the lecturer on the Holy Land had 'determined to throw his two remaining lectures into one.'

Up until the last few years before Sumter, the lecture system in South Carolina thrived no better after 1845 than it had before. Charleston remained the only city with a lecture audience. When the star system began to develop, that city was usually the terminus for any lecturers who went into the South (though occasionally one would turn westward to Atlanta and finally to New Orleans).

The chief place for visiting lecturers became the Apprentices'

Library. Years before, its audience had been mechanics whom the civic-minded were trying to lead along the path to literature. With the coming of the occasional northern lecturers the audiences changed. Now they were drawn from the sedate middle class and from the fashionable rich who often turned up mainly to see some notable in person. Among the visitors were Agassiz, who spoke on zoology and the glaciers, and Thackeray, who lectured on 'The Four Georges,' but for another group, the Mercantile Library Association. A gentlemen's society called the Conversation Club developed into a sponsor of lectures during this period. Its cultivated audience heard a variety of people, among them the geologist Sir Charles Lyell, Edward Everett, and the oceanographer M. F. Maury.

Although during most of the period Charleston alone paid attention to lecturing, in the late 1850s the whole state became less indifferent to it. Interest in both public-school and adult education mounted. The novelist William Gilmore Simms, aided it is true by local pride, could speak throughout the state at a profit. He made 'his round of lectures at the various villages of South Carolina . . . cleared some money and increased his reputation.' A few other local lecturers earned a little money. A few towns bestirred themselves. Columbia and Cheraw founded their lyceums and Charleston at the same time organized one more, the Palmetto Lyceum. *Russell's Magazine* of Charleston could remark hopefully in March 1858 that 'One of the signs of a slowly awakening consciousness on the part of the people of South Carolina that in all literary respects they are lamentably behind the age is to be found in the general establishment of LYCEUMS, and organized bodies for the discussion of literary and scientific subjects, in many of the towns and villages of the interior.' Yet *Russell's* compliment was at best a left-handed one; and evidence reveals that that was all the state deserved.

In Georgia the restriction of lecturing to the two or three main cities of the state continued. Savannah's Lyceum Hall remained in use. The Savannah Public Library's digest of newspapers shows that three societies sponsored lectures in the city during the 1850s. They were the Young Men's Literary Society, the Georgia Historical Society, and the YMCA. In Augusta the Young Men's Library

Association, started in 1848, 'sponsored great men in lecture courses,' Thackeray among them, according to the Federal Writers' *Augusta*. He gave 'The Four Georges' as a highlight of the Augusta season of 1855–6 (and thriftily offered the same series concurrently in Savannah).

Kentucky hospitality was tasted by traveling lecturers every now and then during the second period of the lyceum. Louisville, Lexington, and Frankfort were cities likely to be visited. Among the lecturers, almost inevitably, was Bayard Taylor, who made at least one trip to Louisville in February 1855, and Edward Everett, who spoke in Louisville on George Washington in May 1857. The Mercantile Library of Louisville was probably the most important sponsor of courses; after 1852 it was joined by the Mechanics' Institute. But most Kentucky communities developed more enthusiasm for debating societies than for lecture courses, and so the records of lectures even in Lexington and Frankfort are rare.

Public education in Tennessee, already feeble, suffered a severe blow in 1844 through the abolishing of the office of state superintendent. Not until ten years later was this blow offset by the passage of a strong public school law. White's *Development of the Tennessee State Educational Organization* ascribes the inferiority of mass education throughout that decade to slavery and the lingering prejudice against public schools as 'pauper schools.' Nashville and Knoxville, and to a lesser degree Memphis, did not suffer as much as the small towns and rural areas; but even in these cities education and lecturing made out rather poorly. The lyceum as such was hit hard. Knoxville, its newspapers show, had a few literary and debating societies; so did Nashville. The remainder of the state continued to be almost barren of anything like lyceum activity.

Similarly, after 1845 few reflections of the lyceum movement were still to be detected in Alabama. Montgomery and Mobile sometimes saw a visiting lecturer, but the national tours of the leading ones seldom if ever included these cities in the itinerary. At long intervals a noted lecturer bound for New Orleans might disembark from his packet at Mobile, or else break up his tedious journey by land to New Orleans with a stop at Montgomery.

Thackeray, for example, delayed his march through the South long enough to lecture on two of his four Georges in Mobile. In spite of rainy weather the elite of the city (in the eyes of the *Daily Advertiser*) came out to hear him with rapt attention. Some local lecturers made their modest circuit also, yet even they were few. As a matter of fact, the closest thing to a lyceum that Alabama favored was the literary club where the gentlemen members read papers to one another.

The definite interest in the lyceum which Mississippi cultivated in the late 1830s was lost by the next decade. Activity became confined to a handful of societies. The Philo Alethian Club of Aberdeen was listening to lectures in 1846 on 'The Varieties of the Human Species' and 'The Economy of Labor.' And the Woodville Lyceum Association was still alive in 1848. But that was about all. If Natchez or Jackson saw northern lecturers during the 1850s, it was probably because they paused briefly on their way to New Orleans. Compared to the period before 1845, the one following it proved bare.

The lyceum movement in New Orleans shone all the more brilliantly because of the surrounding darkness. In almost every southern state—and even in Louisiana itself aside from its main city—the conditions that would stimulate lyceums simply did not exist. In New Orleans they existed abundantly. This is not to say that the record of the lyceum there was one of complete fulfillment; as a matter of fact, more than one good citizen complained about his city's cultural shortcomings. But relatively, if not absolutely, the over-all record was impressive.

As the second period of the lyceum opened, the People's Lyceum was sponsoring courses of rather elevated lectures—'The Relation of Harmony between Man and the Creation' is a sample —given by distinguished local men. During the season of 1845–6 such lectures were supplemented through the arrival of two noted lecturers from outside. One was the famous astronomer, Professor Ormsby Mitchel, who gave a series on his specialty. The other was the eloquent little Down-Easter, Henry Giles, whose subject was English literature. The succeeding seasons of 1846–7 and 1847–8 showed a recession, although Mitchel returned for a second series. The next season saw a slight recovery marked by a course of ten lectures for the benefit of the Asylum for the Relief of Destitute Females. The lecturers in most cases were either benevolent professors from the newborn University of Louisiana or else men from the local Protestant ministry.

In 1849–50 the Library and Lyceum Society took the center of the stage, with help from the Second Municipality. The Second Municipality continued to foster public education up to 1852 when the three municipalities became one. It ordered the building of the Lyceum Hall, which the Honorable T. H. McCaleb dedicated in an elaborate address on 18 December 1849. McCaleb criticized his city for what he righteously regarded as its previous indifference to culture. Other cities, he said, 'have long ceased to discuss the question whether such institutions as lyceums for the delivery of popular lectures be *necessary* and are daily and hourly projecting new schemes . . . to . . . perpetuate the blessings they diffuse.' He then outlined the advantages of literary and scientific knowledge, and concluded with an apostrophe to 'mental and moral excellence.'

With this impetus the Lyceum Society could go on to sponsor three courses, one on astronomy by Mitchel (his third course in New Orleans), one on geology, and one on meteorology. New Orleans' *Picayune* approved. In the issue of 21 December, three days after the dedication, it made clear that it liked 'courses in . . . natural science—mere literary lectures are not to our taste. . . . We have no objection to a reasonable quantity of metaphysics, but we highly approve the decision of the committee to make the Lyceum the means of popularizing science.' The *Picayune* sounded like a voice from the past.

An assortment of lecturers, local and otherwise, offered courses during the ensuing seasons. These were in addition to the ones sponsored by the Library and Lyceum Society. Among the far-traveled speakers to appear in the early and middle 1850s were P. T. Barnum (he talked on 'The Advantages of Temperance'; 'a merrier audience had never been seen'), Agassiz, and Thackeray ('hums of assent,' 'outbursts of laughter,' 'rounds of applause'). But many an outside lecturer was solicited and declined; many another promised but never came. The *Daily True Delta* jealously scolded the Lyceum Society in 1855: 'Let the committee discard the idea that there is no talent in the South and that no person is capable of lecturing here unless he comes with a foreign or northern endorsement.'

A new organization, the Mechanics' Institute, dominated the 1853–4 season with a free course mainly on science but with some other topics thrown in. It had a library and a cabinet besides lectures. Its courses continued annually. Two years later the YMCA was sponsoring lectures, for the relief of 'destitute young men.' In 1858 the Mercantile Library Association began to compete in spite of the economic depression which 1857 had brought. Only with the advent of the war did lecturing dwindle and practically disappear.

The topics New Orleans liked best through all these years were scientific (first by a wide margin), pseudo-scientific (especially phrenology), and inspirational—with an occasional dash of French literary history and other mild spice.

Halfway up the great river, the other outstanding lyceum city of the Mississippi Valley remained second to New Orleans but managed on the whole to hold its own. In Missouri, St. Louis continued to be the cultural focus of the state and the one place where eastern lecturers were apt to stop. Yet its record was a mixed one. The St. Louis Lyceum minutes through 1849 show that enthusiasm for lecturing ebbed although interest in the debates and library survived. The St. Louis Mercantile Library Association opened up and gained its charter in 1846. It had a committee on lectures from the outset. The lectures lost money during the season of 1846–7 and so were abandoned for two years. However, they were resumed in 1849 and thereafter generally produced a profit. The annual reports printed throughout the next decade show that lectures became increasingly significant though they never displaced the reading room as the most important part of the society. During the 1850s the St. Louis YMCA began to compete with the Library Association, running lecture courses too. Both societies found that they could offer respectable courses but that it was at times a struggle to do so.

The lecturing situation illustrated the influence of location perfectly. Most eastern lecturers simply did not wish to travel as far as St. Louis. They either made excuses to an association's committee or else failed to answer its invitation. When they did come, they had to make their journey worthwhile; so they customarily gave courses instead of merely single lectures. Even in Iowa and certainly in Illinois single lectures were the rule, for the lecturer could travel fairly quickly from one community to another. There were enough receptive towns to assure him of a tour. But because St. Louis was the one place in Missouri for lecturing (Bayard Taylor called the rest of the state 'the Missourian wilds'), it had to give those lecturers who visited it unusually firm support. And it did so on the whole, with the net result that although the city heard relatively few lecturers, it heard a good many lectures. Emerson's schedule in the season of 1852–3 was typical. He gave six lectures for the Library Association on 'The Conduct of Life' and then threw in a seventh on the Anglo-Saxon. 'One of the best furnished literary men of America' was the slightly ambiguous verdict on him of the president's report for '53.

The small beginnings of the lyceum in Arkansas, finally, came to nothing. The system failed to take firm root. When the Little Rock Lyceum was established in 1848, the writer who described it for the *Arkansas Democrat* made the point, in passing, that 'there is not in the whole state a public library deserving of the name as such.' That was only one token of the condition of Arkansas culture in the second period of the lyceum; others show the same thing.

The principal reason, as a matter of fact, for founding the Little Rock Lyceum was to develop a public circulating library. When the young members proposed a course of lectures, it was mainly to raise money for books (as was often done by library societies). It is probable that the proposed course was never given. By February 1851 even those books already collected were 'scattered hither and thither,' according to a newspaper item of the time.

The state remained, understandably, in terms of our working definitions, more southern than midwestern; and so many of the conditions that at this time strongly favored the lyceum in the Midwest were not to be found here.

14

The Midwest:
Eastern Stars for Western Associations

IN the years after 1845 New England culture remained alive in northern parts of Ohio, Indiana, and Illinois, and the southern parts of Michigan and Wisconsin. 'I have found a population of Yankees, out here, and an easy welcome for my Massachusetts narrowness everywhere,' wrote Emerson to his wife in February 1854, after a lecture tour through the region.

The New England culture Emerson encountered had by this time experienced some important modifications but, paradoxically, it was all the more assertive of its Yankee qualities because of that. The more it was forced to change, the more it clung to some of the symbols of New England. Its contact with southern culture had plainly left a mark. In testimony to the strength of the South, most of the remainder of Ohio, Indiana, and Illinois was characterized by a mingling of cultures in which the original southern predominated. The frontier too had modified New England culture when it met it. And so, lastly, had the passing of time itself. Each generation included fewer people who kept their awareness of what New England meant. Yet those who did remember often found their devotion to New England culture strengthened partly because they shared it with the few rather than the many. If this devotion showed itself at certain times mainly as an interest in genealogy or antiquated furniture, it showed itself at others as an interest in the lyceum as well as other New England institutions, old or new.

There is no doubt that the midwestern places where the New

England stamp was still most marked stayed the best ones for the lyceum. And New England itself was ready to do its part. As transportation and communication progressed, more and more eastern lecturers readily undertook tours into the Midwest. They brought the aura of New England with them, regardless of their topics, though the older settlers sensed it more than their offspring did. In this difference in attitude between the generations lay, incidentally, the seeds of further change.

As these lecturers from New England (and from metropolitan New York, to a lesser extent) came out in increasing numbers, the Midwest showed a mixed attitude toward them. We have the fullest data about that in Ohio. Already by 1840 the third largest state in the Union, Ohio felt its cultural strength. On the basis of a comprehensive study of Ohio newspaper accounts, David Mead has suggested in his *Yankee Eloquence in the Middle West* that Ohioans were eager to see the bearers of famous eastern names in person but were also ready to be antagonized by what they said. No criticism of the West was welcomed. The northern side of the Ohio Valley was in general striving to shape its own culture—and not only in the image of New England—so it reacted as defensively as the whole country had a generation earlier. The yearning for a national literature now saw its diminished counterpart here in the yearning for a western one.

The touchiness of the West is perfectly illustrated by two issues of the *Sandusky Commercial Register* during the fall of 1854. The first, for 29 September, prints a list of eastern lecturers available for the coming season. The *Register* says it does so for the convenience of western associations but grumbles that the easterners' fees are far too high. Last season Emerson charged fifty dollars per lecture—'this winter the threat is that more will be charged! If such really be the case, we emphatically say don't hire Ralph Waldo Emerson.' But the list is packed with attractive, nationally known names. Probably only one would have drawn blank looks from western audiences; that was the name of Greeley's friend, Henry Thoreau of Concord. And the presence of Thoreau's name can be explained by the fact that the *Register* apparently copied its list from Greeley's *New York Tribune*.

The other issue of the *Register*, for 7 October, printed a complementary list of western lecturers. 'There has been of late,' says the *Register* in preface, 'a shameful neglect of western talent.' Western lecturers were just as good as eastern ones, and besides they cost less. Then the paper stressed the claims both of 'western scholars' (that is, the lecturers) and, significantly, of western 'literatures.' This list, naming sixteen men in all, included only one that was definitely well known throughout the nation, Professor Ormsby Mitchel. The others all had more than a local reputation but hardly a national one. Professors predominated in the group, with ministers and politicians coming next. Perhaps because familiarity breeds contempt, the homegrown talent did indeed cost less. For this particular season the easterners were quoted at about forty to seventy-five dollars a lecture while the westerners ranged from around fifteen to twenty-five dollars. There were also other western lecturers not in this group who would speak for still smaller sums; and there were, finally, the many possessors of local talent who would talk before their townsmen for nothing. But the trouble, too often, was that people valued only what they had to pay for. There lay a genuine dilemma for the lyceum committees.

At any rate, during the busy 1850s lecture tours to the Midwest filled many an eastern wallet. The region was growing with a vitality that astounded the East and dismayed the South. Farms and manufactures were booming; so was the population. Between 1845 and 1860 the population of Ohio increased by one-third, adding well over a million inhabitants. Indiana lagged a little but the remaining midwestern states made up for its backwardness. The farther west and north one went of course, the greater the rate of increase was apt to be. Illinois doubled its population in only ten years; by 1860 the state had 1,712,000 inhabitants. And in the same decade of the 1850s the population of Iowa tripled!

Throughout the Midwest all the trends that aided the lyceum became even more marked. The population increased phenomenally. The number of people in towns and cities grew. The amount of manufactures and commerce went up. The numbers of white children in public schools increased; so did the number of white literates over twenty years old. The number of newspapers and other periodicals multiplied. Transportation by rail, water, and road improved.

To turn to one more trend—and one that cannot be measured numerically—we can see at least in a general way that the members of such upper and upper-middle classes as had emerged were more interested in the lyceum than their peers in the South—although the Midwesterners failed to demonstrate the aggressively intellectual and cultural leadership that had distinguished their counterparts in New England.

With such things in its favor, the lyceum could not avoid flourishing. For at least ten years, from perhaps 1847 to 1857, the lecture system grew better in the Midwest than in any other section of the country. 'We are informed that nearly every town in the West will this winter have one or more courses of lectures.' So said Cincinnati's lively literary magazine, the *Genius of the West*, in November 1854. It struck a note of sweeping affirmation like that of New England itself during the salad days of the lyceum. Only at the end of this period were there signs of a slackening interest. The panic of 1857, a growing sophistication about eastern lecturers, and the nearing of the Civil War constituted the main reasons. But even within this slight general diminution there were individual variations. For example, Ohio became a trifle jaded by eastern names; yet in Illinois and Wisconsin they kept their appeal. The total picture is still one of striking interest in the lecture movement until 1861.

◆

Sons of that Pilgrim race
Were they from whom we trace
Our Buckeye blood,

sang the Ohio bard L. J. Cist in tribute to the original migrants. For all his bathos, he was asserting more than a sentimental truism. He was expressing the sense of cultural heritage which still had its place in the state during the years after 1845.

During the early 1850s the number of lecture-sponsoring associations constantly increased. They built on a broader foundation than the eastern societies were now able to, for Ohio still paid some attention to the mechanic class when it came to making out

the programs. Something of the interest in practical science remained. So did the stress on the lyceum as a moral influence on
young men. In line with these facts, Governor Reuben Wood in
1852 called on the General Assembly to set aside funds for the
promotion of lyceums and literary organizations—and this twenty
years after eastern legislatures had lost their official interest in
the lyceum movement!

Naturally there were exceptions to the general support. The
local newspapers could report poor attendance as well as good.
But the remedy for indifference was, the lecture committees
thought, eastern celebrities. The peak of the demand came in the
season of 1855–6. During that season at least three dozen Ohio
communities, ranging from Akron to Zanesville, imported them.
Eastern lecturers talked in towns whose names in some cases
they had never heard before.

Nevertheless, the smaller towns in particular ran into trouble
at times in scheduling star performers. The idea of a co-operative
system simultaneously emerged in several places. The initial result was two abortive associations. The Bryant Association, named
after the poet and journalist, was organized, in fact, for this peak
season of 1855–6. But the dozen constituent societies soon found
that the scheduling was too easily upset and that the eastern
lecturers did not infallibly make money anyway, so the alliance
fell apart. The second association of local lyceums, managed by
the editor of the *Massillon News*, started in the same season and
failed equally swiftly. If good times had continued, it might
have been a different story. But the depression of 1857 delivered
a strong enough blow to delay co-operative scheduling in Ohio
until after the Civil War.

The hard times from 1857 on resulted in renewed favor for
practical lectures and scientific ones. Science, especially, represented something concrete, something that could do everybody
good. Sprightly E. L. Youmans on 'The Chemistry of the Sunbeam'
and Ormsby Mitchel on the planets could compete if not with
Bayard Taylor then at least with John Lord and his history of the
Middle Ages. However, the arrival of the war inevitably curtailed
lecturing even on science. Many a lyceum hall became deserted.
The long-lived Young Men's Mercantile Library Association of

Cincinnati, for decades a leader among Ohio lyceums, dropped its courses; and a number of other societies followed.

In retrospect, the strength of the lyceum movement in Ohio throughout the second period appeared outstanding. In spite of the relatively mediocre years of 1857–61, Ohio outstripped all the New England states but Massachusetts and all the Middle Atlantic states except perhaps New York.

By the late 1840s some of the noted eastern lecturers were stopping off at Indianapolis but, as a rule, ignoring the rest of the state of Indiana. The young men of that city founded the Union Literary Society and by 1847 were tentatively offering the kind of lecture courses which Ohio was finding effective: a judicious mixture of eastern and western talent. The *Indiana State Journal* for 8 February 1847, for instance, reports that their current course included such renowned easterners as Henry Ward Beecher and such a westerner as the Reverend P. D. Gurley ('Mr. G. is known to be one of the most talented men in the West'). A sample of courses offered by independent lecturers can be found in the *Journal* of 18 November 1849. In that issue an Episcopal clergyman named Thayer, for example, announced that he would give a dozen lectures, the topics ranging over history, self-help, morality, science, and poetry. The course was aimed at young men and presumably offered them a synopsis of human thought through the ages. Other courses were only a little less ambitious and diverse.

Apparently such random courses more than filled the growing city's need, since the Union Literary Society struggled for years to make its courses popular. 'We regret to say that the lecture of Mr. Hudson . . . had again to be deferred Wednesday evening for want of an audience,' the *Journal* for 12 March 1852 complained—and that was typical. The last gasp of the Society came in 1853. By 1855–6, however, the city was finally large enough, and interested enough, to support the courses sponsored thereafter by the newly organized YMCA. The lectures were attractively divided between eastern and western speakers. Among the noted easterners to read lectures there before the Civil War were Parker, Beecher, Gough, Everett, Emerson, Bayard Taylor, and Henry Giles. Among the noted westerners were Professors Youmans and Mitchel.

There was not much lyceum activity to be found outside of Indianapolis. Logansport, La Porte, Evansville, and Terre Haute were the chief places for organized courses during the years before the Civil War. They represented nothing like the almost inexhaustible activity of the lyceum system in Ohio.

The Detroit Young Men's Society remained the leading lyceum in Michigan. It built a hall (which turned out to be hard to pay for), steadily increased its handsome library holdings, and arranged lecture courses which customarily paid a fair profit. Attendance varied considerably, however. In commenting on the lecture season of 1854–5 the Society's report announced with pique that Detroiters were not 'spontaneously' a lecture-going people and that famous names were needed to attract them. The succeeding season illustrated the truth of this observation, for the audiences ranged from sixty or seventy to a closely packed crowd of 500, depending on who spoke. The easterners demonstrated their cash value dramatically. The result was that eastern names gradually crowded out most of the western ones on the course schedules. For one thing, the completion of the Great Western Railway allowed the professional lecturers from the East to reach Detroit much more conveniently than before. Yet it sometimes took hard work to persuade them to make the journey. In point, the lecture committee for the season of 1857–8 wrote to more than a hundred prospects and came up with only six acceptances. One was Herman Melville, who gave a hack lecture on 'Statuary in Rome.' Another was Youmans and a third was Starr King. But the profit for the season, in spite of hard times, was two hundred dollars.

The season just prior to the opening of the Civil War was the best one in the Society's history. It ran from November 1860 to February 1861. Among the sixteen lecturers were Bayard Taylor, Youmans, and the essayist E. P. Whipple. George Vandenhoff performed, giving his usual three nights of readings; the last was the ultrasentimental 'Smiles and Tears from Poetic Fountains.' Taylor cost the Society the most in expenses but, characteristically, gave one of the best attended lectures. The average attendance for all the lectures was 522.

Other lecture-sponsoring organizations of any importance failed to grow up in Detroit. The city lost its remarkable early cultural advantage. Like most other expanding American cities, it did not find its culture increasing in proportion to its population. With some of the smaller communities this was not true. Only two or three of them, though—Kalamazoo and Ann Arbor in particular—made a successful effort to attract eastern lecturers. The others were like Flint, which favored more local speakers. When the Flint Lecture Association advertised a course for the season of 1860–61, for example, the ten speakers listed were drawn mainly from Detroit pulpits and the state educational system.

Lecturing in Illinois expanded after a tentative and discouraging start. With the advent of the 1850s Chicago, now full of vigor, emerged as the western end of the lyceum circuit and probably heard more lectures than any other midwestern city. When Emerson came there in February 1854 to address the Young Men's Association, he was amazed at how the population had risen. He wrote his brother William that he had 'seen wonderful growths of towns and states. But this city of Chicago . . . is the fastest of all.' The Young Men's Association continued as the main lyceum. The Mechanics' Institute kept on with lectures too, but these were naturally more practical or technical and were offered as a rule by local men—'the best informed and most scientific men in the city.' The city also had, in growing numbers, the usual independent courses and lectures.

The *Daily Democratic Press* of Chicago has been indexed; and the file for 1855—to pick a year—shows that lectures are well reported. Next to notices of Chicago and downstate lecturing, there are many notices of lecturing in the East. The picture for Chicago is crowded. Besides the two societies already mentioned, the Metropolitan Literary Union, the Chicago Female Seminary, the Chicago Phrenological Society, and the Chicago Literary Union sponsored courses that year. Almost half a hundred lecturers in Chicago, running from a Mr. Bedford to a Mrs. Young, are listed. The most famous names were those of Beecher, Benjamin, Curtis, Gough, Greeley, Mark Hopkins, Starr King, Lowell, Theodore Parker, Phillips, Saxe, and Bayard Taylor. It is not hard by the way, to construct the typical (though not necessarily the famous) lecturer for the 1850s as Chicago saw him. He was a Protestant minister, lively of address and with an ethical message or else some special sidelight on life to offer his listeners. And he had to come from outside.

Chicago of course attracted eastern lecturers but in the late 1850s the star performers began to visit the small towns too. The same 1855 index to the *Democratic Press* cites lectures in Jacksonville, Equality, Belvidere, Elgin, Rockford, Galesburg, and Aurora, mostly by easterners. There was a good reason for them. Local lecture committees were beginning to write each other, realizing— here as in Ohio—that easterners might come to a number of small towns on a lecture tour but would never come to only one. Now when sending the elegant E. P. Whipple, for instance, an invitation they could promise him a good itinerary. Matched, moreover, with these casual associations of local lyceums were the newly emerging lecture managers, who earnestly (and often inaccurately) insisted that they had no financial stake in their star's engagements. Of these representatives, Henry Ward Beecher's became the most disliked.

This correspondence among the local lecture committees and the efforts of the lecture managers both accomplished something. But the results they all achieved were far surpassed by the efforts of one Chicago man, the civic-minded S. D. Ward. More small towns in his part of the Midwest heard lectures because of him than for any other reason. As secretary of the Chicago Young Men's Association, Ward soon had more than his fill of refusals from eastern lecturers. He decided that the solution was to line up enough other engagements for his easterners so that they would readily agree to lecture for him in Chicago. On his own initiative he began to correspond with the lyceum secretaries and lecture committees in the communities around Chicago. Having enlisted their co-operation, he was able to arrange tours for the eastern stars he wanted—and he did all this without taking a cent for it.

J. R. Brigham, secretary of the Milwaukee Young Men's Associ-

ation, became Ward's chief lieutenant; Brigham's papers, still preserved, include much correspondence from Ward and offer a rich
insight into the business side of lecturing from 1854 to 1857. Although the move toward co-operation among lyceums was failing
at this time in Ohio, it succeeded in Illinois (and Wisconsin) thanks
mainly to the energy and resourcefulness of Secretary Ward.

With their two large societies as the nucleus, Ward and Brigham continued to invite lecturers west and were able to have
the smaller towns of Illinois and Wisconsin join for mutual benefit. The Brigham papers testify that it worked out nicely for all concerned. Noted eastern lecturers appeared as a result in at least
a dozen Illinois towns. Ward made as many as twenty engagements for one of the lecturers, as he unselfishly took over the function that the lecturers' representatives were laboring to assume.

The cities of southern Wisconsin became more hospitable to the
lyceum as they became larger. Milwaukee, favored by the facts
that it was a lake port and had developed good boat connections
with Chicago, supported the outstanding lyceum in the state. This
was the previously mentioned Young Men's Association, organized
in December 1847. Like certain of its counterparts in the East, it
first strove to gather a library for its members and then decided
to have public lectures as an adjunct. Its minutes show that by
January 1850 the Association began sponsoring courses made up of
lectures by 'home men.' Admission was set at a shilling for gentlemen, and ladies free. But eastern eloquence was beckoning. By the
end of the year the society had instructed its secretary to negotiate
with Park Benjamin about a lecture for the next season. How the
trend grew can be demonstrated from the course of 1853-4, which
included Emerson, G. W. Curtis, Horace Mann, Greeley, and Taylor. Help for the trend lay in the fact that the easterners made
money, good money, for the Association. At the end of this particular course the committee could not 'refrain from expressing their
congratulations to the Board at so auspicious a result.'

Throughout most of the decade the Wisconsin man who had
more to do with the securing of lecturers than any other was Brigham. When serving as secretary for the Milwaukee Young Men's
Association he encountered the same difficulties in getting eastern
lecturers that Ward had in Chicago. His solution paralleled Ward's

too, for he began entering into informal arrangements with other lyceums to take the same speakers he wanted. Then he joined forces with Ward. But he lacked Ward's strategic location as well as some of his drive, so his role became a secondary one. Nevertheless, it was important and, after Ward, he deserved more of the credit for bringing in eastern notables than anyone else. Ward's and Brigham's plans worked well. The broad cast on the waters returned in ample amounts, and a score of the best lecturers in the country came to Milwaukee and drew crowded houses.

Other Wisconsin lyceums were encouraged to co-operate. Either through Ward and Brigham directly or else by following their method, Madison, Beloit, Janesville, Kenosha, Racine, Fond du Lac, Waukesha, and Portage all enjoyed eastern speakers that they would never have attracted otherwise. For their part, Beecher, Taylor, Emerson, and many another shivered philosophically in snow-swept inns while touring Wisconsin towns for a substantial fee.

Several other lyceums, in the southern part of the state, grew up and maintained themselves independently. They used local lecturers. In this group Sheboygan was outstanding. It always had some kind of a lyceum. To begin with, it was the Sheboygan Lyceum; then it was the Young Men's Association; then the Young Men's Institute; and finally, as the second period of the lyceum system's development closed, the Sheboygan Lyceum again. The typical program was a full one, for it combined a lecture with a debate. The lecture topics were a miscellaneous lot, 'Education,' 'Liberty in Europe,' 'Men for the Times,' and 'Commerce, Manufactures, and the Mechanical Arts' being examples.

The lyceum came late to Wisconsin but when it finally arrived, in the 1850s, it was greeted with all the enthusiasm that a novelty can command. While a state such as Ohio was a little weary of paying to see eastern faces, Wisconsin was eager to gaze on them. 'The people are infatuated,' said Bayard Taylor writing from Milwaukee on 16 March 1854; and he was right. 'If I lecture next winter,' he added expansively, 'I can spend three months in the west and have engagements for every night.'

In the years before 1845 no typical lyceum of that period—that is, a practical society for mutual education—took root in Iowa.

After 1845 the lyceum system changed, concentrating heavily on lecturing and ultimately on the star system; Iowa, changing too, found the altered institution more to its taste. Culturally the key city was Davenport. Starting in 1847, its Literary Society began to hear lectures. In 1854 the Young Men's Literary Society, another group, entered the lecture field. Spurred on by the local press, it decided to invite eastern lecturers not only for what they might say but also because they would advertise the existence of Davenport. The season of 1855–6 saw the success of the young men's efforts. E. P. Whipple spoke on 'Education'; Park Benjamin read his poem 'Fashion'; Parke Godwin spoke on 'American Social Life'; and Emerson gave a lecture which, the press stated with admiring perplexity, could have been called almost anything. These were the highlights of the course, and doubtless they helped draw attention to Davenport. The courses continued until the end of our period. For the season of 1859–60, it should be added, they were the only ones of their kind in the whole state. When the war came even the Young Men's Literary Society course stopped.

By the 1850s the rest of Iowa still had only a few communities large enough to support eastern lecturers; but of those that could, almost all had the satisfaction of hearing 'wise men from the East.' In the period after 1855, a check of state newspapers shows, Keokuk, Muscatine, Iowa City, and Burlington employed well-known easterners. Sioux City tended to employ local lecturers, on the other hand. Its lyceum listened to home-town talks on such topics as 'Mental Culture,' 'Men of the West,' and 'The Human Machine.'

All in all, the lyceum in Iowa did about as well as one would expect. Its most vital long-run contribution was probably the support it furnished to public libraries. Nearly a dozen of the lecture-sponsoring societies, especially those in the larger towns, established and maintained libraries as their other important activity. In most cases the libraries became public or quasi-public property after the lecture societies died out. In some other states to the east the lyceum and the public school worked together. In Iowa it was characteristically the lecture system and the library.

15

The West:
Outposts of Culture

TODAY we think of Minnesota, Kansas, and Nebraska as midwestern, but if we remember that the frontier was a dimension of time as well as place, they were in the far West when the second period of the lyceum was getting under way. Kansas and Nebraska were not even organized as territories until 1854; they became states in 1861 and 1867 respectively. Minnesota progressed faster, becoming a territory by 1849 and a state in 1858. Its rate of growth during the '50s proved to be outstanding. At the start of the decade it had 6000 inhabitants; at the end it had over twenty-eight times as many, 172,000 in all. The population of Kansas grew much more slowly; it had 107,000 people by 1860, while Nebraska had only 29,000.

Almost all the implications of the population figures in Nebraska and Kansas were against the lyceum. In terms of population density Nebraska was obviously much worse off than Kansas. Kansas, however, was handicapped by the lack of sizable villages which could support lyceums. In the whole territory, as of 1860, there was only a single town above 5000, Leavenworth. Atchison had a population of 2,600 by then, and there was no other place in Kansas with a population even of 2000. Surprisingly enough, the situation in Minnesota was not notably superior; it did not have many more populous towns than Kansas. But what Minnesota did have was a favorable climate for the lyceum in many of its villages.

There were several reasons. Education was better supported there than in Kansas or Nebraska. The actual proportions of children in school to the whole population did not vary much from territory to territory but the fact that Minnesota, with more people, had so many more schools resulted in a school system superior in more than numbers alone. One out of every seven persons attended school in Minnesota as of 1860; one out of every eight attended in Kansas; and only one out of every nine attended in Nebraska. In its low proportion of illiterates, moreover, Minnesota had a slight edge over Kansas. On the other hand, Nebraska had only a handful of them in the whole territory. But the lyceum could reap no advantage from this fact. The frontier was still so strong in Nebraska that it discouraged almost every cultural effort. Conversely, much of Minnesota was past the frontier stage, and since three-quarters of its illiterates were foreign born, that meant a highly literate native population.

In periodical publications Minnesota likewise ranked first. Both magazines and newspapers, and especially newspapers, demonstrated here again that their presence helped the lyceum. Transportation was important too. A prime factor in providing the lyceum system in Minnesota with a favorable environment was the Mississippi River. In the 1850s the amount of railroad trackage throughout the West was gradually rising; but both before and after this decade Minnesota took full advantage of the relatively easy and inexpensive mode of water travel the Mississippi always offered.

That is not to say that throngs of eastern lecturers promptly took river-boat passage to St. Paul. Actually, they were still rare; Minnesota and the remainder of this West lay too far away. The great advantage that improved transportation afforded was general at this time rather than specific and did not extend at once to giving east-coast lecturers a swift, easy journey from Massachusetts to the headwaters of the Mississippi.

Between Minnesota, Kansas, and Nebraska on the one hand and the West Coast on the other, there was for the lyceum nothing. But at the coast itself California, riding high on the gold rush, was beginning to establish a culture where lecturing could play a part. With a population that rose from 92,600 in 1850 to almost

380,000 in 1860, California's activity during the decade was feverish in the extreme. Wealth was the be-all and end-all for its people throughout most of the 1850's; yet without blinking at that fact, the people established schools, published periodicals, and improved transportation. And some definite signs of New England culture could be detected. Caught, however, in the cross-currents, the situation of the lyceum was still rather precarious. After the Civil War the trends in California would be hospitable to lecturing, but before 1861 they varied.

Since it was the capital of Minnesota, St. Paul listened to a good deal of lecturing from the early 1850s on. Both local and itinerant lecturers, including an unusually large number of quacks, spoke their piece. Among the first organizations to appear was the Young Men's Association and Lyceum, founded apparently in 1851. It soon encountered hard times but reappeared with gathered strength in the fall of 1854, along with the Literary Association of the City of St. Paul. Meanwhile, in 1853 to be precise, the territorial legislature, meeting in St. Paul, passed an act which allowed the incorporation of lyceums, as well as colleges and libraries, and thus provided a token of the interest of the territory in intellectual developments. The YMCA, organized in the summer of 1856, sponsored lectures immediately. Its season for 1857–8 included 'The Problem of India,' 'Social Prejudice,' 'Lord Bacon and His Works,' and 'Aaron Burr,' all read by local men. The Library Association, incorporated in 1857, typified the book-gathering group which also sponsored lectures.

Nor was this search for improvement on the eastern model confined to the capital alone. An impressive list of little towns which had lyceums or literary associations in the late 1850s includes Austin, Cannon Falls, Hastings, Mankato, Red Wing, St. Anthony, Stillwater, Taylor's Falls, and Winona. And Minneapolis, though by no means the competitor of St. Paul that it is today, also had its lyceum at least temporarily in operation by 1854. But eastern lecturers for any of these communities, small or large, were infrequent.

The history of Kansas before it entered the Union was so notoriously sombre and tumultuous that it is a wonder any lyceums existed there. Yet a handful did, all of them, as far as we know, operating in the late 1850s. One was the Athenaeum in Lawrence. It received occasional newspaper publicity. A card in the *Kansas Herald of Freedom* in early January 1855, for instance, announces an evening meeting at St. Nicholas Hall. 'The introductory lecture of the course will be delivered by the president, J. S. Emery, Esq. Subject: "Popular Eloquence."' Later issues mention a gift of books from the East for the library of the infant society, as well as the third (but not the second) lecture in the course, on 'Thought,' by a local man named John Hutchinson.

The Leavenworth Lyceum was alive in 1857. The *Kansas Weekly Herald* of 10 January reported, 'We attended the meeting of this society on Monday evening and were very agreeably disappointed at the ability displayed by its members.' The program consisted of the reading, by the secretary, of 'an exceedingly rich and racy article from the budget-box,' an address upon 'The Growth and Destiny of Our Country,' and a debate.

In Nebraska, as in Kansas, it was not until the late 1850s that the lyceum ventured near. During these years the Omaha Library Association tentatively offered some lectures to the public, but by December 1860 the *Omaha Nebraskian* had to announce that 'The usual lectures . . . will not be delivered the present winter.' Instead, the paper reported, the Omaha Lyceum was being formed. Its object was debating, however, and in that respect it was characteristic of the scattered associations in the Nebraska Territory. Here too, debates were the frontier's favorite.

The Territory had, however, at least one other organization which conformed to the eastern pattern. It was the Everett Institute of Nebraska City. A brief article in the *Nebraska City News* of 6 August 1859 gives the society's aims as the establishment of a reading room and lecture courses; later it added debating. The article notes that a lecture course had been given the previous year. Lectures announced for the season of 1859–60 included 'The Anglo-Saxon Race, Their Past, Present, and Future,' 'Loyalty to Truth,' and 'Icebergs.' 'Our only regret,' the *News* for 24 December said of the last one, 'is that more persons did not hear it.'

For the lyceum as well as other cultural institutions, San Francisco was the heart of California. Throughout the 1850s it continued to support some form of lyceum life. In December 1851 the *Alta California* announced what it believed to be the first course of lectures ever sponsored in the city. Opened by a local minister who gave at least two lectures, both of them on the resources of California, the course was sponsored by the Western World Institute. The Mercantile Library Association, incorporated in January 1853, soon saw the advisability of sponsoring lectures in order to make money. Its books and debates seemed more important, doubtless, than the lectures; but the lectures turned the profit. They were designed to appeal to an assortment of tastes. The *Alta California* for 1 December 1856, for instance, announced the current course, with 'The Internal Connection and Mutual Dependence of the Various Occupations of Man,' 'The Beautiful in Poetry and the Poetic in the Beautiful,' 'Arabia, the Arabs, and Mt. Sinai,' 'Types, Ink, and Paper,' and 'Chemistry' numbered among the miscellany of subjects. Tickets for the course were five dollars, a gold rush price. Perhaps the peak of prewar activities, by no means surprisingly, was Bayard Taylor's series in 1860. It was not only that his appearance for the association was lucrative; it was also that the famous traveler was again visiting the California he had previously celebrated and would doubtless celebrate again.

The Mechanics' Institute, whose charter was adopted in March 1855, recalled the old lyceum, with aims that included the collection of a cabinet and the procurement of scientific apparatus. This organization devoted itself to mutual education less by lectures, as it turned out, than by other means. Its most widely publicized activity became the holding of annual mechanics' and manufacturers' fairs.

In the other parts of the state only a handful of references to lyceums are to be found. There was far less activity in Los Angeles than in San Francisco; inland, in Sacramento—primarily because it was the state capital—there was a little more cultural life. The proposed exercises of the Sacramento Lyceum were announced in 1854 as 'discussions, lectures, and the reading of essays.' The Sacramento Mercantile Library Association sponsored lectures during 1851 which Thompson and West's *History of Sacramento*

County considered 'valuable and interesting.' Tickets for the course were, again, five dollars.

Elsewhere throughout the growing nation, in other states and territories, the lyceum movement as we have defined it did not exist. That somewhere or other a group might have organized itself into a lyceum is certainly true, but one swallow does not make a summer. Throughout the Rocky Mountain area and in the Pacific Northwest the conditions which stimulated lyceums in particular and social culture in general would not be established until after—and sometimes considerably after—the end of the Civil War.

Facets of the Lyceum: II

16

The Economics of the Lyceum

THE slowly changing economics of the lyceum might be summed up in a set of symbols. For the first stage an orrery and a door key might be appropriate. They would represent the cost of the 'philosophical apparatus' that many lyceums bought to begin with and the cost of hall rent. For the second stage we might use a few dollar bills and a pocketful of loose silver. These would stand for the modest travel expenses of the earliest lecturers from out of town and then for the first modest fees. For the third stage we would use a well-filled wallet, a dog-eared timetable, and a busily corresponding lyceum secretary. These would represent the last stage of the lyceum system, the heyday of the star lecturer on tour from town to busy town.

In shaping the economics of the system at the outset, no one played a more vital part than Holbrook. It was he who suggested just how the money was to be gotten and how it was to be spent. He proposed that the budding lyceums buy the scientific apparatus that was so important to their early aims; when he saw how costly the apparatus was, he set up his own firm for making and selling it. He advertised his wares well, both in his own lyceum publications and in the pages of others. He did his work so effectively that his name on scientific apparatus for schools ultimately became a household word; and it was legally decided, after a long lawsuit, that *Holbrook* when applied to such apparatus was in the public domain and could be used by any manufacturer.

Directions for founding a lyceum are bound in with the printed

Proceedings of the meeting of the national lyceum in 1831. The problem of financing, with solutions according to Holbrook, receives due attention there. The instruments available from his firm are described too. To us the list of them looks long and dull— there is nothing exciting about the specifications and price lists of old-fashioned scientific apparatus. The eolopile, the arithmometer, even the orrery, mean little today. But to the lyceums who bought them and the audiences who saw them used they were the keys to a new world. The vistas they opened up were limitless. Much of the scientific instruction in the early lyceum was practical—a knowledge of 'mechanical powers,' for instance, would make a better machinist. Some instruction, however, was far from practical; it was liberal and humane. Of this kind the orrery, a small clockwork model of the solar system, was the best example. Its lessons included little that the mechanic could use at his bench but much that would allow him to understand the heavens he saw above him and the universe he inhabited.

The first step suggested in the specimen directions is the levying of modest dues. No figure is proposed, but the idea itself was almost universally adopted and nearly every society did have dues. A dollar or two a year was all that was apt to be asked of the members during the first decade of the lyceum system. After that the dues rose slowly, reflecting the increase in costs. Dues should be spent, advised the American Lyceum pamphlet, 'partly for mutual improvement and partly for the general diffusion of knowledge.' The tools of knowledge, that is, lyceum apparatus, should be purchased promptly. The apparatus would include 'visible illustrations,' specimens in natural history (especially geological specimens for the cabinet), and books. The cost of this would be about $75.

If a local lyceum had less to spend, it could still get, besides an orrery, a set of geometrical apparatus (twenty-six solids, several transposing figures, and two sheets of diagrams), an arithmometer or numeral frame with 144 balls, and a globe. This collection by itself was priced at only $10 and was recommended for elementary schools. More complicated and consequently more expensive instruments of the same sort were recommended for lyceums and academies. An unusually handsome orrery, with 'tide dial, instruments for showing the change of seasons, eclipses, the cause of the earth being flattened at the poles, revolution of the moon, etc.,' cost $18. A set of 'mechanical powers,' constructed to show the principles of the lever, pulley, wheel and axle, screw, inclined plane, and wedge (and including a hydrostatic bellows), cost $15. In the field of chemistry Holbrook stood ready to sell for a total of $25 a pneumatic cistern with two gas holders and a compound blowpipe, a pyrometer, an eolopile, a conductometer, a pair of concave reflectors, a lampstand, flexible and glass tubes, retorts and flasks, and finally a 'small collection of materials not commonly found in druggists' shops.'

For the geological cabinets, dearly beloved of most early lyceums, Holbrook offered a set of twenty specimens of common rocks, each labeled, for $3 while a set of fifty including the 'elements of rocks' cost $5. To start the lyceum library a series of his *Scientific Tracts* was recommended. Two journals, the *Education Reporter* and Professor Silliman's *American Journal of Science*, were likewise suggested and along with them a small group of useful books.

The other main cost of the lyceum turned out to be extremely variable. This was hall rent. It might be five, ten, or twenty dollars a season; it might be substantially greater or nothing at all. The place where the lyceum met might be a church basement (donated), a room in a village hall, or an office in the village's two-story ancestor of an office building. Or the lyceum might convene in its own hall, for an occasional lyceum was able to rent an entire building from the start, while some lyceums here and there financed the erection of their own building after the first few years. Typically, this last was done through bonds; and a high proportion—it may be hazarded—of the lyceums that borrowed also staggered as a result of the load. Yet construction was cheap a hundred and twenty-five or even a hundred years ago. A lyceum hall which suited the purpose could be built for about a thousand dollars. A proud community might spend much more. The Salem Lyceum hall was finished in 1831 at a cost of slightly over $3000. Much more impressive than the average lyceum hall, it could hold 700 persons in semicircular tiers of seats around the speaker's platform. To take away the heated air, the hall had a ventilator in the center of the ceiling, decorated with a picture of Apollo in his chariot ushering in the Morn. The outside of the hall was a boxy adaptation of Greek classical. However, such pretensions were far beyond the average lyceum. It was much more apt to rent than to build—and to rent, understandably, as cheaply as possible.

The lyceum evolved two ways of meeting its expenses. The first was to charge outsiders for admission to the lectures but to allow the admission of members to be covered by their annual dues. The second and somewhat more usual practice was to consider that those dues paid for other privileges of the society and consequently to charge everyone, both members and nonmembers, for admission to the lectures.

Regardless of which method was adopted, we can make some generalizations about admission costs. The price of a single lecture throughout the first twenty years of the lyceum was generally set at twenty-five cents. That paid for one seat at one lecture. Tickets for a whole course cost (per lecture) much less. The range for the course during this same period of time was as a rule between $1 and $2.50, with the most frequent sum perhaps being $1.50. At the start, it should be remembered, the lecturers came free; yet the cost of course tickets was often able to remain relatively low in later years because the audiences were large and the original overhead had been paid off. Here are a few sample prices from Maine. During 1843 Bangor sold course tickets for $1, Kennebunk for fifty cents, and Camden (this was exceptional) for twenty-five cents. Portland, like Bangor, charged $1 and offered a family ticket for $3. The situation was comparable in other states. The Young Men's Institute of Hartford, Connecticut, as its minutes for the autumn of 1839 show, charged $1 for tickets for the course if three or more members of the same family would buy them and $1.50 otherwise. Single tickets for one evening cost twenty-five cents (the next year it was raised to fifty). Longer seasons meant higher prices. When the New Orleans Library and Lyceum announced the course for 1850–51, forty lectures were anticipated instead of the usual dozen or so, and family tickets (admitting three) cost $8 while single tickets for the entire course cost $5. Single tickets for a single lecture cost fifty cents.

From the lecturer's point of view the lyceum provided at its outset only nonmarketable satisfactions. This changed, as we know, with a gradually accelerating motion.

Wanted: 'lecturers who add to a thorough acquaintance with astronomy, geology, chemistry, etc., a faculty of speaking to an audience with plainness and perspicuity; salaries are offered to such gentlemen.' Such was the request of many lyceums as reported in the *American Journal of Education* for January 1830 in its sketch of the history of the lyceum movement. Rather frequently, in fact, we can read suggestions elsewhere that good lecturers be employed by county lyceums and then make their rounds among the different town lyceums within the county. It is clear that the lyceums had soon discovered that not every local citizen who was willing to lecture could lecture well. The curators turned to the neighboring towns with anticipation. They had heard that in these towns there were several speakers of remarkable talent. The rub, they were forced to realize, was that the outside speakers would at least want their expenses paid. Noble examples to the contrary appeared every now and then, but the number diminished season by season, month by month. This 1830 mention of salaries in the *American Journal* is one of the first hints that some lyceums were willing early to face the facts of economic life.

For an analysis of lecture costs and fees, we might take Concord, Massachusetts, as an example of the lower range and neighboring Salem as an instance of the higher one. Incidentally, the minutes book of the Concord Lyceum shows that one of the first things it did, upon its founding in January 1829, was to resolve to procure 'a cabinet of minerals, a library, and an apparatus for illustrating the sciences.' Concord listened to lectures from the beginning of its existence. It had a remarkably intellectual community to draw on, and the result was that it enjoyed better than average lectures at a lower than average cost. Emerson, who tried out most of his lectures on his fellow townsmen, did so gratis and—since he was Emerson—gave his hearers far more than most of them would have gotten from other lecturers even by paying generously.

By 1831 the Concord Lyceum was reimbursing outside speakers for their modest expenses but not feeing them. For the season of

1833–4, to select one at random, twenty-two lectures were given; roughly half were delivered by local people and half by outsiders imported at a total cost of $33.88. Concord continued to be able to be thrifty. Within a short ride of its boundaries it had an even richer source of lecturers than in the town itself. Boston and Cambridge stood ready to supply them and so allow Concord the privilege of a total lecture disbursement annually (including hall, heat, etc., as well as lecturers' expenses) of only about a hundred dollars. By 1843, though, even Concord had to concede that conditions were changing. In the Lyceum's Cash Book which covers the years from 1829 to 1859, the lecturing fees that were paid begin to be entered. In the mid-1840s the standard sum was $10, and the travel expenses were supposed to come out of that. As well known a platform figure as E. P. Whipple was still receiving only that much when he lectured in Concord. When the 1850s opened, the cost crept up. Concord's annual budget was by now $120. H. N. Hudson gave his 'Falstaff' at a charge of $12, while a new high was set by the witty Dr. Oliver Wendell Holmes, who took $15 from the Lyceum's treasury. Two years later, however, Dr. Holmes' fee of $15 had become the average. By the time the season of 1855–6 came around, the average fee for outside speakers had risen to $20; and the treasury was confronted with a surplus of only $4.69. In the autumn of 1858 stern measures were taken (this was in the wake of the panic of 1857) and fees went back to $15. And there, with an occasional exception, they stayed as the Civil War put a conclusion to the second period of the lyceum system.

The Salem Lyceum provides a different set of figures. In his history of the Salem society H. K. Oliver says that after 1836 the local citizens who lectured 'seemed to have received $20 a lecture.' But he gives no evidence, and his statement is to be doubted. Nevertheless, we can be sure that Salem treated its speakers, whether native or not, with relative generosity. The Lyceum Cash Book for 1841–57 shows that $15 per lecture was the normal fee for the first season it covers. Among those paid that amount were John Pierpont, John Lord, R. H. Dana, and Holmes. The next season the fee went up to $20 and there it stayed until 1845–6. That season had two exceptions, where $25 was paid. By 1847–8 there were three cases of two lectures by the same man, with the price being $35 per lecture. And Louis Agassiz gave a total of six lectures for the handsome fee of $250. In the course for 1848–9 Daniel Webster broke all precedents by receiving $100 for his 'History of the Constitution of the United States.' Henry Thoreau, however, who lectured in the same course, on 'Student Life in New England, Its Economy,' received the customary $20.

Slowly, as the seasons passed, the average of Salem's fees went up. The thirty-first course, given in 1859–60, illustrates the point. George Sumner was paid $30 for 'Lessons from Spain,' Grace Greenwood $50 (apparently) for 'The Heroic in Common Life,' W. W. Silvester $25 for some readings, Carl Schurz $30 for 'The French Revolution of 1848,' T. M. Clark $35 for an unspecified lecture, W. A. Norton the same amount for 'The Comet of 1858,' A. G. Browne, Jr., $25 for 'Utah and the Mormons,' Emerson the same for 'Manners,' Beecher apparently a resounding $100 for 'The Head and the Heart,' T. W. Higginson $25 for 'Physical Education,' A. L. Stone $20 for 'At Home and Abroad,' and Wendell Phillips $50 for 'Law and Lawyers.'

The trend so far described continued throughout the last decade of the lyceum before the Civil War. It reached its summit in the Midwest. The desire of the lyceums there to have the most famous lecturers visit their platform meant that they had to pay for them. High fees, in turn, meant a greater element of risk for the lyceum managers and curators. They realized that they must provide lecturers who were drawing cards or else their society would have to suffer financial consequences. Their cardinal principle ultimately became not providing the best instruction, as it had often been in the former days of the lyceum, but providing the most popular instruction. The swing from practical knowledge to family entertainment was to become still more pronounced after the Civil War; notwithstanding, a good many newspaper editorials pointed it out sourly even during the 1850s.

In this determined attempt by the small towns as well as the large, in the West even more than the East, to attract noted lecturers, transportation was the key factor. A town such as Concord had little trouble because it was so close to where many of them lived. A town such as Crestline, Ohio, or Peoria, Illinois, found it impossible to bring in any famous men independently except by the rarest chance. In the first place it could not afford to pay them a lecture fee and their expenses too; but in the second place even if it could have, most of the eastern lecturers would not have come.

One reason the South fell behind in supporting popular education and the lyceum was poor transportation. The rapid growth of the canal system, the increased use of natural waterways, the inauguration of the railroads, and above all the general improvement of the dirt roads benefited the East and the Ohio Valley much more than either the South or the extremely rural parts of New England and the Midwest. Not that transportation had to become remarkably good. From the point of view of the early lyceum that might have been a disadvantage, since the audiences could have traveled around enough to look at their local efforts at uplift and improvement with some condescension. In New England, for instance, easy transportation would have helped the Boston lyceums but would have hindered those of Worcester, Cambridgeport, Salem, and the like. Transportation had to be just good enough so that the lyceum audiences could easily travel short distances and the lyceum lecturers—once local talent had been exhausted—could travel longer ones without too marked an effort.

And that was the way it developed. At first the stagecoach furnished the answer for the lecturer; horseback and carriage, or farm wagon, solved the problem for such of the audience as lived a short distance from town; and walking, of necessity, was the favored method for the townspeople themselves. There were a few corduroy roads, made of logs laid crosswise to the course of traffic. The rest were dirt. Most of the roads were bad by today's standard but at least in New England and the Middle Atlantic states they existed in fair numbers. In the South and of course on the western frontier, they did not exist in any number at all.

As transportation improved, the lyceum system grew. Before 1830 the railroad was only an experiment but ten years later there were about 3000 miles of track. Stage transportation too became better. The National Road, the famed interstate highway between the eastern seaboard and the Middle West, was the chief east-west artery during the second quarter of the century according to Dunbar's *History of Travel in America*. It furnished the exemplar for many of the other, smaller coach roads. During the years of the lyceum it was adorned by a rich variety of drivers, hostlers, and assorted characters; and Dunbar gives some of their names with relish: David Bonebraker, Caldwell Slobworth, Frank Ear-locker, Samuel Sidebottom, and John Smasher among them. They and their fellows must have enriched lyceum travel.

Then, in the second period of the lyceum, came the quickened expansion of the railroad system, spreading its filaments through all parts of the East and Midwest. By 1860 there were 30,626 miles of trackage, with the East North Central states having the most for any section (nearly 10,000 miles) and the West South Central having the least (only 680 miles). River, lake, and coastwise traffic also increased. For the lyceum lecturer the most popular route in water-borne transportation remained the Ohio River.

But in spite of the improvement of transportation, some communities were still too inaccessible to lure the lecturers they wanted. For them the obvious thing to do was to co-operate. A speaker who would never come to one Ohio or Illinois town might be persuaded if there were several that wanted him. Regular associations of societies which wished to employ lecturers would not thrive until after the Civil War, but Mead in his *Yankee Eloquence* cites two short-lived alliances—those mentioned in Chapter 14—formed in Ohio in the middle 1850s. One was the Bryant Association, named in honor of William Cullen Bryant. It started in Sandusky in October 1855 with delegates from half a dozen Ohio towns as well as one from Adrian, Michigan. These delegates passed a resolution to the effect that the Association could 'with certainty and at fair rates procure good lectures' for their organizations. The Association expanded during the autumn and secured Theodore Parker as its first speaker on the circuit. But he was a failure, financially, and helped to bring the infant Association down with him.

The other co-operative society to appear, which Mead dubs the 'Massillon Association,' started at the same time. Lecture-sponsoring groups from nine more Ohio towns including Massillon met and attempted to make joint arrangements. They agreed, by the way, that $50 per lecture was more than any community was able to pay and that the maximum should be half that amount. Emerson, Parke Godwin, and Theodore Parker (who apparently tried a combined arrangement with both associations) were among the lecturers engaged. But local organizations canceled some of the dates; itineraries were at times unsatisfactory; and at least one lecturer, Emerson, broke off relations with the Massillon Association because of these cancellations by member societies.

The problem remained a pressing one, however. Other expedients were explored. Some of the noted lecturers dealt directly with the lyceum secretaries, mainly in the larger communities. Bayard Taylor, for one, when giving fatherly advice to I. I. Hayes, the explorer, who wanted to break into the lecture field, wrote him on 1 March 1856 and reeled off the names of the lecture 'officers' for the nine community lyceums in Pittsburgh, Cleveland, Detroit, Cincinnati, Chicago, Milwaukee, St. Louis, Buffalo, and Madison, Wisconsin. Taylor assured Hayes that the thing to do was to get in touch with those men, adding that he could probably get engagements in the smaller Illinois towns through the secretary of the Chicago Young Men's Association, S. D. Ward.

Taylor's method worked well enough, but there was another expedient which proved like the co-operative to be ahead of its time. This was the use of the lecture agent, or rather the lecture agent doing his zealous best to be made use of. To many lyceums Henry Ward Beecher became particularly odious through hiring such an agent. Cries of wrath pursued Beecher in Ohio when he tried to make more money by channeling his lecture engagements through his agent's hands. The correspondence addressed to J. R. Brigham, secretary during the middle 1850s of the Milwaukee Young Men's Association, also casts a cold light on Beecher and his agent. By this time one of the most sought-after of all lecturers, Beecher on the platform was characterized as the 'forty-parson power' speaker. His biographers have tried to defend him from the charge of avarice but the Brigham papers refute them. There we see the reflection of a man who knew his platform renown and intended to squeeze as much money out of it as he could.

The agent who aided and abetted him was a Chicagoan, E. S. Wells. Operating under the shadowy title of the Metropolitan Literary Union, Wells handled Beecher's lecturing during this time. The technique was simple. To the organizations which wanted him and wrote to him, Beecher made no answer. He turned the correspondence over to Wells instead, and Wells swiftly applied the screws. But he went too far, as the Brigham papers show, and earned for his portly client the reputation of a grasping, ruthless man. Wells acquired another star to manage in John B. Gough, and the Brigham papers include a copy of the fancily printed announcement dated 8 November 1856, and sent from Chicago, in which Wells states that all 'friends of temperance' who want to hear Gough must do it through him. 'I have,' he adds nobly, 'no pecuniary interest whatever in Mr. Gough's lectures.' But perhaps because his client was not interested in money as Beecher was, Wells was able to employ the same techniques in exploiting Gough's fame without arousing widespread resentment.

The method which then worked out best was not of course the agent method as Wells practiced it but an informal arrangement among lyceum secretaries. The East, not being faced with the problems of distance and transportation, failed to evolve such a system. The West, however, began to; and the method developed most usefully in the hands of Ward and Brigham. Both were prominent and forceful men who made an outstanding success of their secretarial posts.

What Ward did, it may be recalled, was primarily to act as an agent for lecturers but without pay. His reason was that by making arrangements for a series of lectures by a given man he could be sure of getting him for his Chicago society. It was enlightened self-interest on Ward's part. Brigham became his most constant associate, and the Milwaukee organization benefited correspondingly. So, in their wake, did the lyceums of two dozen small towns in Illinois, Wisconsin, and even Iowa. They could fill out the tours that the two cities had arranged and in this way be able to hear lecturers from the East whom they could not possibly have listened to otherwise.

Such is the development that constitutes the last chapter in the economic side of the lyceum before the Civil War. To see that development in specific human terms, the best thing is to look at the letters (preserved in his papers) which Brigham received for a given year. Eighteen fifty-five is an excellent one.

The first item for the year is the typed copy (as some of them are) of a communication to him from John G. Saxe dated 1 January. 'Unluckily Tuesday the 20th of February is booked for Detroit,' he writes and goes on to suggest alternative dates for Milwaukee. The third paper (the second is another from Saxe) is a brisk note from Ward which begins 'Telegraphed you today.' It is about the tour of Starr King, who was currently giving 'Substance and Show' to northern Illinois lyceums. In addition to the fees, Ward says that the Chicago association will pay part or all of King's fare from New York while the other towns will pay from place to place. In other words, Rockford will pay the fare to Freeport, Freeport to Dixon, and so on. That such arrangements failed to work out perfectly is evident from the hurt tone of Ward's next letter. He has tried to supply 'country places' with lecturers but some of those little towns are acting unreasonably. Milwaukee, however, he assures Brigham, is a city and not at all unreasonable. He proposes to Brigham that the two communities work together next year and offer eastern lecturers $150 in all for two lectures, one in Chicago and the other in Milwaukee.

The letters that follow work out King's transportation problem and throw light on Saxe's. Midwestern snow and ice, it turned out, blockaded Saxe in Michigan and hindered transportation for other lecturers elsewhere too. Correspondence from Horace Mann now enters the picture. He is willing to lecture in Milwaukee, giving 'Young Men' and 'Women' perhaps. Both lectures, he adds, have been printed and reported in the East but they ought to be unknown in this part of the country. In other letters James Russell Lowell's itinerary is arranged. Then in spring the letters show that Ward was re-elected secretary, and he suggests plans for the next season to Brigham. A paragraph dated 4 April on Beecher is clear testimony to his drawing power. 'Last winter we offered Beecher $250 for a single lecture. . . . This year I shall propose to him $50 or $75 for one lecture to go in course and then $200 for the second lecture, keeping it secret that he was to deliver more than one until the first had been delivered.' Ward knew the public —and ministers as well, for he adds a warning to Brigham, 'Where you have clergymen you better keep them from preaching *before* they lecture, as many go and hear them then and see them and won't pay to hear a lecture.'

In the next months the correspondence is filled with famous names. For the new season Ward and Brigham desire nothing but the best. Agassiz, Beecher, Wendell Phillips, Holmes, Chapin, and Curtis are among the leading names which appear. Brigham now, it is evident, suggests that the fee of $75 which Ward had proposed to pay every noted lecturer is high and that those whose lustre is a trifle less bright than the rest ought to be offered only $50. Ward agrees. In another letter, of 31 July, he explains more about his technique to Brigham: 'I do not generally offer a price at first but tell gentlemen they will be invited elsewhere hereabouts if they will accept, and that they can have a fine opportunity of visiting the western places.'

Early in August Brigham receives the first of several letters of a kind. It is a proposal from a would-be lecturer, a man named Stebbins. He has, he affirms, a panoramic lecture on 'The West' and a moral one on 'The Old and the New.' 'Now, Sir,' he says, 'as I visit other places I would like also to visit Milwaukee.' He will bear the financial risk. If his appearance makes money, he will ask the usual fee which the Milwaukee Association pays; if he fails to draw, he will not ask that sum. Other unknowns, with less modesty than Stebbins, also wrote to Brigham. Ward had similar experiences. 'We are bored horridly with these applications,' he complains.

By this time the parallel courses for Chicago and Milwaukee had begun—but only begun—to take shape. Ward lists about thirty names of notables who had either accepted, declined, or not answered so far. There were considerably more declinations than acceptances. But Wendell Phillips, Starr King, and the Harvard classicist C. C. Felton gave at least a tentative yes, and a well-drawing course could still be worked up out of the men who had not yet answered. Then Ward comforts Brigham, 'Am afraid you are getting a little blue. Don't think of getting discouraged this two months yet.' But it is evident that fees were not holding down as Ward and Brigham wanted. However, they came to accept the fact with good grace. Dr. G. W. Bethune is to get $100, 'most cheerfully' (he is 'a splendid "fellow"'). Even to a lecturer named D. P. Brown, not a famous person, 'we would readily give him $75 and perhaps $100 rather than not get him,' Ward admits. But Beecher's case is a little different. Ward wrote to Brigham that he had offered him $100 but that Beecher had somehow 'understood that amount I spoke of was $125.' 'But I know,' Ward says bluntly, 'he said $100 per night and it is enough in all conscience.' He adds, with a rush, 'It is annoying for have spent a great deal of time and written a great many letters and had a plan all prepared which was sent to Beecher weeks ago but not a word was heard until Wells had called and made his offer.'

Ward wrestles with the matter again in a letter to Brigham of 30 August. Now that the West can be easily reached, $50 is enough for most lecturers and $100 is enough for any man. But the rub is that Beecher, even at $125, can make a profit for the Chicago Association. Turning to the case of Dr. Bethune, Ward says that the doctor probably will not accept less than $100 per lecture and suggests that one more lecture at a bonus of $50 ought to cover Bethune's expenses to the Midwest and back. He appends a dry comment about an upstart lecturer: 'George Bradburn is the man I spoke to you about. Think 150 other men we could get would do better than he.'

The strain involved in making ends meet for the lyceum is clear in a question Ward asks as a postscript to the letter of 30 August: 'Don't you propose season tickets? A little hard work selling them is a good investment and saves a deal of anxiety afterward.' Lecturers as well as lyceum secretaries had their devices. On 1 September Ward mentions a Dr. Hitchcock, for example, who 'hints somewhat about part of his expenses being paid as he has to support his family mostly by lecturing.' Two weeks later Ward writes an indignant letter about the meanness Beecher and his agent Wells had just shown. 'Oh! most noble Mr. Beecher!' Ward exclaims sardonically, 'generous, kindhearted man, the young man's true friend! . . . Money has no charms for thee; never dost thou debase thyself by letting thyself out to be exhibited by a showman as would a lion, bear, or monkey. Richly dost thou merit canonizing for all thy virtues.'

But the fact of Beecher's platform appeal was persuasive, more so to Brigham than were his colleague's satiric flings at the man. When Wells assured Brigham in September that he still could have the spellbinding minister at $125 plus a twelfth of his expenses for the tour—which would probably be about $8 and would certainly not go over $10—Brigham agreed, we can deduce, for on 4 October the agent Wells wrote to him briskly, 'In regard to the pay, you will please forward draft for amount ($135) on Monday 15th.'

Meanwhile the news was circulating that the renowned William Makepeace Thackeray might be prevailed upon to tour the West. The fees he asked and received broke through all previous ceilings, yet his reputation was so great that the lyceum secretaries seldom did more than murmur. Ward was willing to pay him $200 a lecture, he told Brigham, though he wanted to pay only $150 if he could. In another letter, dated 10 October, Ward repeated that $200 was too much 'but guess we had better pay it rather than not have him.'

In November the activity reflected in the Brigham papers became exceptionally agitated, but the program somehow straightened itself out for both the Milwaukee and the Chicago associations as well as their auxiliaries. The actual season began well. Almost all the lecturers who had promised to come did so, and a fair number of the previously undecided ones made up their minds and likewise journeyed to Illinois and Wisconsin. On 27 November Ward wrote that Phillips had given 'The Lost Arts' before 1,400 people. 'Everybody was delighted.' But on a succeeding night he gave an anti-slavery lecture to an audience of at least 600 less. On it Ward comments wryly, 'Good in delivery and language but sentiment not so pleasing.' By December the shuffling of dates and the shifting of itineraries eased off. Things seemed to be running smoothly and promised to continue so. The correspondence decreased in volume and intensity, while the shrewdly pragmatic estimates of this or that lecturer's earning power lessened in number. The back of the lecture season had been broken; most, though not all, of the work of the season was over.

In all this interplay of the economic with other forces of the lyceum, it is evident that the economic side became more and more influential. The earlier the lyceum the less it had to worry about meeting its financial obligations. The days of the orrery and neighborly instruction gave way to the days of small fees and slight travel expenses. Those times in turn yielded to a much more commercial period. The lecture fees went up, but the quality of education did not. The quality of the performance, of the form as opposed to the content—which too often reduced itself to entertainment—alone improved under the hand of the professionals. After the Civil War the trend continued with doubled speed, for the lecture bureaus had not only to keep audiences happy but to keep themselves alive. Other factors too are chargeable with the further deterioration of the lecture in America, but the economic one is certainly important. After the time of the bureau managers Redpath and Pond, came the Chautauqua, which made some attempt to bring back education. It failed when the day of the radio arrived; and in the second quarter of the twentieth century the movies and then, after World War II, television displaced the lecture in public popularity with such decisiveness that it would probably never return to its previous place.

17

Platform Gallery: II

'The lyceum is my pulpit,' Emerson once said. . . . When Starr King was asked what he lectured for he answered 'FAME—Fifty And My Expenses.' . . . Oliver Wendell Holmes remarked to Herman Melville and some others that 'a lecturer was a literary strumpet, subject for a greater than whore's fee to prostitute himself.' There is the range.

IN the lyceum before 1845 it is hard to pick out any considerable number of widely known individuals; after that time the problem is instead which ones among many to select. The total number of lecturers was now much smaller but the proportion who became platform celebrities was large.

Ormsby Mitchel: Napoleon of Space

The lyceum always, particularly in the West, retained some of its original love for popular science. Living in Cincinnati, Ormsby Mitchel became the most famous Western apostle of science on the lecture platform. A short man with the same stern expression and shock of hair that Andrew Jackson had, he began and ended as a soldier, graduating from West Point in 1829 and returning to the service as a general in the Civil War. But in between lay the long years when he made himself a nationally respected astronomer and lecturer. Largely through his efforts the Cincinnati Observatory, which mounted the second finest refracting telescope in the world, was completed in 1845. His work with it and his studies as professor at the Cincinnati College earned him the respect of scholars, while his lecturing made him famous among the public.

Horace Greeley's *Tribune* printed one of the most successful of Professor Mitchel's courses. It was given at the Broadway Tabernacle in December 1847. The six lectures were taken down 'phonographically,' word for word, by the *Tribune* and then distributed in pamphlet form. Clear, logical, tactful, they show why he proved so popular. The third lecture, to single out one of them, gives the flavor of all. The synopsis is printed in the pamphlet: 'Adherence to established notions of nature's laws . . . Natural laws the expression of God's will . . . Difficult to conceive the object of creation . . . Perpetuity a design . . . A simpler system possible . . . Perturbations difficult to calculate . . . A higher design than mere stability . . . Newton's calculations— orbitical curves—figure of the earth—centrifugal force resulting from rotation—inclined plane and centrifugal force equal . . . Other orbs kept within limits of perpetuity . . . Elliptical figure of orbs affects their motion . . . The equinoctial points,' and so on. It was a meaty exposition, which his New York hearers had to follow with care. But they did, and twice interrupted him to applaud an especially well-put explanation.

An idea of the kind of pleasure Mitchel's astronomy gave audiences can be gotten from the *Tribune's* preface to the pamphlet; it calls the astronomy 'this beautiful Science.'

John Lord: History in Color

Puffy-eyed John Lord, after a brief and unsatisfactory career as a minister, began lecturing with a fair amount of success in the early 1840s. History, particularly ancient and medieval, became his field; and he represents both the semiprofessional historian who provided a gloss of culture for the programs of the lyceum's second period and the aggressive performer who sought lyceum engagements instead of waiting to be asked.

A trip to Europe, 1843–6, furnished him with a good deal of local color, which he thereafter used lavishly in his lectures. Other items in his stock in trade were vivid characterization and, fundamental to that, the interpretation of history through its leading personalities. He belonged to the 'Carlyle-ish' school of historians but without any of Carlyle's insight or scholarship. A *Modern History*, published in 1849, was one of the textbooks Lord wrote out of his lectures. In its preface he said, justly, 'In preparing this history I make no claim to original and profound investigations; but the arrangement, the style, and the sentiments are my own.' The sentiments he alludes to constituted the other elements in his success. He loved to make history a series of homilies, and he would frequently append some pious reflections to his description of a historical act.

His thickest work, put into print long after the lyceum, was the *Beacon Lights of History*, in eight volumes. Here his lecture notes of the preceding decades are organized and collected. Volume II, *The Middle Ages*, includes the germ of some of his most frequent lectures. The book is set up, as one might expect, almost entirely in terms of great men. The chapters are headed 'Mohammed,' 'Charlemagne,' 'Alfred the Great,' 'Hildebrand,' 'Saint Bernard,' 'Saint Anselm,' 'Thomas Aquinas,' 'Thomas Becket,' 'The Feudal System,' 'The Crusades,' 'William of Wykeham,' and 'John Wyclif.'

Though Lord solicited many a lecture committee for a place on the program, the lyceums that acceded showed, more than once, a financial loss instead of a profit. However, as the years went along, Lord managed through both his books and lectures to become well known. By the time the shrewd lyceum managers such as Brigham of the Milwaukee Young Men's Association began to play an important role, Lord had accumulated enough reputation to keep on having engagements whether or not he earned money for the local societies that sponsored him. One reason for the fact that Lord sometimes made a bad showing lay in his platform mannerisms. In Armstrong's *An Artist Historian*, which is in general a lavish eulogy of the man, the admission is made that Lord was 'a lecturer whose person was diminutive, whose gestures were erratic movements of the arms ignoring all co-ordination with his thought, and who read his notes in a frayed, unmusical voice interrupted with a periodic thoracic sneeze.' He even stammered.

To his audiences, however, he gave through the years, in content if not in presentation, the sort of popularized history—history almost at the folk level—that will always draw the crowds.

E. P. Whipple: the Verbal Acrobat

Judged by many of his audiences to be second only to Emerson among the literary men who made lecturing their other occupation, Edwin Percy Whipple was celebrated for almost a generation as 'our American Macaulay.' He was a public success from the start. In September 1840 at the age of twenty-one he delivered an original poem before the Mercantile Library Association of Boston which the *Transcript* for the 30th announced was 'full of playful humor, lively sallies, and satirical hits in which [he] cut up and used up, with the skill of an old master, the numerous humbugs and abstractions which are emptying the pockets and turning the heads of so many people of the present generation.' He delighted his auditors, the *Transcript* added, and drew forth 'peal upon peal of rapturous and hearty applause.'

With such a start Whipple found it easy to be invited to speak elsewhere. During the years from 1843 to 1849 he toured the New England states with a repertory of six lectures, 'Authors in Their Relations to Life,' 'Novels and Novelists—Charles Dickens,' 'Wit and Humor,' 'The Ludicrous Side of Life,' 'Genius,' and 'Intellectual Health and Disease.' The first one sets the tone. It is a yeasty presentation of the difficulties famous writers encountered in their 'relations to their age, to booksellers, and to domestic and social life.' In a characteristic judgment Whipple remarks of the age that Dryden lived in that he 'was its pander and parasite.' And when he treats of the authors' domestic life, Whipple does so with a smirk. 'We now come,' he begins, 'to a delicate part of the subject, which every prudent man would wish to avoid.'

Henry Thoreau heard Whipple in 1847 at the Concord Lyceum and took his measure at once. 'We have had Whipple on Genius,' Thoreau wrote Emerson, who was then in England, 'too weighty a subject for him, with his antithetical definitions new-vamped— what it *is*, what it is *not*, but altogether what it is *not*; cuffing it this way and cuffing it that, as if it were an India-rubber ball.' Audiences, however, enjoyed the Macaulayan antitheses which

Thoreau scorned, and they chuckled at humor which would have left Thoreau stolid as an Indian.

Whipple polished these lectures and published them in a slim volume, dated 1850, as *Lectures on Subjects Connected with Literature and Life*. Once they were committed to print he had to compose a fresh set; and until 1856 he used an equally popular series on individual and national character. They were entitled 'Character,' 'Heroic Character,' 'Eccentric Character,' 'Intellectual Character,' 'The American Mind,' and 'The English Mind.'

His reputation as a critic grew, both on and off the platform. Although his fame was to die before he did, he impressed many a man who should have known better. Emerson, Lowell, Agassiz, and Holmes all thought well of his talents. Margaret Fuller was more cautious, saying in her *Memoirs,* 'He is among the first of the second class of men.' The Civil War marked the end of his most popular period.

In *Off-Hand Takings,* G. W. Bungay, one of the thousands who heard him, provides a characteristic picture of him in action, 'Mr. Whipple speaks distinctly, in a sharp, nervous, energetic manner, with a graceful yet monotonous gesticulation, emphasizing every dozen words with a jerk of the head and a swing of the arm, as though he were pumping the blood from the vitals of the brain.'

Wendell Phillips: the Two-Edged Crusade

Wendell Phillips had all the iron and strength that Whipple lacked. Like Whipple he sprang into notice as a young man (in 1837) on the basis of a single outstanding public appearance, but there the similarity ends. Whipple read a clever set of verses while Phillips poured out his protest against the mob murder of Elijah Lovejoy, the abolitionist printer, in the teeth of hisses, heckling, and cries of 'Take that back' (as well as applause from his partisans). One of the notations in the printed text of the speech adds, 'The uproar became so great that for a long time no one could be heard.' The portrait prefixed to the 1863 edition of Phillips' speeches, lectures, and letters shows a man high-nosed and narrow-faced, with an expression of idealism so conscious as to be almost unpleasant.

Nobody on the lecture platform had a more bitter tongue than

Phillips. He cursed the Constitution and called Lincoln a slave-hound, and sometimes went further still. Dedicated to abolition-ism if any man was, he spoke on that angry subject wherever audiences would consent to hear him. When the time came that lecturers were paid fees, he offered local lyceums these alterna-tives. If they would listen to him on abolitionism, there would be no charge; if they wanted a noncontroversial subject, he would have to be paid for it.

As a matter of fact, his noncontroversial lectures became almost as renowned as the other kind. 'The Lost Arts,' first given in the season of 1838–9, grew to be (according to the preface of the 1884 edition) 'the most popular and the most charming lecture ever delivered from an American platform.' It was not quite that; nevertheless, it was a remarkable tribute to Phillips' versatility that he could be thoroughly refreshing as well as vituperative. This does not mean that Phillips composed 'The Lost Arts' out of sugary platitudes. The reverse was true. His aim was an as-tringent one: to upset American self-conceit by showing that in the very field, practical science, where America prided itself most, it had been outdone time and time again by the ancients. The forging of a steel that was strong, flexible, and safe from rust; the making of glass that would bend and not break; the grinding of pigments that would not fade—these were some of the things, Phillips pointed out with anecdotes and unfamiliar examples, that had once been well understood but now were to us lost arts.

His speech 'Surrender of Sims' delivered in 1852 at Faneuil Hall in Boston represents his powerful controversial lectures. Like most others, it had to be given before an anti-slavery group rather than a regular lyceum because of its fiery nature. It was a bitingly sarcastic attack on the chief opponents of abolitionism. Phillips lampooned Daniel Webster as 'Sir Pertinax M'Sycophant, who all his life long has been bowing down to the Slave Power to secure the presidency.' He likened Rufus Choate fidgeting on a platform to 'a monkey in convulsions.' And when a heckler shouted, 'Three cheers for the Union,' Phillips retorted to great applause, 'Feeble cheers those!'

His lectures of both kinds had a crusading force, a fluency, a directness and familiarity, and a sharpness of wit that made them equally famous and notorious. Other lecturers might soothe the American audience; Phillips' purpose was the opposite of that.

Park Benjamin: Poetastical Wit

A minor poet at best, Park Benjamin did not become a success in the lyceum until his already slight creativity was on the wane. Born in 1809, he was lamed from the age of three by a shrunken leg. How much that gave an edge to his tongue and pen is impossible to say but it doubtless had some effect. For a good many years he edited or helped to edit various periodicals which had one thing in common—they all failed. The one to last longest under his leadership was the *New World*, which he ran from 1839 to 1845. In addition he managed to publish many of his lyrics in other and better known magazines. In the early 1840s he discovered a kind of verse which gave him both free scope in choice of subject and an outlet for his often caustic attitude toward contemporary life. It was the satire, written in an imitation of the heroic couplet of Dryden's time.

As Benjamin used it the form was almost devoid of polish but it had a rapid movement; it allowed a quick change of tone; and its couplets proved once again that they were the best medium for epigram. Although he tried the form tentatively before 1849, M. M. Hoover, who has compiled the standard edition of his verse, says that it was after that year that his considerable success with it really began. His wife (he was married in 1848) understood the potentialities of the lyceum for her new husband and persuaded him to concentrate on it. He chose such subjects for his verse as 'Fashion,' 'Hard Times,' 'Modern Society,' 'True Independence,' and 'The Age of Gold.' Hoover suggests that he usually appeared on the same program with a serious lecturer; the records we have found show that this was the exception not the rule. Since he was crippled, he ordinarily read his verses from a stool placed behind the lectern. This,' Hoover points out, 'raised his large torso to [a] commanding position, with resulting effectiveness for his eloquence.' In spite of his handicap he toured New England, New York, and the Ohio Valley and even ventured briefly into the South.

His satire 'The Age of Gold,' which he first read in 1849, ex-

emplifies the kind of thing that audiences liked. Its hurrying
couplets begin with the discovery of America and then briskly
characterize 'Five mighty ages, since Columbus stood / On the dry
land and saw that it was good.' They are the Ages of Discovery,
Learning, Science, Invention, and Progress. Now there comes a
sixth, the Age of Gold.

> Few marvels now the busy mind engage
> In this gold-seeking, gold-discovering age,
> When Love himself forsakes his bowers for mines
> And all our firesides turn to Mammon's shrines.

Benjamin sketches the greed and shortsightedness of the '49ers
as well as of the stay-at-homes. He seasons his lines with mock-
epic similes, with a dash of sentiment (the gold-seeking lad who
forgets his true love, whom he left behind), and a little sermon
for the audience's soul. He closes with magniloquence.

> He, whose firm soul resists Temptation's wile,
> Sees every firmament above him smile . . .
> He need not seek for treasure-teeming mines,
> Beneath his feet more precious metal shines.
> In conscience clear, in duty, virtue bold,
> Here is his placer, *now* his Age of Gold.

Parke Godwin: Grandiose Reform

In the limbo of American culture lie Park Benjamin and Parke
Godwin—totally different personalities but at times confused if
for no other reason than that their first names are much alike.
They both were editors and journalists, but there resemblance
stops. Godwin married the daughter of William Cullen Bryant and
for many years was connected with his noted New York *Evening
Post*. For the lyceum movement Godwin represents the political
liberal who found the platform a rewarding place as long as he
spoke from it in general terms. If he talked about the United
States as a political whole instead of about its individual warring
parties, he was well received.

Born in 1816, he acquired a sympathy with socialism by the
time he reached young manhood. When the most noted native
socialist community, Brook Farm, opened he was exactly the right

age to be fascinated by it. The social gospel side of New England Transcendentalism continued to interest him even after Brook Farm met with failure. The numerous magazine articles he published, as time went on, were generally about economic and social subjects. His political orientation can be seen by the fact that he was a liberal Democrat for many years and then became a radical Republican who fought for Abraham Lincoln. If any single condition made him change his party it was the long series of compromises by Jacksonian Democracy with the South and slavery, for Godwin developed into a devoted abolitionist.

The political gospel he preached ordinarily avoided the inflammatory subject of abolition, however. One of the most popular lyceum lectures of the 1850s was Godwin's 'Manifest Destiny,' which he alternatively called 'The Future Republic.' Excerpts from and summaries of the lecture show that it was a broad evaluation of the country's merits and faults, with the merits inevitably predominant. He expressed a low view of politicians and a high one of the people. Perhaps his philosophy is best epitomized in the introduction to the lecture *Democracy, Constructive and Pacific*, printed in 1844, where he asserts: 'We are about to speak of Democracy, but in no party sense; not as it is spouted in ward meetings nor slavered through the columns of newspapers; but of Democracy as a God-ordained principle of social government.'

Such was the most notable sentiment that Godwin uttered on the platform. His praise and blame he distributed in a style that was literate and a little heavy. The newspapers frequently agreed that he was no orator but that his manner was pleasing. During his years in the lyceum he had a profusion of prematurely white hair and beard. He looked like a good grandfather in a day when grandfathers were in fashion, and it may be that audiences accepted bluntness from a man like him where they would not have from a callow, barefaced one.

Starr King: Facile Emerson

With the kind of homeliness that attracted hearers instead of repelling them, Thomas Starr King emerged swiftly as one of the most renowned lyceum lecturers. He was born in 1824, educated himself, and from the start displayed the talent for being listened to and believed that made him into a clergyman and speaker of national standing. His wide, mobile mouth and his luminous eyes distinguished him; his slightness always made him look rather young. Near the end of his short life—he was not quite forty when he died—he went to California to take a pastorate. There the merchants and the miners all admired him. One miner, for instance, at the edge of a crowd King attracted, listened to him with delight and exclaimed to his companion, 'I say, Jim, stand on your toes and get a sight of him! Why, the boy is taking every trick!'

In California King lectured widely but his great reputation was already made by the time he arrived on the west coast. The most notable pulpit he had occupied was that of the Hollis Street Unitarian church in Boston. To its congregation he had preached a positive, active social gospel. An abolitionist and critic of both major political parties, he used his pulpit for more than theology. It was from 1848 when he went to Hollis Street to 1860 when he moved to California that King occupied one of the top places among the royalty of the lecture platform. His engagements took him from Boston up north to Bangor and from Boston out west to Chicago. His sensationally popular address 'Substance and Show' ranked second only to Wendell Phillips' on the lost arts. Other topics, almost as celebrated, were his 'Socrates,' 'Sight and Insight,' and 'The Laws of Disorder.'

Lecturing, however deeply he enjoyed it, took a toll of his slender strength. Not only the strain of speaking but all the discomforts of travel—the sharp changes in temperature, a poor appetite or poor food, the tedious train rides, and the concern about the parish he was currently separated from—these too wore Starr King down.

When we look more closely at his lectures the witticism about FAME which heads this chapter seems less than just as an index to him. His lectures show him to be, in fact, a kind of poor man's Emerson. 'Substance and Show' is the best example in point. Its thesis actually echoes one tenet of Emerson's Transcendentalism, that ideas are more real than things. King is quoted in the introduction to this and the other printed lectures as saying, 'The aim of ['Substance and Show'] is . . . to break down, in the popular mind, the inveterate association of strength and permanence with the visible side of the world and the things we can "sense." ' 'Let us look at ideas as substantial things,' he proposes in the lecture itself. To do so he uses popular science as his most effective aid. As he explains, again in the introduction, 'The illustrations from science are taken to buttress faith in the invisible and intangible as being the causal and productive agencies.' An iron ball, a grape vine, a lily, a historical incident or character are among the common examples he uses to impress on the audience his uncommon doctrine of the nature of reality.

Thus, though King was also a theologian and a strong voice for abolitionism, he was most widely appreciated on the lyceum platform for his simplified philosophy. An apostle of philosophic idealism, he became the lyceum's everyday Plato, Bishop Berkeley, and Emerson.

John B. Gough: the Rewards of Reformation

Purely on the basis of the emotional appeal he made to the audience, no lyceum lecturer ever surpassed John B. Gough. Wendell Phillips often stirred his hearers, especially when he spoke violently for abolition, but there was always a political and intellectual content to his addresses. Not so for Gough and his temperance talks. He was, to begin with, the platform speaker most gifted with the common touch. Added to that was the fact that he rode at the head of a crusade, the crusade against drink. Social statistics of a century ago are more or less approximate, but there seems little doubt that there was a great deal more of both public and private drunkenness then than now. When Gough, after a short though successful career as a popular singer, made his appearance in the temperance movement in the early 1840s, he used the wave of mounting public indignation (and helped to crest it too) about the liquor traffic. A reformed drunkard himself, he learned to wring the last drop of emotion out of the audience as he told the vivid story of his conversion. He found the same sympathy and support that today's reformed radical experiences when he explains how he came to see the light.

Many a scurrilous tale was circulated about Gough as soon as he achieved prominence: he was a secret drinker, he was a lecher, he was a gambler. They added to his audience appeal instead of detracting from it. Most if not all of the stories were untrue but it is doubtful whether it would have made any difference to his excited hearers one way or the other.

In opening his book *Platform Echoes* Gough says frankly, 'The public do not expect from me a literary entertainment, an intellectual feast, or a logical argument.' He was right. The public wanted and received a highly personal, anecdotal, and rhetorical account of the evils of drink. This is a sample passage on the drunkard: 'Once purity was his garment; now he is appareled in the filthy livery of his tyrant master. He bartered his freedom for a lust, and now endures an unutterable thraldom. He sold his birthright for a pleasure, and now is cursed with a heritage of woe. He dissolved his pearl of price in the cup, and drank it. Thus he rushes on, scorned and despised by his fellow-men, his better nature loathing the thing he has made himself, carrying a foretaste of the undying worm within his breast, wrapped in dull despair, or shouting in fearful wildness, or laughing in the glee of the maniac, shrinking, shivering, dreading, yet wilfully approaching, he staggers on the brink, shrieking, cursing, reeling on the edge. With one look upon the past, the mighty deluge of sin rolling after him, he clasps his poor, swollen hands, and in mad despair plunges into utter ruin.'

Lyman Abbott, in his introduction to *Platform Echoes*, describes Gough the lecturer. He mentions his small stature, thin melancholy face, and flashing eyes. 'His fluent language,' he goes on to say. 'his dramatic action, his intense and impassioned earnestness, his suppressed feeling, and the lightning-like rapidity with which he changed the moods of the audience with his own from the humorous to the pathetic, took all audiences by storm.' Other reports, less impassioned, agree with Abbott on every score except that of suppressed feeling. Here instead was a surplus of it. During his lectures, which were longer than average and took about two hours instead of the customary one, he made use of an 'unbroken succession of contortions and antics,' as Pond says in his *Eccentricities of Genius*. Gough worked so hard on the platform that in winter he had to wear two overcoats when he left the lyceum for his hotel. When he got back to the hotel,

he always had a valet rub him down—as if he were a race horse—
and then he ate a bowl of bread and milk. His endurance was
remarkable when we realize that he made about three hundred
platform appearances every year from 1842 on to the end of our
second period.

Henry Ward Beecher: Platform Magnate

There is a full-face portrait of Henry Ward Beecher in his
prime which is perhaps more revealing than it was intended to be.
With his heavy head thrown back and his mane of white hair,
he looks like a dissipated lion. A portly man who loved many of
the good things of secular life, he became one of the most talked
about ministers in the country. He faced down a great scandal
(which broke after the Civil War) as well as charges of avarice
to keep his reputation as a peerless orator for the lyceum.

Born in 1813 of a distinguished ministerial family, he did mediocre work in college and then held a number of pastorates cul-
minating in the famous one at the Plymouth Church in Brooklyn.
At each of his churches he demonstrated a remarkable flair for
preaching coupled with a lack of zeal for his other ministerial
duties. His first lectures, delivered in 1840 while he was in charge
of an Indianapolis church, were an example of that popular
vehicle for ministers, the lectures to young men. Beecher composed a set of seven. He titled them 'Industry and Idleness,'
'Twelve Causes of Dishonesty,' 'Six Warnings,' 'The Portrait
Gallery' (the Wit, the Libertine, etc.), 'Gamblers and Gambling,'
'The Strange Woman,' and 'Popular Amusements.' By 1847 he
had become a widely known public lecturer. He discovered that
the platform gave him the free rein which a pulpit, even the most
informal, could not. His love for theatrical effects, his humor,
and his general flamboyance made the lyceum his appointed
place. Yet the kind of impression Beecher made on his hearers
ought not be oversimplified. Charlotte Forten, an unusually dis-
criminating young Negress, heard him in Salem in 1855. He spoke
on 'Patriotism' and she admitted in her *Journal,* 'I thought the
lecture extremely interesting, and many parts of it very touching
and beautiful. His manner is not at all polished or elegant, but he
says so many excellent things with such forcible earnestness or

irresistible humor, that we quite forget it.' And she ended by praising his sincerity.

From the Salem Lyceum he took away $50 (for two renditions of the lecture) but so did several other men in the same course. His total profits were, however, probably unsurpassed. His lecture fees from 1847 to 1857 are estimated in Howard's life of Beecher at a total of $30,000; and in the next decade they doubled.

The anger aroused when in the mid-1850s Beecher put himself in the hands of a close-fisted lecture agent and tried for still higher fees was bitter. In 1855 when Beecher returned to Ohio for one of his lecture tours, the average admission still cost twenty-five cents. Now, to pay Beecher, it would sometimes have to be doubled. The sarcastic newspaper announcement of Beecher's lecture which the *Daily Clevelander* printed at this time was set up under the heading of GRAND LITERARY CIRCUS, while the *Cleveland Leader* of 24 October said, 'Mr. Wells, the Chicago showman, will let his fifty-cent lion roar at Concert Hall tonight. The smooth walls of that hall are excellent for the reverberations of the lion's voice, and we hope there will be few woolen coats and silk dresses to deaden it.'

'Patriotism,' 'Beauty,' 'The Ministry of the Beautiful,' ' The Christian Commonwealth': such were the lay sermons he preached in Ohio and other states throughout his years in the lyceum. He generally used an exclamatory, often extravagant style, set off with rather homely illustrations. If he saw any contrast between what he practiced and what he preached, he gave no evidence of it in those elaborate addresses.

Dr. Boynton: Science en Masse

Far removed from the great lyceum personalities of the period after 1845, whose names grew literally into household words, were the itinerant free-lance lecturers. No lyceums sponsored them as a rule. All that these travelers did was to go from town to town, insert a little card in the local newspaper saying that they would arrive and give a course ('admission $1, first lecture free') on this or that titillating topic, and then open their mouths. As often as not, the men were charlatans; sometimes they were mere eccentrics; occasionally they were apostles of radical causes; but at any rate they failed to fit into the lyceum pattern.

Nonetheless, in terms of total lectures given, the itinerants bulk large. A leader among them was a popularizer of science named Boynton—'Dr. Boynton,' the announcements always say simply, no first name, no initials. He managed early to build up a certain reputation, even in the South. 'We feel pleasure in announcing that Dr. Boynton, who is celebrated as the most interesting and instructive lecturer upon the subjects of electricity, electromagnetism, and the theory of the earth intends to visit Norfolk in a few days,' says an item from the *Norfolk Herald* for 30 September 1847. Just prior to his coming to Norfolk, Boynton lectured in the other Virginia cities of Richmond and Petersburg.

His first Norfolk lecture was about electromagnetism, with particular emphasis on Morse's telegraph. Boynton knew the value of demonstration and experiment, and his audience 'manifested great interest,' the *Herald* stated afterward. He began with a small audience but the second and third lectures of the course were better attended. In fact, Boynton was enough encouraged to offer another course. Its four parts were announced as (1) electricity and magnetism of the globe, (2) formation and geology of the earth, (3) electricity of the human body, and (4) electricity of the vegetable, mineral, and animal kingdoms and (a shrewd climax) the application of electricity to the cure of diseases. The *Herald* for 9 October characterized the lecture on geology as of 'intense and absorbing interest' and observed two days later that Boynton 'displayed the powers of a master mind and the graces of elocution.' Boynton kept on with his lecturing in Norfolk until he determined, apparently, that he had exploited public interest to the full. Then he moved on to the next town.

He continued his lecture tours and consolidated his good standing. An item in the *Richmond Enquirer* in January 1859 shows that the doctor was still in business after more than a decade. There a course of eight lectures on geology is announced, to be given 'in compliance with the invitation of a number of distinguished citizens' and to be illustrated with a 'series of large and splendid paintings, which cover over 3000 feet of canvas and were executed at a cost of more than $4000.' The pictures represented everything from scenes of California to animals of the pre-Adamite world. 'A view of these paintings alone is worth more than the price of the whole course. Tickets . . . $2.' As a climax to the course Boynton advertised a 'scientific exhibition.' In it he promised to suspend a bar of iron without anything touching it, to load a cannon with water and have it fire an icicle, and to lift up a boy by electricity. It is not hard to see why he made more money than the general run of itinerant lecturers. Essentially, he did quite well what most of them did rather poorly.

As we can understand, he was flourishing more than ever in the late 1850s. By that time he had widened his circuit to include the richer fields of the Middle Atlantic states, New England, and finally the Middle West. When he came to Evansville, Indiana, early in 1860, the Library Association which sponsored him issued a four-page leaflet advertising the event and eulogizing him. According to it, Boynton was scheduled for two lectures, 'Evidences of Design by the Creator in the Structure of the Solar and Terrestrial System' and 'The Thickness of the Earth' (with three 'beautiful paintings' of volcanoes). The first lecture obviously presented the kind of science which ministers and their congregations would find most edifying, while the second was filled with pictures of liquid fire. Half of the leaflet is devoted to testimonials of Boynton's ability. One, written by a dull but respectable ex-president of the United States, Millard Fillmore, praised the lecturer's 'earnest enthusiasm,' his use of the 'oral instead of written' lecture, and his 'plain, familiar language.' Another, reprinted from the *Springfield* [Massachusetts] *Republican* for 5 March 1856, is equally revealing. Summing up its good report of Dr. Boynton (and Professor Ormsby Mitchel, incidentally) in contrast with most other lecturers in that particular field, the newspaper remarks of Boynton and Mitchel that 'they *entertain* their audiences, and this fact, and not their bare scientific revelations, makes them popular.'

Oliver Wendell Holmes: the Urbane Cynic

The wittiest man in the lyceum was Oliver Wendell Holmes. His early lectures appealed less to the sense of humor than did his later ones; he started out with scientific topics and ended with almost pure entertainment. As a matter of fact, he recapitulated the shift in lecture topics which characterized the lyceum as a whole. Not that his change was entirely undeviating; he had one or two early lectures which were not on science and an outstanding later one which was. Over-all, however, he fitted the trend. Moreover, he did so consciously. He himself once explained apologetically to Emerson, 'I am forced to study effects. You and others may be able to combine popular effect with the exhibition of truths. I cannot.' Increasingly Holmes tailored his lectures for the public. As it became lighter-minded, so did he.

Throughout the 1840s Holmes gave lectures such as 'The Natural Diet of Man' and courses such as 'Scientific Mysticism.' For the season of 1848–9 he composed 'The History of Medicine.' In the 1850s, however, he presented such unscientific subjects as 'Lectures and Lecturing' and 'Lyrical Passion.' He abandoned science and history in favor of literature, rather trivially treated. In a representative itinerary, for 1851–2, we see that Holmes offered his audiences three lectures, the one on the history of medicine, the one on lectures and lecturing, and a third called 'The Love of Nature.' That season he gave 'The History of Medicine' eight times, 'Lectures and Lecturing' twenty-two times, and 'The Love of Nature' forty-one times!

Bayard Taylor: the Byronic Traveler

Dressed in his colorful Arab costume with a scimitar at his side, Bayard Taylor came late to the lyceum but found as ecstatic a welcome as any lecturer could wish. He catapulted into popularity in 1854 shortly after his return from a world tour which included being with Commodore Perry when he finally broke through the barriers against American trade with Japan. This and other adventures Taylor related in a series of letters to Horace Greeley's *Tribune*. Taylor was already known as a self-reliant traveler who had gone through Europe and, in this country, overland to California on the trail of the '49ers. Then too, he had published three books of poems. His first full lecture tour, which began in January of '54, was astoundingly successful. He was overwhelmed with invitations, and it was clear that he had caught the public fancy. In triumph he went up and down the east coast, through New York state, into the Midwest, and then even into the wilds of Wisconsin and Missouri.

If there was anything needed to consolidate his success, to keep it from being a flash in the pan, it came in the form of the publication, later this same year, of two romantic travel books. *A Journey to Central Africa; or, Life and Landscapes from Egypt to the Negro Kingdoms of the White Nile* appeared in August, while *The Lands of the Saracen; or, Pictures of Palestine, Asia Minor, Sicily, and Spain* came out in October. Add to this the fact that from its earliest days the lyceum exhibited a liking for travelogues, a liking which time magnified instead of reduced, and the reasons for the long-continued deluge of lecture invitations to Taylor are evident. Once audiences saw him, their feminine part especially, they were all the more eager to see him again. Before them stepped no stout, elderly gentleman full of moral observations, but a hawk-nosed, handsome world traveler who was also the writer of exotic ballads such as the 'Bedouin Song.'

Two groups of six lectures apiece made up his most popular platform efforts. In the first group were 'Japan and Loo Choo,' 'India,' 'Life in the North,' 'Moscow,' 'Russia,' and 'The Philosophy of Travel.' In the second were his efforts at a geographical approach to man and his social criticism of Americans. He gave these lectures until he was wearied out. He disliked lecturing from the beginning; he did it—and in his letters at least he made no secret of it—simply because he wanted the money. Every time he stepped on a platform he got fifty dollars. He could clear $5000 each season and so pay for the fine mansion he wanted out in the country as well as the things that went with it.

One rainy night as he sat in his room at a Niles, Michigan, inn while waiting to speak, he described his tribulations:

> Comes a rapping, tapping
>   At my chamber door,
> But, unlike Poe's raven
>   Crying 'Evermore!'
> 'Tis the new Committee

Any one can tell,
Come to see the lecturer:
   'Hope you're very well!' . . .

Finally they leave me,
   I'm alone, again, . . .
When again a rapping—
   (Hope you will not laugh)—
School-boy with an album
   Wants an autograph!
Next a solemn gentleman,
   Unctuous of face:
'What's your real opinion
   Of the human race?' . . .

Thicker than the deluge
   Pouring out-of-doors,
Comes a rain of questions
   From the crowd of bores;
'Where's your lady staying?'
   'What's your baby's name?'
'Do you find Society
   Everywhere the same?'
'Where are you going to travel?'
   'What's your future plan?'
'Do you think you'll ever
   Be a settled man?'
'Ain't you now the greatest
   Traveler alive?'
'What's the land where turnips
   Seem the best to thrive? . . .'

   Oh, I want to be
Where, for information,
   No one comes to me.
I'd be a bloody whaler
   Among the Kurile Isles,
A tearing, swearing sailor
   Whom the Captain riles,
Anything but Taylor
   Lecturing in Niles!

Edward Everett: the Noble Roman

The type of the classic orator and statesman was Edward Everett. His was from the beginning a brilliant record. He always lacked depth (Emerson put it more kindly, saying he had 'a popular profoundness') but it would take decades to find that out. The youngest member of his Harvard class of 1811, he graduated with highest honors. In 1815 Harvard made him professor of Greek literature. He spent the next years abroad preparing himself for his professorship and returned to Harvard in 1819. Young Emerson was a Harvard student then; many years later he still recalled Everett's 'radiant beauty of person' and his 'voice of such rich tones, such precise and perfect utterance, that, although slightly nasal, it was the most mellow and beautiful and correct of all the instruments of the time.' But Harvard could not contain him. Embarking on a long career of public service, he was elected to Congress in 1824 and thereafter spent most of his time in official life. He was governor of Massachusetts, minister to England, secretary of state, and United States senator before he retired.

His orations were famous from the outset. The printed form in which they survive reveals an ornamental, balanced style—the work of a man on whom formal rhetoric had made a deep impression. Many of the sentences are long; they roll in periods and are adorned with images. Their rhythms are swelling ones. Without a doubt, his audiences knew they were listening to stateliness. Everett's collected addresses are titled *Orations and Speeches,* and the term *Orations* is indicative.

The lyceum, however, was exposed to little of this eloquence except at the opening and at the end of Everett's career. He took part in the founding of the early Boston lyceum called the Society for the Diffusion of Useful Knowledge and had some contact with Holbrook. But he was already in Congress, and the Boston Society received nothing but the leftovers of his attention. This proved to be even more true for the national lyceum. Beginning in 1831, he was elected a vice-president each strenuous year throughout the 1830s, yet his actual contribution was negligible. Only his name meant something. During the 1840s too he found scant time for the lyceum. But starting in 1855 he repeatedly delivered one of the most famous addresses the country was to hear. It was on the character of George Washington and was for the benefit of the Ladies' Mount Vernon Association, which was trying to preserve Washington's home. He gave it, by one estimate, 135 times; audiences customarily greeted it with 'rapturous and prolonged applause.' Newspapers commented fondly on his 'chaste eloquence and grace.' He read the oration all over the country, and the results were flatteringly alike.

In 'The Character of Washington' Everett describes Washington's return to Cambridge at the start of the war in a paragraph which is illustrative of the rest: 'This was the second visit of Washington to this part of the country—his second appearance in a high national capacity before the people of the Union. Years pass by; the august plan of Providence ripens; the beloved and revered chieftain, aided by his patriotic associates, carries the bleeding country through another seven years' war, hard apprenticeship of Freedom; the great European antagonist and rival of England, revenging the loss of her American colonies and moved by the persuasive ardor of Lafayette, throws her sword into the scale—thirteen independent state governments succeed to as many colonies—peace crowns the work—the wounds of the Revolution are slowly healed—America takes her place in the family of nations—and a constitution of confederate union, the bright consummate flower of our political growth, is formed.'

Ralph Waldo Emerson: the Magnitude of Mind

In any study of the lyceum there is bound to be much talk about popularity but little about greatness. Emerson is perhaps the only lecturer in the movement who could unhesitatingly be called great. The amazing thing is that he was also enormously popular. He did not entertain audiences; on the contrary he sometimes irritated them. Frequently the newspaper reports pointed out that he was, after all, a Transcendentalist—and even as late as the 1850s that was a term of reproach. Yet the demand to hear him remained at a peak for nearly twenty years. His integrity, his love of mankind, and his genuine charm were so apparent to audiences that they invited him back again and again in spite of the fact that they plainly did not always understand what he said.

Emerson did not break new paths for the lyceum; he traveled

the existing ones but traveled them as a philosopher. His first lectures, in the fall of 1833, were on the study of natural history and on 'The Relation of Man to the Globe.' In January of the next year he spoke before the Boston Mechanics' Institution on 'Water.' Though these were scientific subjects, it should be added that there is little doubt that he widened them and interwove at least a little philosophy. A little later he spoke on 'Italy,' and by 1835 was using biography, another popular lecture form, as the basis of a course before Boston's Society for the Diffusion of Useful Knowledge. His letters tell us that he read it 'Tests of Great Men' to begin with and followed with 'Michelangelo,' 'Martin Luther,' 'John Milton,' 'George Fox,' and 'Edmund Burke.' Every now and then, in after years, biography again provided him with a fruitful source of material. But by January 1837 he was embarked on the kind of course which made his fame; its subjects became the stuff out of which he prepared his essays. These lectures were now on general topics, wide in their application and devoid of structure. They could be altered or interleaved without the audiences being much the wiser about it. 'Society,' 'Manners,' and 'Ethics' were among the lectures in this course. Here for the first time his listeners got the Emerson who became famous. From then on, his subjects and his attitude changed little.

What he said thereafter is now embodied in his published essays, and the function that the lecture phase performed in his literary process will be discussed in the next chapter. But the place of Emerson on the platform and the relation of the audience to him are also important. Far more often than not his hearers felt themselves—if we can judge from their diaries, their letters, and the newspaper reports—to be in the presence of a truly remarkable man. They always found something to admire in him. Here is how one girl responded to his words. Coming home after listening to him at the Salem Lyceum on 11 February 1857, Charlotte Forten wrote in her *Journal*, 'One of the most beautiful and eloquent lectures I ever heard . . . —Most beautifully did the "poet-philosopher" speak of the earth and sky in many figures.' She added several more sentences in the same vein and then could not help exclaiming, 'Oh, how deeply do the words and the presence of such a man as Emerson make us feel the utter insignificance, the great inferiority, of ourselves.' But Charlotte Forten had far more than an average share of sensitivity. How would a phlegmatic newspaper reporter look at Emerson and react to him?

There is a mass of newspaper references about him from almost every state he spoke in. Although they vary considerably in tone and stress, there is much that they agree on. If any one newspaper comment were to be picked out as the common denominator, it might be the article, quoted by Mead, in the *Cincinnati Times* for 28 January 1857 (two weeks before Charlotte Forten made her comment).

There Emerson is described as 'tall, angular, loose-limbed, with an olive complexion, large features, especially the nose, and a blue or grey eye that has a mysterious and undefinable light in its depth. He looks and dresses soberly, and has a quaint look, bearing, and manner that remind us . . . of Anatomy-of-Melancholy Burton. . . .

'His elocution, like his diction and himself, is peculiar, emphatic, abrupt, sharp, impressive, and oracular. He is not graceful but he carries a weight grace and culture alone never could supply. He stands at an acute angle toward his audience, and limberly, and has barely a gesture beyond the motion of the left hand at his side, as if the intensity of his thought were escaping, like the electricity of a battery, at that point. . . .

'His voice is full, strong, and rich, but he speaks with a sort of hesitation, not unpleasant but the contrary, as if he were struggling with a thought too great for immediate utterance.

'His lecture is not to be reported—without his own language, his manner, his delivery, it would be little—to essay to reproduce it would be like carrying soda-water to a friend the morning after it was drawn, and asking him how he relished it.'

18

The Lyceum and Literature

'A lecture is a new literature, which leaves aside all tradition, time, place, circumstance, and addresses an assembly as mere human beings, no more'—Emerson's journal for 5 July 1839.

WHEN the lyceum system began to pay its lecturers, and the professional lecturer began to appear, literature and the lyceum became enmeshed. The lyceum offered the writer a means for making money and for trying his shorter works on a captive, though also captious, audience. As soon as the time came for him to write new lectures, he could send the old ones—now polished as a rule into essays or chapters—to publishers with the assurance that there would be more of a market since he was a platform personality. So his works were printed, and today our libraries still hold them. We do not have the precise form of the lecture version, granted, in most cases. Consequently, we cannot determine just how much revision there was. Some people, such as Wendell Phillips, altered their manuscripts up to the time the printer snatched the page proof from them. Others made various changes, while a few made almost none at all. We can, however, go on the basis that most of the lectures now published were substantially as given aloud.

Differing markedly in subject and skill, a few of the printed books which emerged are literature in the highest sense of the word. The bulk are not. But their importance in helping to give a broad picture of American culture is patent. A good many books came out thanks partly to the lyceum; scattered through the mid-nineteenth century are the marks that it put on the reading of the time.

One day when the second period of the lyceum's development was starting, Henry Thoreau scribbled a paragraph which summed up his method of composition. 'From all points of the compass,' he wrote, 'from the earth beneath and the heavens above, have come these inspirations and been entered duly in the order of their arrival in the journal. Thereafter, when the time arrived, they were winnowed into lectures, and again, in due time, from lectures into essays.'

What held for Thoreau held for a hundred others who strode on the lecture platform. The lecture for them represented an important intermediate step in the process of composition. It was generally the place for experimentation and revision. Emerson remarked in his journal for 1834, 'When a village lyceum committee asks me to give a lecture, and I tell them I will read one I am just writing, they are pleased. Poor men, they little know how different that lecture will be when it is given in New York, or is printed. I "try it on" on them; *"The barber learns his trade on the orphan's chin."* ' Emerson meant exactly what he said, as any close study of his texts will show. Up to the moment of print, he shifted paragraphs and shuffled pages with—it sometimes seemed—an Olympian indifference to the structure of his writings. Thoreau, with more of a sense of structure, seldom cared to attempt such wholesale alterations. Nor did he need to. He realized his work required polishing instead of reorganizing. Yet even this was not always true for we can tell at times that the polishing amounted to almost a major operation. At times it did not, and then the only changes on the manuscript may be the scratching out of the *you's* and the substitution of *he's* since the audience was no longer being directly addressed.

To his 'auditory' Thoreau usually read either early versions of his essays or excerpts from the manuscripts which later became books. His very first lecture, given before the Concord Lyceum, was—with perfect anticipation—against 'Society.' A decade after-ward, in the late 1840s, his most frequent one was on the 'Life in the Woods' theme. At the beginning of the following decade he gave several lectures which sprang from his excursions to Cape Cod, and he also used his excursion to Canada as a subject. These were partial drafts of future books. Among the single essays, 'Walking' was the nature essay he tried out most often before New England audiences, while 'Getting a Living' (a preliminary ver-sion of his famous 'Life without Principle') was a 'Transcendental' essay he often gave. Toward the opening of the Civil War, he had the opportunity to read his John Brown essays, his 'Wild Apples,' 'The Succession of Forest Trees,' and (the last one he ever gave) 'Autumnal Tints.'

The reception of these lectures varied, and it is evident that they are better read to oneself than heard. As a rule Thoreau thought little of his audiences and, as a rule, they retaliated. None-theless. through their very indifference they helped him to sharpen his words and to give added point to his ideas. He was often busy at his revising anyway, but it is a fair guess that he would have been less so had the audiences shown much admiration for the drafts they listened to.

With Emerson it was different. Almost every audience felt to-ward him something close to veneration. From his first tentative lecture to his last tragic attempt, they realized that here were the words—obscure or badly organized though they might be—of genius. His method of writing his lectures changed from the bold revisions of his prime to the random gathering of pages in his old age, but his hearers remained respectful and receptive.

In estimating the relation of Emerson's lecturing to his printed works, the question is not how many of the essays were lectures first but rather how many were not. Fully three-quarters of his published writing began as lectures. With the important excep-tion of most of the *Essays, First* and *Second Series,* published in 1841 and 1844 respectively before the lecture system had reached its peak for Emerson, almost all his earlier essays were lectures to begin with. An example is 'Man the Reformer,' a lecture read before the Mechanics' Apprentices' Library Association in Boston in 1841 and separately printed at their request. In 1849 *Nature,*

Addresses, and Lectures came out. In this collection 'Man the Reformer' was also included along with a good half dozen similar pieces. In the same year *Representative Men* appeared (although its official date was 1850). It had been given as a course to audiences before it went to the printer; its subtitle is, in fact, *Seven Lectures*. They must all have had a familiar ring to the readers who had heard him. As published, the lectures were: 'Uses of Great Men,' which acted as the introduction, and one lecture each on Plato, Swedenborg, Montaigne, Shakespeare, Napoleon, and Goethe. When *English Traits* came from the presses in 1856, it had the same sort of history. Lecture audiences would read its pages with more than a gleam of recognition. In the case of Emerson's next volume, *The Conduct of Life,* though we cannot be sure, it is probable that he did not lean on his lecturing to quite the same heavy extent. We come across most of the individual chapters, in lecture form, in the newspaper announcements and reports printed not long before the book itself went to press; but the impression remains that Emerson altered these lectures for publication more extensively than the previous ones.

After the Civil War, as Emerson neared the end of his long years of productive thinking, it became his habit not to follow the original lecture form of an essay at all when putting it into print. Now, however, it was no longer a matter of extensive revision but instead of selection—selection from his pile of manuscript pages of lectures of all sorts. With his creative fire nearly dead, it was all he could do to pull out from the various lectures whatever sheets dealt with the same general theme and thus could go to the printer under the guise of a new essay. Formerly, Emerson had done bold things with his pages and paragraphs but the shifts had ordinarily been confined to the compass of a single lecture. His essay on 'Intellect' would be based on his lecture on 'Intellect' instead of being a haphazard aggregate of two dozen pages on philosophical intellectuality from as many different lectures. He found himself less and less able to write transitional material, so that three-quarters of the essays in the final volumes are conglomerations rather than entities.

His daughter Ellen once summed up the final phase of Emerson's method when she remarked about the printed version of

'Fortune of the Republic,' 'This is a collection of every general remark on the country from many lectures of many dates, each full of the moment when it was written and so adapted to that occasion and no other that scarcely a page entire could be saved.' She was speaking over a decade after the end of the war but the eclectic process—then much accentuated by Emerson's mental decay—had begun years earlier. *Society and Solitude,* published in 1870, *Letters and Social Aims,* dated 1876, *Lectures and Biographical Sketches,* published in 1884, the *Miscellanies,* dated the same year, and the *Natural History of Intellect,* published in 1893, all have, in a greater or lesser degree, the same provenience. All plainly bear the marks of lecturing, and of his eclectic method and waning powers. In some cases the lecture manuscripts were as much as forty years old; most were not quite that of course but nevertheless many an earlier lecture had served as grist for the essay mill. The details of this tangled history of Emerson's lectures and addresses require almost a hundred pages in the *Memoir* of him written by James Elliot Cabot. The sheer bulk of the section throws light on the importance that the lyceum had for Emerson the literary man.

Behind him and Thoreau, and a long way behind, it must be said, came a number of other essayists. In general their mode of operation was the same. The lectures were tried out on the public, served their turn, and then went to the publisher after more or less polish had been added. The content was inevitably of many different sorts.

The most popular topic of all was, as has been suggested before, the good spiritual life. It was the natural field for ministers. Those who mounted the lecture platform were well aware of the need to be tactful about doctrine but aside from that they encountered few restrictions. The Reverend Orville Dewey's *Discourses on Human Life,* published in 1847, is a valid example of this very popular kind (except for its superior thoughtfulness). One discourse is entitled 'Life is What We Make It,' and it gives a suitable taste of the remainder. In this series the basic problems are dealt with not unsuccessfully. Dewey's discourses are above average specifically in that he has a firm grasp of the religious principles which, to him, underlie the solutions of those problems. Moreover, he is ready to suggest a definite religious answer that later lecturers—and some who were not late but lacked his firmness—declined to give in order not to antagonize any element in their audience. Beneath the rather banal surface of 'Life is What We Make It,' to return to that example, there is first of all an emotional conviction of the importance of Christ. But in addition there is a serious statement of the proofs for philosophical idealism. Dewey actually tries to show his audience, in philosophic terms, that mind is the only true reality. He does so in a fashion that reminds one strongly of Emerson's Transcendentalist manifesto, *Nature*.

The related problems Dewey attacks in this collection of lay sermons are indicated by their titles: 'The Moral Significance of Life,' 'That Everything in Life is Moral,' 'Life Considered as an Argument for Faith and Virtue,' 'On Inequality in the Lot of Life,' 'On the Miseries of Life,' 'On the School of Life,' 'On the Value of Life,' 'Life's Consolation in View of Death,' 'The Problem of Life, Resolved in the Life of Christ,' 'On Religion, as the Great Sentiment of Life,' 'On the Religion of Life,' and 'The Voices of the Dead.' All these discourses are orderly in their organization and strong in their rhetorical appeal. But their style is plain, with none of the verbal embroidery that marked many a pulpit utterance of the day. They impress by emphasis rather than ornamentation. A few sentences from 'Life is What We Make It' can show this well enough: 'There are no blessings—and it is a stupendous truth that I utter—there are no blessings which the mind may not convert into the bitterest of evils; and there are no trials which it may not transform into the most noble and divine of blessings. There are no temptations from which the virtue they assail may not gain strength instead of falling a sacrifice to them. I know that virtue often falls. I know that the temptations have great power. But what is their power? It lies in the weakness of our virtue. Their power lies not in them but in us, in the treason of our own hearts.'

Although the sort of lecture, on the good life, that the Reverend Mr. Dewey read was the most popular of all, a remarkable variety of successful lectures in other fields were eventually put into print as essays and books. One is linked to Dewey's field; it is the finger-shaking, cautionary lecture course for young men. A sidelight on its enduring vogue can be gained from the fact that Henry Ward Beecher's series—perhaps the best known of the kind—was reprinted, in expanded form, by the G. H. Doran Company as late as 1925.

Much different in tone and content but second to the lay sermons in long-run popularity was the lecture on science. One of the most famous collections of scientific lectures, an enduring favorite, was Agassiz's *Methods of Study in Natural History,* published not long after the opening of the Civil War. Based on his prewar Lowell Institute lectures, it had nineteen editions in one generation! The process these lectures went through is explained by Agassiz in the preface. They were originally delivered without any thought of publication. 'Notes were, however, taken of them at the time, and I very willingly assented to the suggestion of some of my listeners that they should be recorded in the form of articles for the *Atlantic Monthly.* They still retain something,' he added significantly, 'of the repetition which is needed in a public course of scientific lectures in order to keep the connection of the subjects clearly before the mind of a popular audience.' Agassiz's style is lucid and simple, with only a minimum of technical vocabulary to confuse his public. The organization too is clear, with a good many points being numbered, one, two, three, and so on. The images come from everyday life, and rhetorical questions are frequent.

Lectures about history, solidified in book form, constitute another important connection of literature with the lyceum. Perhaps the best known instances are the books about European history which the Reverend John Lord evolved and which are discussed in the previous chapter. Such history, heightened, colored, and simplified, unquestionably gained a far wider circulation than the more workmanlike and learned history by scholars such as John G. Palfrey.

The love of the past is only one aspect of the love of the out-of-the-way. The lyceum audience enjoyed hearing about the distant or unusual people of the present just as much as it did about the people of the past. The traveler who brought back his tales could generally count on prompt engagements. The most sought after of them all was Bayard Taylor, but he was only the head of a numerous company. Another traveler of note was the Arctic explorer, Dr. Elisha Kent Kane. His highly popular lectures found their printed form in *The U. S. Grinnell Expedition in Search of Sir John Franklin,* which came out in 1853. But the suspense-filled nature of his lectures is better shown by the title of the abridged version: *Adrift in the Arctic Ice Pack.* More representative of the average traveler in popularity was a handsome Indian chief named George Copway. A fairly frequent lecturer, he appealed both to the interest in the remote and to the slowly growing humanitarian concern about the Indian now that he was no longer in the white man's way. In his introduction to *The Traditional History and Characteristic Sketches of the Ojibway Nation,* Copway explained that his intent was to 'awaken in the American heart a deeper feeling for the race of red men and induce the paleface to use greater effort to effect an improvement in their social and political relations.' In his book, as in his lectures, he describes the life of his tribe, its wars with the Hurons and the Iroquois, its legends, language, government, and religion.

His manner of writing is odd but understandably so. He tells about his tribesmen in a generally plain style but mixes into it something that he must surely have gotten from his contact with the whites and their reading—and that is a touch of neoclassical rhetoric. He likes to use elegant personifications, for instance. He will sketch the outcome of an Indian battle and then announce that 'Death made a throne of the bodies of the slain, and arm in arm with his hand in hand, friend Despair ascended and ruled the day.' Or he will quote from Alexander Pope.

The printed essay on education, mainly for the teacher but also for the public, was often another outcome of the lyceum system. Especially in the early days of the lyceum, lectures on school keeping were manifold, as were those pointing out the advantages of public education to a democracy. Probably the most notable example of either kind was Horace Mann's *Lectures on Education,* first issued in 1850. As the decades of the lyceum went on, the lectures on education as related to democracy diminished and almost entirely disappeared—in fact, it is a reasonable deduction that the total number of lectures on general education from any point of view went down—and only the more technical, methodological lectures on education remained. The kind of thing that the American Institute of Instruction listened to from the early 1830s —'On School Discipline' by the noted 'teacher of teachers' S. R. Hall, for example—dominated the field by the beginning of the second period of the lyceum. The more general lecture was crowded out. Not entirely of course but even when it did find a place on a program during the 1850s, it was apt to be the program of an educators' group. Samuel Bates's *Lectures on Mental and Moral Culture* fall into this category. The titles of the individual lectures, lectures which Bates said he gave before teachers' institutes during the five years preceding publication, are 'inspirational' rather than 'practical.' The first lecture is on the 'Dignity of the Teacher's Profession,' while later lectures include 'The Power of Spoken Thought,' 'Popular Education,' and 'Education and Democracy the True Basis of Liberty.' But such subjects became rare.

Compared to the good life or travel or education, the criticism of literature was not very appealing to lecture audiences. On the other hand, the number of available critics was small, so their difficulty was not too great and they seem to have filled their share of engagements. Furthermore, a satisfyingly high proportion of the literary lectures found their way into print. At times the lecturers approached literature as a part of culture; at times they concentrated on the biographical approach. Often their literary criticism was impressionistic if not historical. Seldom if ever did it become formal or esthetic.

Illustrations of Genius in Some of Its Relations to Culture and Society, which Henry Giles published in 1854, is an excellent instance of the general cultural kind. These are the lectures he assembled in the volume: 'Cervantes,' 'Don Quixote,' 'The Scarlet Letter,' 'Fiction,' 'Public Opinion,' 'The Philanthropic Sentiment,' 'Music,' 'The Cost of a Cultivated Man,' 'Conversation,' 'Wordsworth,' 'Robert Burns,' and 'Thomas De Quincey.' In their conversational manner, their brief, direct sentences, they show the style most useful to Giles in maintaining his platform popularity. He avoids the ornate abundance of a good many rhetoricians and is far less guilty of overwriting.

Among the lectures dealing primarily with literature, H. N.

Hudson's series on Shakespeare is a noteworthy example. In their printed form he still refers to them as lectures rather than essays. Typically, he does not deal with Shakespeare as Shakespeare, with Shakespeare for his own sake. One of the watchwords of the lyceum throughout the years was Usefulness. In Hudson the lyceum found what it wanted, for he says in his preface, 'The peculiar excellence of the poet's works is in their unequaled ability to instruct us in the things about us and to strengthen us for the duties that lie before us.' There, in essence, is the justification for the audiences' hearing about Shakespeare. It is not literature for pleasure but for instruction—and quite explicit instruction at that. Hudson's style is the sort that audiences considered appropriate for an expositor of literature because it was 'literary' too. 'It was out of this dark, pestiferous, and lethiferous imbroglio of earth and heaven, of dirt and divinity, that the myriad-minded genius of England was to create the bright, breathing, blossoming world of a national drama, the finest and noblest ever seen.' So said Hudson, with a flourish, in a sample sentence from the first lecture in the book.

Not the least effect of the lyceum was, then, to furnish an audience for a number of literary critics. It is true that the only first-rate critic to lecture—and then with some distaste—was Lowell, but several others who only afterward were recognized as second-rate made the platform their home. They read their criticism glibly to audiences and then passed it on to the printer.

It can be fairly said that the lyceum was kind to the essay as such although it too often put a premium on shallowness and easy wit. On the other hand, the lyceum was a blight to all serious poetry. Only the jester or epigrammatist in verse, the Park Benjamin, that is, won any place in the lecture system. There were very few humorous versifiers, to begin with, whom the lyceum curators or managers would invite. This was still before the vogue of the slapstick comic poet; the current fashion was satire. Next to Benjamin, the Vermont poet John G. Saxe was the most prominent member of the small group. Although he was influenced by the poetry of Oliver Wendell Holmes, the most popular verses he read to the lyceum were much like Benjamin's. 'Progress: a Satire,' published by Saxe in the late 1840s, has the same loose heroic

couplets, the same mock-heroic devices, and the same flings at
some of the silliness in American life. That there is little real progress is Saxe's conclusion; and before he arrives at it he makes fun
of false progress in philosophy, education, science, fashion, politics, and communitarianism. On the last he writes:

> Hail, Social Progress! each new moon is rife
> With some new theory of social life,
> Some matchless scheme ingeniously designed
> From half their miseries to free mankind;
> On human wrongs triumphant war to wage,
> And bring anew the glorious golden age.

And so forth, through similar stanzas. Feeble though the poetic
efforts of Saxe were, their support by lyceum audiences showed a
certain interest in formal literature which disappeared swiftly
after the Civil War.

On the whole, however, there was little demand for poetry even
in the best days of the lyceum; the demand was for the prose lecture. Within that *genre* the range was wide but there were, as
we can see repeatedly, certain strong preferences that audiences
had. The prose that they preferred they usually obtained.

The minutes of a sizable number of lyceum committee meetings show that the curators wished to please their general membership. The existence of marked preferences among the 'auditory'
must have had some effect on the very subjects that potential lecturers chose. It would not mean that an explorer would propose
to his audiences to read them an original poem; Elisha Kane and
Park Benjamin would never change places. But in the marginal
instances, where a lecturer hesitated between two topics, his
hearers' likes and dislikes might well become decisive.

To be specific, it is highly probable that the subjects of some
of the printed books which made a place for themselves in nineteenth-century American culture were chosen originally because
of their appeal to lyceums and that here is another way in which
literature was connected with the lyceum. Emerson himself, it may
be remembered, started out among the lyceums by talking on
science when science was fashionable. In his 1833 lecture on 'The
Relation of Man to the Globe,' for instance, he gave science a

cordial emphasis and added his own philosophical doctrine of the correspondence between the world of the senses and the world of thought. In the years that followed he and lyceum audiences continued to find themselves generally in agreement on the topics to be discussed. One of his later books, published in 1860, was called *The Conduct of Life,* and it epitomizes the most attractive kind of lyceum subject. In Emerson the measured shift from one subject to another was the result, certainly, of his personal growth. Yet even he felt pressures working upon him at times. The best testimony is his admonishing himself to say what he ought to say, regardless of audience reaction. There must have been occasions when other, weaker lecturers decided to pick the popular topics, to climb on the bandwagon.

Another kind of carry-over from the lyceum to literature had its own importance. Whatever the literary form, whether popular or unpopular, prose or poetry, one of the most pervasive influences of the lecture system on it was in the awareness of the reader. When the lecturer read his manuscript he had the audience squarely in front of him and probably could not have forgotten its members had he wished. Later, when he printed his manuscript, the same awareness was seldom revised entirely away. The direct address to the reader and the attitude, often, of informality were certainly sanctioned by the tradition of the familiar essay; but they received strong psychological support from the lyceum. In general the style too retained the marks of the lecture form. There was a slow change, clear enough by 1845, from the orotund sentences of the early lecturers—the fine language of the Fourth of July orations—to the brisker and more intimate simplicity of the later professionals. It is the difference between Daniel Webster and Wendell Phillips, between the elaborate periods of Webster's 'Second Bunker Hill Address' (1843) and the astringent directness of 'The Lost Arts' (delivered first in 1838 but demanded by audiences all through the second period of the lyceum). By the late 1850s Edward Everett's florid speech on the 'Character of Washington,' popular though it was, represented a vanishing rhetorical tradition.

The omnipresent audience—the symbol of the lyceum—also

acted as an influence on literature that was by no means wholly good. Even at the beginning of the lecture system the audiences failed to be as serious minded as the best men on the platform wished. As time passed, the intellectual leaven diminished. Audiences wanted to learn, or so they asserted doubtless without exception, but they also wanted to be amused. They called more and more for the light touch. Thoreau wrote bitingly in his journal for 1845, 'What a grovelling appetite for profitless jest and amusement our countrymen have. . . . Curators of lyceums write to me, "Dear Sir: I hear that you have a lecture of some humor. Will you do us the favor to read it before the Bungtown Institute?" ' For this sort of invitation Thoreau had nothing but scorn, but his attitude was exceptional. Even Emerson, as was just mentioned, had sometimes to steel himself to avoid making concessions to the audience in front of him. Do not, he firmly advised himself in his journal for 1834, give them 'what they will expect to hear, but what is fit for me to say.' Still another of the major New England writers, Oliver Wendell Holmes, viewed the matter more casually. As befitted a man of wit, he shrugged and gave the audiences what they wanted. They enjoyed the verbal fireworks he set off. Notwithstanding, he had his set of values and demonstrated the fact by refusing to let a single one of his 'fireworks' lectures be published.

For the great bulk of writers, for those gifted with only an average amount of talent, there was not the same problem. They did not have to stoop so far to reach the audience. But they still had to bend a bit. There was always apt to be an adjustment, downward, particularly in the later years of the lyceum. Yet by and large there may have been some gain in clarity and directness to compensate partly for the loss in subtlety and seriousness. Among the general run of writers the effect of the lecture system varied. It probably did Park Benjamin, for instance, more harm than good by cheapening his wit, but the reverse was true for such a man as John Lord, whose style benefited from the platform.

One final influence of the lyceum on literature was of a different kind than the rest. It was economic. The lyceum was a fruitful source of income to authors. Then as now, literature paid its practitioners badly indeed. Lowell, for instance, had better luck with publishing his poems than perhaps any of his contemporaries of the middle 1840s, yet he could hardly support his wife Maria and himself on the less than $1000 he was able to garner in a year. Emerson and Thoreau made no financial profit of any size on their publications during the lyceum period (Thoreau, in fact, lost money). But even Thoreau could gain a few dollars on the platform while Emerson was able to do far better than that. He had little love for the discomforts of his various tours during the 1850s but he thought himself well paid for them. One tour to New York, Brooklyn, Newark, Paterson, and Philadelphia, for example, gave him a profit of about $630. On a trip through the West, his most productive stop was Cincinnati. There he received $471.71, more than twice his expenses for the entire trip. In Boston he gave half a dozen lectures, including the one on 'Beauty,' and netted $772.36. In a single year such as 1856 he made about $1,700 in lecture fees. He was not quite in Bayard Taylor's class but that was a tribute to his Transcendentalism.

Smaller literary men than Emerson—aside from a few such as Taylor—did not do as well financially, but they still made a living in some cases and supplemented their normal income in all cases. Though lecturing did not always please them, they also knew that there were a good many things more distasteful. The alliance, economic as well as otherwise, of literature and the lyceum was an uneasy one; it was a marriage of convenience, no doubt; but it was a marriage.

19

The Lyceum and the Library Movement

'Calling into Use Neglected Libraries, and Giving Occasion for Establishing New Ones'—from Holbrook's list of promised advantages of the lyceum.

Out of the massive democratic impulse that manifested itself during the second, third, and fourth decades of the nineteenth century came the social library as well as the lyceum and the public elementary school. After the social library came the public library much as we know it today. Its official beginning might be set in the spring of 1854 as well as any time, when the now famous Boston Public Library first opened its doors. But before that spring some at least of the groundwork had been laid for the public library movement by the American lyceum system itself.

In the organized attempts, made around the middle of the century, to give the American people more library facilities, the lyceum had an important part. Authorities quarrel about the exact extent of its importance but a core of agreement can be found. In his wide-ranging history of American education Edwin Grant Dexter, for instance, saw only two major forces behind those attempts. The first was the increased leisure that people began to have. The second was 'the prevalence of the lyceum,' 'bringing the masses, as it did, into new fields of thought.' On the other hand, a pair of recent writers on the library movement assign the lyceum much less of a role than Dexter. Sidney Ditzion in his *Arsenals of a Democratic Culture* and J. H. Shera in his *Foundations of the Public Library* both minimize the effect of the lyceum. But they limit their view of the lyceum severely by confining it to the early, Holbrook-inspired stage of the movement. With allowance for that fact a common ground between them and Dexter can be established.

The best way, perhaps, to gauge the effect of the lyceum is chronologically, since factors of various sorts rose to importance with the passing of time and then fell.

Long before the lyceum, private libraries reached the American continent. The earliest settlers of New England, particularly the ministers, brought over books with them; so did a few of the southern gentry a little later. These seventeenth century libraries might well be represented by the collection of four hundred volumes gathered by Colonel Ralph Wormeley of Virginia. His shelves were filled with theology, law, history, English literature, and a sprinkling of the classics of Greece and Rome. Doubtless their fine brown-calf bindings reflected the book-loving man of means.

Though Colonel Wormeley and his urbane kind were too early to permit any connection with the lyceum, their private libraries were the distant ancestors of those public ones which found the lyceum an ally. After these private libraries came the subscription libraries. Benjamin Franklin founded the first one, motivated by the same kind of zeal for spreading knowledge that would have made him a leader in the lyceum movement. In 1731 he and some of his friends raised £100 and bought books with the money. They called their group the Library Company of Philadelphia. It was agreed that the books could be taken out instead of having to be read on the premises. To do the clerical work they secured a male librarian but not until after some difficulty, it may be, for the genial Franklin himself was pressed into service for three months.

Another step forward came with the appearance of a number of societies which by both listening to occasional lectures and collecting libraries for the use of their members anticipated the lyceum. Often the library and the lecture derived from the same educational interest; they were but the two sides of the coin. Before the rise of the lyceum, it was the library side. Afterward, though the emphasis shifted at times, on the whole the lecture side dominated.

The earliest place, shortly before the lyceum movement was under way, where the lyceum and the library touched each other was in the mechanics' and apprentices' societies. They heard their lectures in the 1820s on the practical application of science and in addition got together whatever technical books they could find. In *Public Libraries in the United States of America* (1876), one contributor to the volume, F. B. Perkins, lists both the mechanics' and apprentices' societies' libraries that he found and their date of establishment. They include the Boston, Portland, and New York Apprentices' Libraries, the Salem Charitable Mechanic Association, and the Philadelphia Apprentices' Library Company, all of which were inaugurated in 1820. The Portsmouth Mechanics' Association is listed as of 1826, the Lancaster Mechanics' Library as of 1828, and others follow. The bulk of them come during this second decade of the century.

Signs of the spread of these organizations, with their alliance of lectures and libraries, can be found on every hand. In the city directories alone, of the 1820s and 1830s, at least two dozen such apprentices' societies can be found. The Charleston, South Carolina, Apprentices' Library Society, listed in the *Charleston Directory*, is representative. Its one to two hundred young members were scheduled to spend two nights a week at the library and two at lectures.

Another, slightly different, kind of situation from that of the regular apprentices' libraries is represented by the New Haven social library which was opened to apprentices in 1827. After some haggling its books were bought by the Young Mechanics' Institute a little more than a decade later. In 1840 this organization, strengthened by its new library, changed its name to the Young Men's Institute—and under that title led a long, healthy existence characterized by a sound balance of reading and listening.

Meanwhile, many a regular lyceum had been springing up, with a constitution that stipulated the gathering of a library as one of the aims. The lyceum in Concord, Massachusetts, begun in January 1829, became one of the many to follow that pattern. Another was the New Bedford Lyceum, born a month earlier. By 1832 its delegate to the American Lyceum could report that his organization had 'a handsome building, a library, and a philosophical apparatus.' The Orange, New Jersey, Lyceum, formed in 1832, offered the usual exercises to its members, including lectures and debates, and owned a library. So did the Buffalo Lyceum and the Newark Mechanics' Institute and Lyceum.

The mercantile library association was the next of the strands connecting the library movement with the lyceum. It differed from the mechanics' apprentices' library society primarily in the kind of people who belonged, for ink-stained young clerks rather than grimy apprentices borrowed books from the mercantile association. Out of the difference in background of the two groups came a difference in the kind of books they wanted to read. Naturally enough the apprentices had more use for manuals of applied science. They thumbed the pages of such a volume as Overman's *Mechanics for the Millwright* or Rees's little *Mechanic's Second Book of Philosophy*. The clerk, on the other hand, was more apt to reach for books on trade and accounting or else in the field of general culture. Foster's *Clerk's Guide* or Coffin's neat *Exercises in Bookkeeping* or, for culture, Cobbett's tendentious *History of the Protestant Reformation* looked good to him.

As a rule the mercantile libraries themselves, like their parent mercantile associations, started after the mechanics' and apprentices' groups. Perkins lists mercantile libraries and their date of founding for New York (1820), Boston (1820), Philadelphia (1821), Cincinnati (1835), Baltimore (1839), St. Louis (1846), Pittsburgh (1847), Portland (1851), Portsmouth (1852), San Francisco (1853), Peoria (1855), and Brooklyn (1857).

Many of these associations offered courses of lectures and so got into the lyceum movement through a side door. The most successful associations in the early 1850s sponsored a series every year. 'Next to the library,' according to a report on 'Mercantile Library Associations' in *Hunt's Merchants' Magazine* for October 1853, 'the chief feature of these institutions is the course of LECTURES.' The article goes on to give a shrewd enough summary of the reasons for having lecture courses along with the library.

Among the most significant is the fact that lectures can attract wide attention. If a library association needs to be advertised—and most do—a stimulating series of talks, given by noted men, is a far better source of publicity than a collection of good books. Then too, hearing an interesting lecture may lure men into reading when they would not otherwise do so. According to *Hunt's* the brisk sequence of cause and effect runs like this: 'The lectures incite to reading and thought; from the lecture hall [these men] pass to the library, and perhaps to the classes, becoming efficient members of the association.' Moreover, the lecture courses will make money if capably managed. That was a telling point, and *Hunt's* proceeded to document its assertion. In the past year New York's Association had netted $1,593, the Boston Association $1,585, the one in Cincinnati $581, the one in St. Louis $470.

These profits ordinarily went first into books and then into the building of association halls. Like the schoolmen earlier, the mercantile library people saw in the lyceum a useful instrument, so they seized it. And in general it helped the associations to establish themselves successfully.

Still later, as a rule, than the mercantile library associations came the regular library associations, which were designed for the public rather than for clerks and merchants. These library associations reached adult stature in the 1850s, about the same time as the young men's associations. It was the practice for the general library associations, like the mercantile libraries, during the second period of the lyceum to sponsor lectures in the hope of raising money for books. In that way those associations entered the lyceum movement too. A good example is the Orange Library Association, which was formed in 1858.' As a local history says, 'Two annual courses of popular lectures were given by the Association which added materially to its finances and justified a further expenditure for books.' Other instances among a number about this time include the Alexandria, Virginia, Library Company and the Franklin Library Association of Cambridgeport, Massachusetts.

The athenaeum was another, somewhat less related, kind of society. Normally it acted as a literary or scientific club and often owned a library. A minority of the athenaeums offered lectures and had other characteristics of the lyceum. Intended mainly for gentlemen, athenaeums had a long history in this country. There were a few of them in colonial days and more, a good many more, during the first half of the nineteenth century. They were predominantly urban, flourishing on the east coast and being found in the West only here and there in large towns.

The South often found the athenaeum a more congenial kind of club than the lyceum. The Natchez Athenaeum, started in 1821, is a case in point. Its object, the constitution averred, was the intellectual improvement of all ranks and professions; but the stated requirements for membership show otherwise, for annual dues were set at ten dollars and life membership at one hundred dollars. Provisions for a library of books and periodicals were included in the constitution. The Adams Athenaeum, also in Mississippi, was a library society active in the later 1820s. An illustration of the continuing strength of the athenaeum in the South was the establishment of the Columbia, South Carolina, Athenaeum in 1856. Its constitution shows this to be mainly a library society but lectures were also included in the scheme.

Most notable of all athenaeums was Boston's, incorporated in 1807 and still open, which fought a pitched battle in the 1850s to keep from being absorbed by the Boston Public Library. It represented the acme of the gentlemen's social library. The Boston Brahmins used it oftenest but even Transcendentalists were allowed. Emerson, shortly after his first marriage, subscribed to the Boston Athenaeum and began a long contact with it. Bronson Alcott, Ellery Channing, and James Freeman Clarke were other Transcendentalists who took advantage of its resources. The historians Bancroft, Prescott, and Parkman and such literary lecturers as E. P. Whipple and Oliver Wendell Holmes gladly borrowed its volumes too. Hawthorne was given a tour of it in 1850 and was impressed. 'The library is in a noble hall,' he wrote afterward in one of his notebooks, 'and looks splendidly with its vista of alcoves.'

In spite of the importance of the athenaeum to a general history of the library movement in the United States, it must have less prominence in any study of the connection between the lyceum system and the library movement. This is true primarily because, as was just remarked, the proportion of athenaeums which also acted as lyceums was small. Such societies as the Brooklyn Athenaeum and Reading Room, reported in 1858 as having lectures as well as a library, were the exception. Much more significant was the relationship of the young men's associations to libraries.

The young men's associations, the last distinctive variety of the lyceum before the Civil War, began in the mid-1830s but did not reach full popularity for a decade. Once they attained their popularity, however, they held it well. These associations were literally lyceums without using the name. When, in 1856, Bayard Taylor sent his letter of advice to the neophyte lecturer I. I. Hayes, every lecture-sponsoring society he recommended in it called itself a young men's association. Some of these associations also acquired libraries. Perkins noted that in Albany, Buffalo, Troy, and Milwaukee there were young men's associations which had them. His list could be swelled without much trouble, particularly by adding such smaller towns as La Crosse, Wisconsin. But the bigger communities had the more active associations.

The Young Men's Association of Buffalo was a flourishing example of the kind. It strongly supported both its library and its lecture programs. In 1856 it spent almost $2000 on new books. By the books it ordered, the Association revealed the interests of its membership—and they were by no means those of the apprentices' associations of former times. History was the most popular subject, with science, in its various branches, next. Then came fiction—a strong third—and travel was fourth. Clearly, the same interests dictated the selection of lecturers and their topics. Half the lectures were historical; William Gilmore Simms on 'South Carolina in the Revolution,' for instance, E. H. Chapin on 'Columbus,' and George Sumner on 'Spain and Her Revolutions' each gave their hearers a type of spoken history which was close kin to the history books being ordered for the reading room. These lectures likewise catered to the interest in travel. Science was represented by the address of the noted oceanographer M. F. Maury, on 'The Winds and the Sea.' Fiction alone failed to find a place in the program, and this was because the time-hallowed maxim of the lyceum that a lecture must teach something stood in its way. No good could be gotten, the lecture audiences still felt, out of listening to a made-up story. But the correspondence in popularity of the other subjects was close. It illustrated a psychological connection between reading and listening that worked to the advantage of the library—as, on a lower level, did the fact that this particular lecture course made a profit of hundreds of dollars for the book fund.

There are two other ways in which the library and the lyceum showed a historical connection. The first is through the fact that a substantial minority of lyceums as they withered or died left their books to the library in their locality and thus strengthened its holdings. In his book Shera cites ten new Massachusetts public libraries created in the years between 1851 and 1854 alone. These were either actual or potential caretakers for the libraries of decaying lyceums. The details of how this worked can be seen in Haverhill. Sponsored by the Haverhill Mechanics' Debating Society, the Apprentices' Library opened in 1825. The Mechanics' Library Association began in 1831. The Haverhill Athenaeum (which had a library) was incorporated in 1852, while the Haverhill Mechanics' Institute (which had a library too) was incorporated in 1856. In 1859 the Athenaeum and the Mechanics' Institute combined and pooled their libraries. The combination, when chartered the next year, called itself the Haverhill Library Association. 'With the opening in 1875 of the Public Library, the first free library in Haverhill, the Haverhill Library Association was discontinued and its books turned over to the new library.' So says one official report. Out of this conglomerate of private library-owning societies, some with lyceum characteristics and some without, came the public library of the community. What happened in Haverhill happened, not infrequently, elsewhere.

Sometimes a lyceum turned into a library. That was the second way in which the library movement and the lyceum system showed a historical affiliation. Perhaps a lyceum's lecture program atrophied, as did its other oral activities. The speakers and discoursers disappeared but the books did not. They might be dispersed—that happened in some cases—but generally they seemed tangible enough property to be kept together and to invite use. Accordingly, the books were the sole bond that held the membership together. A comment in *The Chicago Public Library* describes such a case: 'In 1868 the Young Men's Association had changed its name to [the] Chicago Library Association, an indication of the extent to which the conduct of the library had superseded all other activities.'

That the connection between the library movement and the lyceum was constant and close, no one would be apt to argue. It varied, in fact, from place to place, as state and local histories show. In Alabama and Kentucky, for instance, the connection was tenuous. In Massachusetts it was substantial. And in New York state, according to Frank Leland Tolman, the lyceum 'was a vigorous force in the establishment of popular libraries.' Over all, the conclusion must be that in the country as a whole there was indeed a connection, a relation sometimes direct and sometimes roundabout, between the lyceum and the library movement.

————◆————

20

The Configuration of the Lyceum

O N 15 April 1861, President Abraham Lincoln declared officially that an insurrection existed in the country. He called for 75,000 volunteers to enlist for three months and put it down. Four years later almost to a day came the surrender of General Lee to General Grant. In those four bitter years, the nation laid aside the lyceum as if it were a tool now nearly useless. In spite of a few local lyceums, such as those of Concord or Evansville, which kept on with their normal activities, the movement as a whole disappeared. All adult education suffered deeply from neglect, but it was a neglect on the basis of first things first. Though lecturing itself continued as a form of activity within the American culture, its aim on both sides of the Mason-Dixon line shifted to helping win the war.

Despite the fact that lyceum records for the North are far fuller than those for the South, we know that for both sides the Civil War had become a crusade. In the North it was to some degree based on the moral energy aroused by abolitionism, and by humanitarian feeling in general, partly through the lectures of men as varied as Beecher, Taylor, Phillips, and Saxe. Even Emerson reflected something of the war in his lectures. If anyone on the platform retained an unworldly point of view as a rule—above controversy—Emerson was the man. Yet in the 1850s he felt this particular moral conflict increasingly. In the last years before Sumter his public sympathy for abolitionism ripened even if he gave no anti-slavery lectures. When the actual conflict came, there was no doubt where he stood. Being Emerson, he consistently avoided a narrow patriotism, however. In speaking, for example, in Boston about 'Moral Forces' on the first anniversary of Sumter, he took what became his characteristic wartime position. Only the victories that would benefit all mankind would benefit the North, he said firmly. He added, however, that if we deemed our common and popular sympathies to be sound and safe (that is, if the North was really in the right as Emerson believed), then much good could come out of the war.

In the South the war was felt to be a crusade even more deeply. Its politicians sounded even more fiery than those of the North. But its lyceum system had always been rudimentary at best, so lecturing now played a very minor role. Notwithstanding, the South had a few lecturers, and they spoke out with intensity for the 'peculiar institution' and the region that clung to it.

Most lecturers on both sides confined themselves to the blunt but by no means surprising assumption that their side was entirely right; and they did their best to incite the patriotism of their hearers. Whether they spoke in Boston or New Orleans, Marietta, Ohio, or Oxford, Mississippi, they interpreted the war simply. It was a struggle in which they were Christian and the enemy was infidel. From this assumption the South tolerated no deviations. The North allowed a few, depending on place and circumstance. In the North the pure individualist, the pacifist, and even the Copperhead could mount an occasional platform and talk against fighting the South; but not often. The direct result for the lecture system—or rather such small parts of it as could maintain themselves—was of course that lecturing became propaganda instead of education or even amusement.

Once the war was finished, all lecturing began to increase again. But it was thereafter far more commercialized and much more an entertainment than it had ever been before. 'A year or two after the war,' Major J. B. Pond recalled in his chapter on the lyceum in *Eccentricities of Genius,* 'when over a million men had returned from military strife to civil pursuits, . . . there came an unprecedented demand for entertainments and amusements.' The quondam patriotic lecturers of the North 'were sought after for lectures all over the country' (except in the prostrate South). The demand proved particularly strong in the Middle West. The Associated Western Literary Societies started by 1865 and grew into the leading organization, in the decade after the war, for booking eastern lecturers on midwestern tours. It succeeded where the Bryant and Massillon confederations could not. During the late 1860s the lecture bureaus likewise began. Among them were the American Literary Bureau and the Williams Lecture and Musical Bureau. But the most notable one was founded by an enterprising ex-war correspondent and abolitionist, James Redpath.

In 1868 he established the Boston Lyceum Bureau, later called the Redpath Lyceum Bureau, with the help of a man named G. L. Fall. Redpath capitalized on his energy, his tact in dealing with platform celebrities, and his shrewdness in handling local associations. It was a rich harvest that he reaped for his celebrities, and he retained 10 per cent of it for himself. Other promoters too saw a golden opportunity. By bidding against one another they emerged with 'Star Courses,' now systematized, which set new highs in lecture fees as well as in profits for the promoters. A decade later Major Pond's own career as a manager began. He ultimately achieved an eminence second only to Redpath's. His *Eccentricities of Genius* is a rambling, anecdotal but refreshing story of his contacts with the star lecturers up to the turn of the century. It has, however, only the faintest of reflections of the adult education movement in it—and that is perfectly natural. Education had pretty well deserted the lecture platform despite the fact that a rather distinguished minority of the prewar names could be found in the postwar courses.

With the coming of the Chautauqua movement in the first quarter of the twentieth century, education of a kind returned to the platform; but though it bore more resemblance to the lyceum system than did the star courses of the lecture bureaus, the differences were still much greater than the similarities. A good deal of distance remained between the lecture rooms of the lyceum and the brown canvas tents of Chautauqua.

When, exactly, did the lyceum movement end? Out of the bulk of evidence we have accumulated, it would certainly seem that it ended with the Civil War. Yet at least two other interpretations of the evidence could be made, and it would be less than just not to note them here. One is that the lyceum in the sense of a local, public, adult-education movement was finished by about 1840. It is true that by then the cabinet of curiosities, the interchange of information among neighbors, and the close connection with the public elementary-school movement were largely gone. But against that interpretation is the fact that the most important element remained. It was the people's desire to be educated, and it manifested itself principally through attendance at society-sponsored lectures. The lecture furnished the continuum. Furthermore, although the lecture topics themselves changed as time went on, public recognition of any marked alteration in the lyceum system was tardy. The public still thought of the lyceum in its original form long after certain educational aspects had faded away. Here we have a case of cultural lag—something which as a rule can be dismissed as a preliminary to getting down to practicalities. In the case of a social institution, however, the public's idea of it is very important. To an unusual extent the institution is what the public thinks it is; the social concept has a working reality even though the concept itself may be an example of cultural lag.

The other interpretation goes to the opposite extreme. It would extend the life of the lyceum system, perhaps indefinitely, instead of cutting it short after the end of the 1830s. This second interpretation, dwelling on the lectures alone, suggests that the American habit of listening to lectures continued through the Civil War, into the '70s, '80s, and '90s, and then into the twentieth century. Obviously, to this very day we have lectures, lecturers to give them, and a few lecture bureaus to make needed arrangements. Yet of the characteristics of the lyceum movement—in the shifting cluster that constituted it—today there is little if anything left.

Those once more or less closely related characteristics have all been redistributed. Management of the lecturing has long since been taken over by the bureaus. The practical adult education has been re-formed in the mold of extension courses, vocational schools, night schools, and in-service training. The museums and some of the public schools have absorbed any cabinets of specimens. The educational use of scientific apparatus has been transferred too. The public libraries have taken over the collecting of books and the whole library function. In the sphere of entertainment—even entertainment mixed with a bit of instruction—the mass media of radio, motion pictures, and television have triumphed unconditionally over the lecture.

What is strikingly true nowadays was also true, though to a smaller extent, a generation ago. In the busiest days of the Chautauqua some of the marks of the lyceum developed but not enough to constitute an extension of the life of the lyceum movement. Moreover, if we go back beyond the Chautauqua days of the 1920s and into the last quarter of the nineteenth century, we can see that the major signs of the pre-Civil War lyceum had already disappeared. The adult education and the relatively serious purpose—both of which were diminishing in importance in the lyceum system but were certainly not gone by the time the Civil War came—meant little to the postwar promoters, whatever they meant to a few of their greatest lecturers.

And in place of the things which had vanished during the war there were two or three new and brassier ones. Chief among those was the deepening stress on entertainment that has already been cited. Though deficiencies existed in the old lyceum system, it never catered to such clumsy comics as Artemus Ward and Petroleum Nasby. They represented a degree of rustic mirth which the prewar audiences would have found unseemly. J. G. Holland editorialized about the matter in *Scribner's Monthly* for February 1872. 'There was a time,' he wrote, 'when a lecture was a lecture. The men who appeared before the lyceums were men who had something to say. . . . Now, a lecture may be any string of nonsense that any literary mountebank can find an opportunity to utter. Artemus Ward "lectured"; and he was right royally paid for acting the literary buffoon. He has had many imitators; and the damage that he and they have inflicted upon the institution of the lyceum is incalculable.'

Another change, at first glance at any rate much more palatable than the rise of the comedians, was the introduction of music. The lyceum, at times to its own loss, had almost ignored music. Now, however, the lecture bureaus discovered that choruses, bands, and soloists could attract many an audience. This or that family of singers, this group of Swiss bell-ringers or that one, would often mean overflow attendance. That may have been well and good, but it was not characteristic of the lyceum as an educator.

After all the qualifications have been made, all the reservations entered, it still seems that the lyceum as an American social institution began in the late 1820s and ended with the Civil War. And so too a number of its most sagacious participants thought. The postwar lecture period they themselves considered to be different and less valuable. Granted that some allowance must always be made for the tendency of the past to look better than the present; nonetheless, when veteran lecturers like Holland and G. W. Curtis praised the prewar lyceum and indicted the postwar period they did so with a specific enough bill of particulars.

Writing in the 'Editor's Easy Chair' of *Harper's* for April 1887, Curtis pronounced the epitaph of our lyceum as feelingly as anyone. 'The lyceum of the last generation is gone, but it is not surprising that those who recall . . . its golden prime should cherish a kindly and regretful feeling for an institution which was so peculiarly American, and which served so well the true American spirit and American life.'

I HAVE omitted individual footnote references. To provide the reader with the necessary leads to my source materials, I have customarily cited the sources in the text itself and supplement them with the bibliographical note which follows.

The only published work on the American lyceum is a seventy-two-page monograph, Cecil B. Hayes's *The American Lyceum: Its History and Contribution to Education,* printed by the United States' Office of Education in 1932. Three unpublished doctoral dissertations have been completed on the topic. Kenneth White's 'The American Lyceum' was submitted in history at Harvard University in 1918; Paul Stoddard's 'The American Lyceum' was submitted in education at Yale University in 1947; and James Kelso's 'The American Lyceum: an American Institution' was submitted in history at Harvard in 1952. I have been allowed to examine the first two. A few master's theses which attempt to survey all or the greater part of this extensive topic have also been written.

Likewise, there are several sketches of the history of the lyceum which have appeared in print in the form of articles. Of these John Munroe's 'The Lyceum in America before the Civil War' in *Delaware Notes* for May 1942 is representative.

Though these works are all supposedly studies of the lyceum on something close to a national scale, they are actually in the main studies of the early development of the lyceum system in Massachusetts and certain parts of the rest of New England. Various other studies, published and unpublished, which deal with the lyceum in the different states and localities will be noted in the proper place below.

For the British predecessors of the lyceum the best source is the *Mechanics'* [or *Mechanic's*] *Magazine* of London from 1823 to 1828. Lord Brougham's speeches are also valuable. No biography of Josiah Holbrook exists; the most useful pictures of his life can

be gained from his son Alfred's *Reminiscences* (1885) and the brief
'Memoir' in the March 1860 number of Henry Barnard's *American Journal of Education*. For the first dozen years of the lyceum
movement the mainstay is the earlier *American Journal of Education*, which in 1831 became the *American Annals of Education*.
In the mass of material appearing there, the most valuable items
are the annual proceedings of the national lyceum. Though repetitious and overly optimistic, Holbrook's own publications—
especially the various versions of the 'American Lyceum' pamphlet and the files of the weekly *Family Lyceum* (28 July 1832–
10 August 1833)—are important sources.

The detailed history of the lyceum movement is to be found
particularly in the local newspapers, local histories, and such
minutes books as have survived. Occasionally there are histories
of individual lyceums, such as H. K. Oliver's *Historical Sketch of
the Salem Lyceum* (1878). For a few states and cities present-day
students have prepared a synthesis of lyceum activities.

Here is the bibliographical breakdown by regions and states:

New England. For Massachusetts there is no state-wide history
of the lyceum but both White and Stoddard devote many pages
to the movement there. Connecticut and Rhode Island lack works
on the lyceum either in those states or in their principal cities.
Grant Herman's Dartmouth undergraduate thesis, 'Tall Talk
in New Hampshire' (1935), affords some information about the
movement in that state. Although we have no over-all guide for
Vermont, for Maine we have Mrs. Barbara Hinds's 'The Lyceum
Movement in Maine,' an unpublished master's thesis which she
submitted at the state university in 1949.

The Middle Atlantic States. Comprehensive accounts, either
published or unpublished, appear to be lacking. For New York
City we have Robert Greef's 'Public Lectures in New York 1851–
1878: a Cultural Index of the Times,' a University of Chicago
doctoral dissertation in English submitted in 1941 and published
in part (Chapter 1) in 1945.

The South. In the southern states only the city of New Orleans
has received much attention. Mary Louise Hamilton's master's
thesis, 'The Lyceum in New Orleans 1840–1860,' was submitted
at Louisiana State University in 1948.

The Midwest. The midwestern lyceum system has, in at least one part, benefited from an unusually thorough study, David Mead's *Yankee Eloquence in the Middle West: the Ohio Lyceum 1850–1870.* Mead's monograph was published in 1951 and is based on a combing of the Ohio newspaper files. Joseph Schick's *The Early Theater in Eastern Iowa,* which made its appearance in 1939, is more useful for us than its title shows, for it really deals with other cultural beginnings besides the rise of the theater. Schick's work takes in the years from 1836 to 1863.

The West. Edna Nelson prepared a term thesis at Hamline University and submitted it in 1927; entitled 'Some Cultural Activities and Associations in Minnesota 1849–1858,' it includes useful data on the lyceum in that state. Accounts of any degree of comprehensiveness of the lyceum in other midwestern or western states during the period from the beginnings to 1861 have not been found at this writing.

The main basis for the chapter 'This Noble National Conclave' is the reports in the *American Annals.* 'The Lyceum and the Public Schools' is the result of original work based on the connection between the two as pictured in the various states. For the chapter of vignettes, 'Platform Gallery: I,' both primary and secondary biographical materials have been used, plus W. N. Brigance's *A History and Criticism of American Public Address* (two volumes, 1943) and W. C. Shaw's *History of American Oratory* (1928). The same basis has been employed for 'Platform Gallery: II.' For 'The Economics of the Lyceum' the major sources are lyceum record books and treasurers' reports (particularly those of Concord, in the Concord Public Library, and Salem, in the library of the Essex Institute), lecturers' personal accounts, the printed leaflets of Holbrook and the national lyceum, and—most important—the unpublished papers, from 18 August 1854 to 11 April 1857, of J. R. Brigham in the Wisconsin State Historical Society's library. The cited material in the chapter on 'The Lyceum and Literature' is drawn from a combination of primary and secondary sources; the bulk of the remainder is original. Information in 'The Lyceum and the Library Movement' is drawn mainly from the writer's files; the other sources that should be named are

Edwin Grant Dexter's *A History of Education in the United States* (1904); in *Public Libraries in the United States of America* (1876), the section prepared by F. B. Perkins; and in the *History of the State of New York,* Volume 9, *Mind and Spirit* (1937), the section prepared by Frank Leland Tolman.

◆

Though at some sacrifice of nineteenth-century flavor, most quotations from all but the great writers have had their spelling and punctuation brought up to date.

Acknowledgments

I T is impossible to thank properly the many librarians and
scholars who helped me while I was gathering my materials.
Like scholars, librarians are notoriously overworked (and under-
paid), yet from them I received a co-operation which must have
cost many hours. Out of all the libraries, the Library of Congress
is the one I used most. Its collections are for the historian of nineteenth century American culture the best in the world. Among the
staff members there to whom I feel especially indebted are Mrs.
B. C. Brown, Mr. Harold Cumbo, and Mr. Elbert Mitchell. I found
the Library of the University of Maryland increasingly useful; Mr.
Howard Rovelstad, its director, and Miss Betty Baehr in particular
earned my gratitude.

My research was facilitated through the helpfulness at the University of Maryland of Dean Ronald Bamford of the Graduate
School, Dean Leon Smith of the College of Arts and Sciences, and
my colleague Professor Charles Murphy, acting head of the Department of English. Through the University and through the
generosity of the American Philosophical Society, I had excellent
research assistance; the bulk of it was provided by Dr. Marie
Harris Henault, Mr. Harry Kroitor, and Mr. Harrison Meserole.
Aid in gaining access to federal library facilities was kindly provided by Congressman John Henderson and Mr. L. V. Monzel.
The students in my seminars on nineteenth century American culture also put me in their debt in one way or another. Mrs. H. J.
Nary and Mrs. Paul Blackmon assisted in the preparation of the
manuscript for the press. I had Mr. Foster Ripley's counsel on
portions of the nineteenth century background.

I wish to acknowledge other, specific assistance. In writing about
the lyceum in Pennsylvania, I drew on a file of newspaper ex-
tracts lent me through the courtesy of the former Assistant State
Historian, Mr. Norman B. Wilkinson. In describing the lyceum in
the South I made use of newspaper and biographical references

provided by Professor Jay Hubbell. For the lyceum in Indiana some of the transcripts of newspaper articles were sent me by Dr. H. L. Heller; Miss Myrtle D. Berry of the Nebraska State Historical Society looked up newspaper references to the lyceum in Nebraska; Dr. Everett Dick and Mr. Forrest Blackburn did me the same courtesy for Kansas. For data on California societies I am obligated to Mr. A. R. Ottley of the California State Library. Professor Louis Budd lent me his manuscript on Emerson in Wisconsin, while Professor John Eidson provided data on the lyceum as it related to Francis Hall in upstate New York.

In several cases I needed to quote from copyrighted materials. Permission was granted me by the University of Chicago Press to quote the definition of *lyceum* in Craigie and Hulbert's *A Dictionary of American English*. From his edition of Park Benjamin's poems Dr. M. M. Hoover allowed me to quote part of a version of 'The Age of Gold.' Professor Ray Billington and the Dryden Press allowed me to quote from the journal of Charlotte Forten. And permission to quote from the J. R. Brigham papers was given by the Wisconsin Historical Society.

Index

The location of a society, other than one formally termed a lyceum, is given after its title, *e.g.* Young Men's Association, Milwaukee (but Chicago Lyceum).